the source

the definitive worship collection compiled by
Graham Kendrick

Kevin
Mayhew

First published in Great Britain in 1998 by
KEVIN MAYHEW LIMITED
Rattlesden
Bury St Edmunds
Suffolk IP30 0SZ

Compilation © Kevin Mayhew Ltd 1998

The right of Graham Kendrick to be identified
as the compiler of this work has been asserted by him in accordance
with the Copyright, Designs and Patents Act 1988.

Words Only	ISBN	1 84003 121 2
	Catalogue No.	1470101
Full Music	ISBN	1 84003 120 4
	Catalogue No.	1470104
Complete Acetate Masters	ISBN	1 84003 119 0
	Catalogue No.	1470201

Cover design: Jaquetta Sergeant
Managing Editor: Katherine Laidler
Typesetting: Louise Selfe

Printed and bound in Great Britain

Foreword

Let the word of Christ dwell in you richly as you teach and admonish one another with all wisdom, and as you sing psalms, hymns and spiritual songs with gratitude in your hearts to God. And whatever you do, whether in word or deed, do it all in the name of the Lord Jesus, giving thanks to God the Father through him.

Colossians 3:16-17

It is to encourage the realisation of this kind of worship lifestyle that we have compiled and published **the source**, not least to facilitate the singing of psalms, hymns and spiritual songs, of which you will find here over six hundred of the best.

As an editorial panel we have sought to discharge our responsibilities as faithfully and generously as possible, believing that diversity was vital to the breadth and richness of the material we were considering. The songs in this book restate the teachings of our faith, explore new insights, proclaim hope, protest, express solidarity with the poor, call ourselves and others to repentance and faith; and in all this we celebrate our God and Saviour Jesus Christ, who, in the words of the writer to the Hebrews, 'became the source of eternal salvation for all who obey him'.

the source has, we believe, several claims to uniqueness.

The content of each hymn and song has been carefully assessed and, while we have still included some material that may be described as 'lighter', we believe that the *overall* balance is more substantial than in previous collections. This attention to substance and breadth has also enabled us to produce a book that will appeal to a broad church constituency.

While compiling **the source** we have been keenly aware of its prophetic dimension. For the first time we were making choices unencumbered by copyright or any other restrictions: the world was our oyster and we have made full use of the freedom offered to us, including songs both new and old which we expect to take their place (or re-take in the case of the older songs) among those loved by congregations everywhere. In this sense we have aspired to be like the kind of teacher Jesus affirmed who 'is like a householder who brings both new things and old out of his treasure-store' (Matthew 13:52).

There is also a sense in which we have been like harvesters; reaping and gathering what has been growing in the 'fields' of diverse worshipping communities. The variety of soils has produced a rich variety of styles and indeed emphasis which we hope will excite, intrigue and challenge the user to appreciate and benefit from the many facets of the jewel of worship expression which seeks to reflect the glory of God in the world today.

We have been careful to use inclusive language in referring to the human race wherever possible. Exceptions were made for clear reasons and after much deliberation. Non-copyright texts have been amended whilst those by living authors were referred back. We are grateful to the authors concerned for their willingness to co-operate.

Another fundamental aim was to make **the source** as *complete* as possible to help congregations integrate the material contained in it into their own worship. Thus, besides the main music book, there is also this words copy, instrumental arrangements for all 610 songs and hymns, a complete set of acetate masters and a recording programme.

the source is also the first major new publication to which the new CCL photocopying licence applies, making its accessibility even more valuable.

It is impossible to undertake a project of this magnitude without the help of many people. We wish to express our immense gratitude to all those whose opinions and assistance we have sought during the compilation of **the source**.

We hope that in this diverse and approachable worship collection we have sown some seeds; that is all we can do. It is in the overflow of worship from hearts which are united in a passionate love for Jesus Christ that these seeds must be brought to glorious fruition.

GRAHAM KENDRICK
Compiler

JONATHAN BUGDEN
Adviser

MATTHEW LOCKWOOD
Assistant Adviser

1 Dave Bilbrough

Abba, Father, let me be
yours and yours alone.
May my will for ever be
more and more your own.
Never let my heart grow cold,
never let me go.
Abba, Father, let me be
yours and yours alone.

2 Henry Francis Lyte

Abide with me,
fast falls the eventide;
the darkness deepens;
Lord, with me abide:
when other helpers fail,
and comforts flee,
help of the helpless,
O abide with me.

Swift to its close
ebbs out life's little day;
earth's joys grow dim,
its glories pass away;
change and decay
in all around I see;
O thou who changest not,
abide with me.

I need thy presence
every passing hour;
what but thy grace
can foil the tempter's pow'r?
Who like thyself
my guide and stay can be?
Through cloud and sunshine,
Lord, abide with me.

I fear no foe
with thee at hand to bless;
ills have no weight,
and tears no bitterness.

Where is death's sting?
Where, grave, thy victory?
I triumph still,
if thou abide with me.

Hold thou thy cross
before my closing eyes;
shine through the gloom,
and point me to the skies;
heav'n's morning breaks,
and earth's vain shadows flee;
in life, in death,
O Lord, abide with me.

3 Graham Kendrick

Above the clash of creeds,
the many voices
that call on so many names,
into these final days
our God has spoken
by sending his only Son.

There is no other way
by which we must be saved;
his name is Jesus,
the only Saviour;
no other sinless life,
no other sacrifice,
in all creation
no other way.

Before we called he came
to earth from heaven,
our maker became a man;
when no one else could pay,
he bought our freedom,
exchanging his life for ours.

Beneath the cross of Christ
let earth fall silent
in awe of this mystery;
then let this song arise
and fill the nations:
O hear him call, 'Come to me.'

4 Donald Fishel

Alleluia, alleluia,
give thanks to the risen Lord,
alleluia, alleluia,
give praise to his name.

Jesus is Lord of all the earth,
he is the King of creation.

Spread the good news o'er all the earth,
Jesus has died and has risen.

We have been crucified with Christ,
now we shall live for ever.

God has proclaimed the just reward,
life for us all, alleluia!

Come, let us praise the living God,
joyfully sing to our Saviour.

5 Dave Moody

All hail King Jesus!
All hail Emmanuel!
King of kings, Lord of lords,
bright morning star.
And throughout eternity
I'll sing your praises,
and I'll reign with you
throughout eternity.

6 Dave Bilbrough

All hail the Lamb, enthroned on high;
his praise shall be our battle cry;
he reigns victorious, for ever glorious,
his name is Jesus, he is the Lord.

7 Edward Perronet

All hail the pow'r of Jesus' name!
let angels prostrate fall;
bring forth the royal diadem
and crown him, crown him, crown him,
crown him Lord of all.

Crown him, ye martyrs of your God,
who from his altar call;
praise him whose way of pain ye trod,
and crown him, crown him, crown him,
crown him Lord of all.

Ye prophets who our freedom won,
ye searchers great and small,
by whom the work of truth is done,
now crown him, crown him, crown him,
crown him Lord of all.

Ye seed of Israel's chosen race,
ye ransomed of the fall,
hail him who saves you by his grace,
and crown him, crown him, crown him,
crown him Lord of all.

Let every tribe and every tongue
to him their hearts enthral;
lift high the universal song,
and crown him, crown him, crown him,
crown him Lord of all.

O that, with yonder sacred throng,
we at his feet may fall,
join in the everlasting song,
and crown him, crown him, crown him,
crown him Lord of all.

8 Noel and Tricia Richards

All heav'n declares
the glory of the risen Lord.
Who can compare
with the beauty of the Lord?
For ever he will be
the Lamb upon the throne.
I gladly bow the knee
and worship him alone.

I will proclaim
the glory of the risen Lord.
Who once was slain
to reconcile us to God.
For ever you will be
the Lamb upon the throne.
I gladly bow the knee
and worship you alone.

9   Graham Kendrick and Chris Rolinson

All heaven waits with bated breath,
for saints on earth to pray.
Majestic angels ready stand
with swords of fiery blade.
Astounding pow'r awaits a word
from God's resplendent throne.
But God awaits our prayer of faith
that cries, 'Your will be done.'

Awake, O church, arise and pray,
complaining words discard.
The Spirit comes to fill your mouth
with truth, his mighty sword.
Go place your feet on Satan's ground
and there proclaim Christ's name,
in step with heaven's armies march
to conquer and to reign!

Now in our hearts and on our lips
the word of faith is near,
let heaven's will on earth be done,
let heaven flow from here.
Come, blend your prayers with Jesus' own
before the Father's throne,
and as the incense clouds ascend,
God's holy fire rains down.

Soon comes the day when with a shout
King Jesus will appear,
and with him all the church,
from every age, shall fill the air.
The brightness of his coming shall
consume the lawless one,
as with a word the breath of God
tears down his rebel throne.

One body here, by heav'n inspired,
we seek prophetic power;
in Christ agreed, one heart and voice,
to speak this day, this hour,
in every place where chaos rules
and evil forces brood;
let Jesus' voice speak like the roar
of a great multitude.

10   Chris Falson

All honour, all glory, all power to you.
All honour, all glory, all power to you.
Holy Father, we worship you,
precious Jesus, our Saviour,
Holy Spirit, we wait on you,
Holy Spirit, we wait on you,
Holy Spirit, we wait on you for fire, for fire.

11   Graham Kendrick

All I once held dear,
built my life upon,
all this world reveres,
and wars to own,
all I once thought gain
I have counted loss;
spent and worthless now,
compared to this.

> *Knowing you, Jesus, knowing you,*
> *there is no greater thing.*
> *You're my all, you're the best,*
> *you're my joy, my righteousness,*
> *and I love you, Lord.*

Now my heart's desire
is to know you more,
to be found in you
and known as yours.
To possess by faith
what I could not earn,
all-surpassing gift
of righteousness.

Continued overleaf

Oh, to know the pow'r
of your risen life,
and to know you
in your sufferings.
To become like you
in your death, my Lord,
so with you to live
and never die.

Knowing you, Jesus, knowing you,
there is no greater thing.
You're my all, you're the best,
you're my joy, my righteousness,
and I love you, Lord.

12 Terry Butler

All over the world,
all over the world,
your Spirit is moving
all over the world.

Your river is flowing,
your presence has come,
your Spirit is moving
all over the world.
You're touching the nations,
you're bringing us love,
your Spirit is moving
all over the world.
You're touching the nations,
you're bringing us love,
your Spirit is moving
all over the world.

Your banner is lifted,
your praises are sung,
your Spirit is moving
all over the world.
Divisions are falling,
you're making us one,
your Spirit is moving
all over the world.

Divisions are falling,
you're making us one,
your Spirit is moving
all over the world.

13 William Kethe

All people that on earth do dwell,
sing to the Lord with cheerful voice;
him serve with fear, his praise forth tell,
come ye before him and rejoice.

Know that the Lord is God indeed,
without our aid he did us make;
we are his flock, he doth us feed,
and for his sheep he doth us take.

O enter then his gates with praise,
approach with joy his courts unto;
praise, laud and bless his name always,
for it is seemly so to do.

For why? the Lord our God is good:
his mercy is for ever sure;
his truth at all times firmly stood,
and shall from age to age endure.

Praise God from whom all blessings flow,
praise him, all creatures here below,
praise him above, ye heav'nly hosts:
praise Father, Son and Holy Ghost.

14 Cecil Frances Alexander

All things bright and beautiful,
all creatures great and small,
all things wise and wonderful,
the Lord God made them all.

Each little flow'r that opens,
each little bird that sings,
he made their glowing colours,
he made their tiny wings.

The purple-headed mountain,
the river running by,
the sunset and the morning,
that brightens up the sky.

The cold wind in the winter,
the pleasant summer sun,
the ripe fruits in the garden,
he made them every one.

He gave us eyes to see them,
and lips that we may tell
how great is God Almighty,
who has made all things well.

15 J. W. Van De Venter

All to Jesus I surrender,
all to him I freely give;
I will ever love and trust him,
in his presence daily live.

I surrender all, I surrender all,
all to thee, my blessed Saviour,
I surrender all.

All to Jesus I surrender,
humbly at his feet I bow;
worldly pleasures all forsaken,
take me, Jesus, take me now.

All to Jesus I surrender,
make me, Saviour, wholly thine;
let me feel the Holy Spirit,
truly know that thou art mine.

All to Jesus I surrender,
Lord, I give myself to thee;
fill me with thy love and power,
let thy blessing fall on me.

All to Jesus I surrender,
now to feel the sacred flame;
O, the joy of full salvation!
Glory, glory to his name!

16 Austin Martin

Almighty God, we bring you praise
for your Son, the Word of God,
by whose pow'r the world was made,
by whose blood we are redeemed.
Morning star, the Father's glory,
we now worship and adore you.
In our hearts your light has risen;
Jesus, Lord, we worship you.

17 Darlene Zschech

Almighty God, my redeemer,
my hiding-place, my safe refuge,
no other name like Jesus,
no pow'r can stand against you.
My feet are planted on this rock
and I will not be shaken.
My hope, it comes from you alone,
my Lord, and my salvation.

Your praise is always on my lips,
your word is living in my heart
and I will praise you with a new song,
my soul will bless you, Lord.
You fill my life with greater joy,
yes, I delight myself in you
and I will praise you with a new song,
my soul will bless you, Lord.

When I am weak, you make me strong.
When I'm poor, I know I'm rich,
for in the power of your name
all things are possible,
all things are possible,
all things are possible,
all things are possible.

18 John Newton and John Rees

Amazing grace! How sweet the sound
that saved a wretch like me.
I once was lost, but now I'm found;
was blind, but now I see.

Continued overleaf

'Twas grace that taught my heart to fear,
and grace my fears relieved.
How precious did that grace appear
the hour I first believed.

Through many dangers, toils and snares
I have already come.
'Tis grace that brought me safe thus far,
and grace will lead me home.

The Lord has promised good to me,
his word my hope secures;
he will my shield and portion be
as long as life endures.

Yes, when this heart and flesh shall fail,
and mortal life shall cease,
I shall possess within the veil
a life of joy and peace.

When we've been there a thousand years,
bright shining as the sun,
we've no less days to sing God's praise
than when we first begun.

19 Carol Owen

Among the gods
there is none like you, O Lord, O Lord.
There are no deeds
to compare with yours, O Lord.
All the nations you have made will come;
they'll worship before you, O Lord, O Lord.

*For you are great
and do marvellous deeds.
Yes, you are great
and do marvellous deeds.
You alone are God, you alone are God.*

You are so good
and forgiving, O Lord, O Lord.
You're rich in love
to all who call to you, O Lord.
All the nations you have made will come;
they'll glorify your name, O Lord, O Lord.

Teach me your ways, O Lord,
and I'll walk in your truth.
Give me an undivided heart,
that I may fear your name.

20 Dave Bilbrough

An army of ordinary people,
a kingdom where love is the key,
a city, a light to the nations,
heirs to the promise are we.
A people whose life is in Jesus,
a nation together we stand.
Only through grace are we worthy,
inheritors of the land.

*A new day is dawning,
a new age to come,
when the children of promise
shall flow together as one:
a truth long neglected,
but the time has now come,
when the children of promise
shall flow together as one.*

A people without recognition,
but with him a destiny sealed,
called to a heavenly vision:
his purpose shall be fulfilled.
Come, let us stand strong together,
abandon ourselves to the King.
His love shall be ours for ever,
this victory song shall we sing.

21 Charles Wesley

And can it be that I should gain
an interest in the Saviour's blood?
Died he for me, who caused his pain?
For me, who him to death pursued?
Amazing love! How can it be that thou,
my God, shouldst die for me?

'Tis mystery all! th'Immortal dies:
who can explore his strange design?
In vain the first-born seraph tries
to sound the depths of love divine!
'Tis mercy all! Let earth adore,
let angel minds inquire no more.

He left his Father's throne above
so free, so infinite his grace;
emptied himself of all but love,
and bled for Adam's helpless race;
'tis mercy all, immense and free;
for, O my God, it found out me.

Long my imprisoned spirit lay
fast bound in sin and nature's night;
thine eye diffused a quickening ray,
I woke, the dungeon flamed with light;
my chains fell off, my heart was free;
I rose, went forth, and followed thee.

No condemnation now I dread;
Jesus, and all in him, is mine!
Alive in him, my living Head,
and clothed in righteousness divine,
bold I approach the eternal throne,
and claim the crown, through Christ my own.

22 Graham Kendrick

And he shall reign for ever,
his throne and crown shall ever endure.
And he shall reign for ever,
and we shall reign with him.

What a vision filled my eyes,
one like a Son of man.
Coming with the clouds of heav'n
he approached an awesome throne.

He was given sovereign power,
glory and authority.
Every nation, tribe and tongue
worshipped him on bended knee.

On the throne for ever,
see the Lamb who once was slain;
wounds of sacrificial love
for ever shall remain.

23 Unknown

A new commandment
I give unto you:
that you love one another
as I have loved you,
that you love one another
as I have loved you.
By this shall all know
that you are my disciples
if you have love for one another.
By this shall all know
that you are my disciples
if you have love for one another.

24 Donn Thomas

Anointing, fall on me,
anointing, fall on me;
let the power of the Holy Ghost
fall on me,
anointing, fall on me.

Touch my hands, my mouth and my heart,
fill my life, Lord, every part;
let the power of the Holy Ghost fall on me,
anointing, fall on me.

25 Peter West, Mary Lou Locke and Mary Kirkbride

Ascribe greatness
to our God, the Rock,
his work is perfect
and all his ways are just.
Ascribe greatness
to our God, the Rock,
his work is perfect
and all his ways are just.

A God of faithfulness
and without injustice,
good and upright is he;
a God of faithfulness
and without injustice,
good and upright is he.

26 Dave Billington

As I come into your presence,
past the gates of praise,
into your sanctuary
till we're standing face to face,
I look upon your countenance,
I see the fullness of your grace,
and I can only bow down and say:

> *You are awesome in this place,*
> *mighty God.*
> *You are awesome in this place,*
> *Abba, Father.*
> *You are worthy of all praise,*
> *to you our hands we raise.*
> *You are awesome in this place,*
> *mighty God.*

27 Martin J. Nystrom

As the deer pants for the water,
so my soul longs after you.
You alone are my heart's desire
and I long to worship you.

> *You alone are my strength, my shield,*
> *to you alone may my spirit yield.*
> *You alone are my heart's desire*
> *and I long to worship you.*

I want you more than gold or silver,
only you can satisfy.
You alone are the real joy-giver
and the apple of my eye.

You're my friend and you are my brother,
even though you are a King.
I love you more than any other,
so much more than anything.

28 Richard Lewis

As the deer pants for the water,
so my soul, it thirsts for you,
for you, O God, for you, O God.
(Repeat)

When can I come before you
and see your face?
My heart and my flesh cry out
for the living God, for the living God.

Deep calls to deep
at the thunder of your waterfalls.
Your heart of love
is calling out to me.
By this I know that I am yours
and you are mine.
Your waves of love are breaking over me.
Your waves of love are breaking over me.
Your waves of love are breaking over me.

29 John Daniels

As we are gathered, Jesus is here;
one with each other, Jesus is here;
joined by the Spirit, washed in the blood,
part of the body, the church of God.
As we are gathered, Jesus is here;
one with each other, Jesus is here.

30 Paul Baloche

Leader	As we lift up your name,
All	as we lift up your name,
Leader	let your fire fall,
All	let your fire fall;
Leader	send your wind and your rain,
All	send your wind and your rain,
Leader	on your wings of love,
All	on your wings of love.
	Pour out from heaven
	your passion and presence,
	bring down your burning desire.

> *Revival fire, fall, revival fire, fall,*
> *fall on us here in the pow'r of your Spirit,*
> *Father, let revival fire fall;*
> *revival fire, fall, revival fire, fall,*
> *let the flames consume us*
> *with hearts ablaze for Jesus.*
> *Father, let revival fire fall.*

Leader	As we lift up your name,
All	as we lift up your name,
Leader	let your kingdom come,
All	let your kingdom come;
Leader	have your way in this place,
All	have your way in this place,
Leader	let your will be done,
All	let your will be done.
	Pour out from heaven
	your passion and presence,
	bring down your burning desire.

© 1996 Integrity's Hosanna! Music/Kingsway's Thankyou Music

31 Dave Bilbrough

As we seek your face,
may we know your heart,
feel your presence, acceptance,
as we seek your face.

Move among us now,
come, reveal your pow'r,
show your presence, acceptance,
move among us now.

At your feet we fall,
sovereign Lord,
we cry 'holy, holy',
at your feet we fall.

© 1990 Kingsway's Thankyou Music

32 Derek Bond

At the foot of the cross,
I can hardly take it in,
that the King of all creation
was dying for my sin.
And the pain and agony,
and the thorns that pierced your head,
and the hardness of my sinful heart
that left you there for dead.

And O what mercy I have found,
at the cross of Calvary;
I will never know your loneliness,
all on account of me.

And I will bow my knee before your throne,
'cos your love has set me free;
and I will give my life to you, dear Lord,
and praise your majesty,
and praise your majesty.

© 1992 Sovereign Music UK

33 Caroline Maria Noel

At the name of Jesus
every knee shall bow,
every tongue confess him
King of glory now;
'tis the Father's pleasure
we should call him Lord,
who, from the beginning,
was the mighty Word.

At his voice creation
sprang at once to sight,
all the angel faces,
all the hosts of light,
thrones and dominations,
stars upon their way,
all the heav'nly orders
in their great array.

Humbled for a season,
to receive a name
from the lips of sinners
unto whom he came,
faithfully he bore it,
spotless to the last,
brought it back victorious
when from death he passed.

Bore it up triumphant,
with its human light,
through all ranks of creatures
to the central height,
to the throne of Godhead,
to the Father's breast,
filled it with the glory
of that perfect rest.

Continued overleaf

All creation, name him,
with love as strong as death;
but with awe and wonder,
and with bated breath.
He is God the Saviour,
he is Christ the Lord,
ever to be worshipped,
trusted and adored.

In your hearts enthrone him;
there let him subdue
all that is not holy,
all that is not true;
crown him as your captain
in temptation's hour;
let his will enfold you
in its light and pow'r.

Truly, this Lord Jesus
shall return again,
with his Father's glory,
with his angel train;
for all wreaths of empire
meet upon his brow,
and our hearts confess him
King of glory now.

34 Graham Kendrick

At this time of giving,
gladly now we bring
gifts of goodness and mercy
from a heav'nly King.

Earth could not contain the treasures
heaven holds for you,
perfect joy and lasting pleasures,
love so strong and true.

May his tender love surround you
at this Christmastime;
may you see his smiling face
that in the darkness shines.

But the many gifts he gives
are all poured out from one;
come, receive the greatest gift,
the gift of God's own Son.

Lai, lai, lai . . .

35 David Fellingham

At your feet we fall,
mighty risen Lord,
as we come before your throne
to worship you.
By your Spirit's pow'r
you now draw our hearts,
and we hear your voice
in triumph ringing clear.

I am he that liveth,
that liveth and was dead.
Behold, I am alive for evermore.

There we see you stand,
mighty risen Lord,
clothed in garments pure and holy,
shining bright.
Eyes of flashing fire,
feet like burnished bronze,
and the sound of many waters
is your voice.

Like the shining sun
in its noonday strength,
we now see the glory
of your wondrous face.
Once that face was marred,
but now you're glorified,
and your words like a two-edged sword
have mighty pow'r.

36 William James Kirkpatrick

Away in a manger,
no crib for a bed,
the little Lord Jesus
laid down his sweet head.
The stars in the bright sky
looked down where he lay,
the little Lord Jesus,
asleep on the hay.

The cattle are lowing,
the baby awakes,
but little Lord Jesus
no crying he makes.
I love thee, Lord Jesus!
Look down from the sky,
and stay by my side
until morning is nigh.

Be near me, Lord Jesus;
I ask thee to stay
close by me for ever,
and love me, I pray.
Bless all the dear children
in thy tender care,
and fit us for heaven,
to live with thee there.

37 Graham Kendrick

Beauty for brokenness,
hope for despair,
Lord, in the suffering,
this is our prayer.
Bread for the children,
justice, joy, peace,
sunrise to sunset
your kingdom increase.

Shelter for fragile lives,
cures for their ills,
work for the craftsmen,
trade for their skills.
Land for the dispossessed,
rights for the weak,
voices to plead the cause
of those who can't speak.

God of the poor,
friend of the weak,
give us compassion, we pray,
melt our cold hearts,
let tears fall like rain.
Come, change our love
from a spark to a flame.

Refuge from cruel wars,
havens from fear,
cities for sanctuary,
freedoms to share.
Peace to the killing fields,
scorched earth to green,
Christ for the bitterness,
his cross for the pain.

Rest for the ravaged earth,
oceans and streams,
plundered and poisoned,
our future, our dreams.
Lord, end our madness,
carelessness, greed;
make us content with
the things that we need.

Lighten our darkness,
breathe on this flame,
until your justice
burns brightly again;
until the nations
learn of your ways,
seek your salvation
and bring you their praise.

© 1993 Make Way Music

38 Morris Chapman

Be bold, be strong,
for the Lord, your God, is with you.
Be bold, be strong,
for the Lord, your God, is with you.
I am not afraid, I am not dismayed,
because I'm walking in faith and victory,
come on and walk in faith and victory,
for the Lord, your God, is with you.

© 1983 Word Music/CopyCare

39 Russell Fragar

Because of your love,
everything's changed,
because of your love,
I'll never be the same.
Your love is perfect,
And I'll never be afraid,
because of your love,
everything's changed.
(Repeat)

I have this confidence
that God is on my side.
All of my days are in your hands.
Love so amazing
that it cannot be denied,
that every day I'm in your plan.

40 Russell Fragar

Before the world began
you were on his mind,
and every tear you cry
is precious in his eyes.
Because of his great love,
he gave his only Son;
everything was done,
so you would come.

Nothing you can do
could make him love you more,
and nothing that you've done
could make him close the door.
Because of his great love,
he gave his only Son;
everything was done
so you would come.

Come to the Father
though your gift is small,
broken hearts, broken lives,
he will take them all.
The power of the Word,
the power of his blood,
everything was done
so you would come.

41 Dave Bilbrough

Be free in the love of God,
let his Spirit flow within you.
Be free in the love of God,
let it fill your soul.
Be free in the love of God,
celebrate his name with dancing.
Be free in the love of God;
he has made us whole.

For his purpose he has called us,
in his hands he gently holds us.
He will keep us and sustain us
in the Father's love.

God is gracious, he will lead us
through his pow'r at work within us.
Spirit, guide us, and unite us
in the Father's love.

42 Billy Funk

Be glorified, be glorified.
Be glorified, be glorified.
Be glorified in the heavens,
be glorified in the earth;
be glorified in the temple,
Jesus, Jesus, be thou glorified,
Jesus, Jesus, be thou glorified.

Worship the Lord, worship the Lord.
Worship the Lord, worship the Lord.
Worship the Lord in the heavens,
worship the Lord in the earth;
worship the Lord in the temple,
Jesus, Jesus, be thou glorified,
Jesus, Jesus, be thou glorified.

43 Geoff Baker

Behold his love.
I stand amazed
and marvel at the God of grace:
that the Alpha and Omega,

the Beginning and the End,
the Creator of the universe
on whom all life depends,
should be clothed in frail humanity
and suffer in my place.
Behold his love
and worship him, the God of grace.

44 Noel Richards and Gerald Coates

Behold the Lord upon his throne;
his face is shining like the sun.
With eyes blazing fire, and feet glowing bronze,
his voice like mighty water roars.
Holy, holy, Lord God Almighty.
Holy, holy, we stand in awe of you.

The first, the last, the living One,
laid down his life for all the world.
Behold, he now lives for evermore,
and holds the keys of death and hell.
Holy, holy, Lord God Almighty.
Holy, holy, we bow before your throne.

So let our praises ever ring
to Jesus Christ, our glorious King.
All heaven and earth resound as we cry:
'Worthy is the Son of God!'
Holy, holy, Lord God Almighty.
Holy, holy, we fall down at your feet.

45 Elizabeth C. Clephane

Beneath the cross of Jesus
I fain would take my stand,
the shadow of a mighty rock
within a weary land;
a home within a wilderness,
a rest upon the way,
from burning heat at noontide and
the burden of the day.

O safe and happy shelter!
O refuge tried and sweet!
O trysting place where heaven's love
and heaven's justice meet!
As to the holy patriarch
that wondrous dream was giv'n,
so seems my Saviour's cross to me
a ladder up to heav'n.

There lies, beneath its shadow,
but on the farther side,
the darkness of an awful grave
that gapes both deep and wide;
and there between us stands the cross,
two arms outstretched to save;
a watchman set to guard the way
from that eternal grave.

Upon that cross of Jesus
mine eye at times can see
the very dying form of One
who suffered there for me;
and from my stricken heart, with tears,
two wonders I confess –
the wonders of redeeming love
and my unworthiness.

I take, O cross, thy shadow
for my abiding place!
I ask no other sunshine than
the sunshine of his face;
content to let the world go by,
to reckon gain as loss –
my sinful self, my only shame,
my glory all – the cross.

46 Graham Kendrick

Be patient, be ready,
look up – the Lord is near.
Be faithful, be fruitful,
until the day that he appears.
Though all things are shaken
and hearts are filled with fear,
keep working, keep praying,
until his kingdom is here.

Continued overleaf

Deep in our hearts there's a cry,
as the Spirit and Bride say:
'Come, Jesus, come, take your white horse
and ride through the heavens. Come!'
(Repeat)

47   David J. Evans

Be still, for the presence of the Lord,
the Holy One is here.
Come, bow before him now,
with reverence and fear.
In him no sin is found,
we stand on holy ground.
Be still, for the presence of the Lord,
the Holy One is here.

Be still, for the glory of the Lord
is shining all around;
he burns with holy fire,
with splendour he is crowned.
How awesome is the sight,
our radiant King of light!
Be still, for the glory of the Lord
is shining all around.

Be still, for the power of the Lord
is moving in this place;
he comes to cleanse and heal,
to minister his grace.
No work too hard for him,
in faith receive from him.
Be still, for the power of the Lord
is moving in this place.

48   Unknown

Be still and know that I am God,
be still and know that I am God,
be still and know that I am God.

I am the Lord that healeth thee . . .

In thee, O Lord, do I put my trust . . .

49   Katharina Von Schlegal trans. Jane L. Borthwick

Be still, my soul:
the Lord is on your side;
bear patiently the cross
of grief and pain;
leave to your God
to order and provide;
in every change
he faithful will remain.
Be still, my soul:
your best, your heav'nly friend,
through thorny ways,
leads to a joyful end.

Be still, my soul:
your God will undertake
to guide the future
as he has the past.
Your hope, your confidence
let nothing shake,
all now mysterious
shall be clear at last.
Be still, my soul:
the tempests still obey
his voice, who ruled them
once on Galilee.

Be still, my soul:
the hour is hastening on
when we shall be
for ever with the Lord,
when disappointment,
grief and fear are gone,
sorrow forgotten,
love's pure joy restored.
Be still, my soul:
when change and tears are past,
all safe and blessèd
we shall meet at last.

50 Irish trans. Mary Byrne and Eleanor Hull

Be thou my vision,
O Lord of my heart,
naught be all else to me,
save that thou art;
thou my best thought
in the day and the night,
waking or sleeping,
thy presence my light.

Be thou my wisdom,
be thou my true word,
I ever with thee
and thou with me, Lord;
thou my great Father
and I thy true heir;
thou in me dwelling,
and I in thy care.

Be thou my breastplate,
my sword for the fight,
be thou my armour
and be thou my might,
thou my soul's shelter,
and thou my high tow'r,
raise thou me heav'nward,
O Pow'r of my pow'r.

Riches I need not,
nor all the world's praise,
thou my inheritance
through all my days;
thou, and thou only,
the first in my heart,
high King of heaven,
my treasure thou art!

High King of heaven,
when battle is done,
grant heaven's joys to me,
O bright heav'n's sun;
Christ of my own heart,
whatever befall,
still be my vision,
O Ruler of all.

© Copyright control (revived 1996)

51 Bob Gillman

Bind us together, Lord,
bind us together
with cords that cannot be broken.
Bind us together, Lord,
bind us together,
bind us together with love.

There is only one God.
There is only one King.
There is only one Body.
That is why we sing:

Made for the glory of God,
purchased by his precious Son.
Born with the right to be clean,
for Jesus the victory has won.

You are the family of God.
You are the promise divine.
You are God's chosen desire.
You are the glorious new wine.

© 1977 Kingsway's Thankyou Music

52 Frances Jane van Alstyne

Blessed assurance, Jesus is mine:
O what a foretaste of glory divine!
Heir of salvation, purchase of God;
born of his Spirit, washed in his blood.

This is my story, this is my song,
praising my Saviour all the day long.
This is my story, this is my song,
praising my Saviour all the day long.

Perfect submission, perfect delight,
visions of rapture burst on my sight;
angels descending, bring from above
echoes of mercy, whispers of love.

Perfect submission, all is at rest,
I in my Saviour am happy and blessed;
watching and waiting, looking above,
filled with his goodness, lost in his love.

53 Kevin Prosch and Danny Daniels

Blessed be the name of the Lord.
Blessed be the name of the Lord.
Blessed be the name of the Lord.
Blessed be the name of the Lord.
For he is our Rock, for he is our Rock,
he is the Lord.
For he is our Rock, for he is our Rock,
he is the Lord.

Jesus reigns on high in all the earth.
Jesus reigns on high in all the earth.
Jesus reigns on high in all the earth.
Jesus reigns on high in all the earth.
The universe is in the hands of the Lord.
The universe is in the hands of the Lord.

54 Gary Sadler and Jamie Harvill

Blessing and honour, glory and power
be unto the Ancient of Days;
from every nation, all of creation
bow before the Ancient of Days.

Every tongue in heaven and earth
shall declare your glory,
every knee shall bow at your throne
in worship;
you will be exalted, O God,
and your kingdom shall not pass away,
O Ancient of Days.

Your kingdom shall reign over all the earth:
sing unto the Ancient of Days.
For none shall compare to your matchless worth:
sing unto the Ancient of Days.

55 Geoff Bullock and Dave Reidy

Blessing, honour, glory to the Lamb.
Holy, righteous, worthy is the Lamb.
Blessing, honour, glory to the Lamb.
Holy, righteous, worthy is the Lamb.

Death could not hold him down
for he is risen.
Seated upon the throne
he is the Lamb of God.

56 Taizé Community

Bless the Lord, my soul,
and bless God's holy name.
Bless the Lord, my soul,
who leads me into life.

57 Edwin Hatch

Breathe on me, Breath of God,
fill me with life anew,
that I may love what thou dost love,
and do what thou wouldst do.

Breathe on me, Breath of God,
until my heart is pure:
until with thee I have one will
to do and to endure.

Breathe on me, Breath of God,
till I am wholly thine,
until this earthly part of me
glows with thy fire divine.

Breathe on me, Breath of God,
so shall I never die,
but live with thee the perfect life
of thine eternity.

58 Janet Lunt

Broken for me, broken for you,
the body of Jesus, broken for you.

He offered his body, he poured out his soul;
Jesus was broken, that we might be whole.

Come to my table and with me dine;
eat of my bread and drink of my wine.

This is my body given for you;
eat it remembering I died for you.

This is my blood I shed for you,
for your forgiveness, making you new.

59   Steven Fry

By his grace I am redeemed,
by his blood I am made clean,
and I now can know him face to face.
By his pow'r I have been raised,
hidden now in Christ by faith.
I will praise the glory of his grace.

60   Noel and Tricia Richards

By your side I would stay;
in your arms I would lay.
Jesus, lover of my soul,
nothing from you I withhold.

Lord, I love you, and adore you;
what more can I say?
You cause my love to grow stronger
with every passing day.
(Repeat)

61   Noel and Tricia Richards

Called to a battle, heavenly war;
though we may struggle, victory is sure.
Death will not triumph, though we may die;
Jesus has promised our eternal life.

By the blood of the Lamb
we shall overcome,
see the accuser thrown down.
By the word of the Lord
we shall overcome,
raise a victory cry,
like thunder in the skies,
thunder in the skies.

Standing together, moving as one;
we are God's army, called to overcome.
We are commissioned, Jesus says go;
in every nation, let his love be known.

62   Matt Redman

Can a nation be changed?
Can a nation be saved?
Can a nation be turned back to you?
(Repeat)

We're on our knees,
we're on our knees again.
We're on our knees,
we're on our knees again.

Let this nation be changed,
let this nation be saved,
let this nation be turned back to you.
(Repeat)

63   Matt Redman

Can I ascend the hill of the Lord?
Can I stand in that holy place?
There to approach the glory of my God;
come towards to seek your face.
Purify my heart,
and purify my hands,
for I know it is on holy ground I'll stand.

I'm coming up the mountain, Lord;
I'm seeking you and you alone.
I know that I will be transformed,
my heart unveiled before you.
I'm longing for your presence, Lord;
envelop me within the cloud.
I'm coming up the mountain, Lord,
my heart unveiled before you, I will come.

I'm coming to worship,
I'm coming to bow down,
I'm coming to meet with you.

64 Matt Redman

Can we walk upon the water
if our eyes are fixed on you?
There's an air of faith within us
for a time of breaking through.
Can we fly a little higher,
can we soar on eagle's wings?
Come and fan the flames of fire
that are flickering within.

Lead us to the promised land,
all that's purposed, all that's planned;
give us eyes of faith again.
Take us on to higher ground
and the greater things to come –
where the eagles soar,
and where we're finding more of you.

Can we walk into the promise
of abundance in the land?
Take us on, beyond the river,
for the harvest you have planned:
let us see your kingdom coming
in a measure we've not seen.
There has been a time of sowing,
could this be a time to reap?

And can we sing the songs of heaven
while we're standing on the earth:
sing within the coming kingdom,
sing and live and breathe and move?

Can we fly a little higher,
can we fly a little higher,
can we fly a little higher,
can we fly a little higher?

© 1996 Kingsway's Thankyou Music

65 Graham Kendrick

Can you see what we have made
for this very special day?
An orange for our planet home,
circling around the sun.

Count the seasons as we sing,
summer, autumn, winter, spring.
Sing to God who sends the rain,
making all things new again.

Candlelight, burning bright,
chase the darkness of the night.
Christ the light, light our way,
live inside our hearts today.

See the food with colours bright,
tastebuds tingle at the sight.
Let's be thankful as we share,
God's good gifts are everywhere.

Why then is the world we made,
wrapped around with ribbon red?
Red is for the ransom paid,
when our Lord was crucified.

There's a world I'm dreaming of,
where there's peace and joy and love.
Light of Jesus everywhere,
this is my Christingle prayer.

© 1997 Make Way Music

66 Graham Kendrick

Celebrate, celebrate, celebrate,
O celebrate Jesus.

Leader	From the far corners of earth we hear music.
All	O celebrate.
Leader	Echoing over the land and sea.
All	O celebrate.
Leader	Sound of the drums awakes a new morning.
All	O celebrate.
Leader	Calling our feet to the rhythms of praise.
All	O celebrate Jesus.
Leader	Out of the West come shouts of rejoicing.
All	O celebrate.
Leader	Out of the East a loud reply.
All	O celebrate.
Leader	Over the nations a voice is calling.
All	O celebrate.

Leader	Worship the maker
	of earth and sky.
All	O celebrate Jesus.

Leader	We have millions of reasons
	to celebrate Jesus;
	and I'll sing you seven
	if you count from one.
	Everybody count:
All	One!
Leader	He gave up the glory of heaven.
All	Two!
Leader	Humbly became one of us.
All	Three!
Leader	Show us the love of the Father.
All	Four!
Leader	Paid for our sins on a cross.
All	Five!
Leader	Rose from the dead victorious.
All	Six!
Leader	Ascended to heaven's throne.
All	Seven!
Leader	Poured out his Spirit upon us.
All	O celebrate Jesus.

67 Gary Oliver

Celebrate Jesus, celebrate!
Celebrate Jesus, celebrate!
Celebrate Jesus, celebrate!
Celebrate Jesus, celebrate!

He is risen, he is risen,
and he lives for evermore.
He is risen, he is risen,
come on and celebrate
the resurrection of our Lord.

68 Eddie Espinosa

Change my heart, O God,
make it ever true;
change my heart, O God,
make I be like you.

You are the potter,
I am the clay;
mould me and make me:
this is what I pray.

69 Sue McClellan, John Paculabo and Keith Ryecroft

Colours of day
dawn into the mind,
the sun has come up,
the night is behind.
Go down in the city,
into the street,
and let's give the message
to the people we meet.

So light up the fire
and let the flame burn,
open the door,
let Jesus return.
Take seeds of his Spirit,
let the fruit grow,
tell the people of Jesus,
let his love show.

Go through the park,
on into the town;
the sun still shines on;
it never goes down.
The light of the world
is risen again;
the people of darkness
are needing a friend.

Open your eyes,
look into the sky,
the darkness has come,
the sun came to die.
The evening draws on,
the sun disappears,
but Jesus is living,
his Spirit is near.

70 Graham Kendrick

Come and see, come and see,
come and see the King of love;
see the purple robe
and crown of thorns he wears.
Soldiers mock, rulers sneer
as he lifts the cruel cross;
lone and friendless now,
he climbs towards the hill.

We worship at your feet,
where wrath and mercy meet,
and a guilty world
is washed by love's pure stream.
For us he was made sin –
oh, help me take it in.
Deep wounds of love
cry out 'Father, forgive.'
I worship, I worship
the Lamb who was slain.

Come and weep, come and mourn
for your sin that pierced him there;
so much deeper
than the wounds of thorn and nail.
All our pride, all our greed,
all our fallenness and shame;
and the Lord has laid
the punishment on him.

Man of heaven, born to earth
to restore us to your heaven.
Here we bow in awe
beneath your searching eyes.
From your tears comes our joy,
from your death our life shall spring;
by your resurrection power
we shall rise.

© 1989 Make Way Music

71 Bianco da Siena trans. Richard F. Littledale

Come down, O Love divine,
seek thou this soul of mine,
and visit it with
thine own ardour glowing;

O Comforter, draw near,
within my heart appear,
and kindle it,
thy holy flame bestowing.

O let it freely burn,
till earthly passions turn
to dust and ashes
in its heat consuming;
and let thy glorious light
shine ever on my sight,
and clothe me round,
the while my path illuming.

Let holy charity
mine outward vesture be,
and lowliness become
mine inner clothing;
true lowliness of heart,
which takes the humbler part,
and o'er its own shortcomings
weeps with loathing.

And so the yearning strong,
with which the soul will long,
shall far outpass
the pow'r of human telling;
nor can we guess its grace,
till we become the place
wherein the Holy Spirit
makes his dwelling.

72 Graham Kendrick

(Leader)
Come, let us return to the Lord;
come, let us return to the Lord;
come, let us return to the Lord,
let us return to the Lord.

As surely as the sun rises,
he will appear, he will appear;
he will come to us like winter rains
and like the spring rains that water the earth.

Come, let us return to the Lord;
come, let us return to the Lord;
come, let us return to the Lord,
let us return to the Lord.

Though he tore us, he will heal us;
though he tore us, he will heal us;
let us return to the Lord.

Come, let us press on to know him,
walk in his ways, walk in his ways,
that we may live in his presence
all of our days, all of our days.

Seek him, find him, know him, love him;
seek him, find him, know him, love him;
let us return to the Lord.

© 1996 Make Way Music

73 Graham Kendrick

Come, let us worship Jesus,
King of nations, Lord of all.
Magnificent and glorious,
just and merciful.

*Jesus, King of the nations,
Jesus, Lord of all.
Jesus, King of the nations,
Lord of all!*

Lavish our heart's affection,
deepest love and highest praise.
Voice, race and language blending,
all the world amazed.

Bring tributes from the nations,
come in joyful cavalcades.
One thunderous acclamation,
one banner raised.

Come, Lord, and fill your temple,
glorify your dwelling-place,
till nations see your splendour
and seek your face.

Fear God and give him glory,
for his hour of judgement comes.
Creator, Lord Almighty,
worship him alone.

© 1992 Make Way Music

74 Martin Smith

*Come on, all us singers, sing
that Jesus Christ is Lord.
Come on, all us singers, sing
that Jesus Christ is Lord.
(Repeat)*

As your people, Lord,
we now stand before your throne.
A sacrifice of praise will be our song.
As your singers, Lord,
we will shout that 'he is good,
for his love endures for ever'.

Come on, all us singers, sing . . .

As your people, Lord,
we will sing with thankfulness.
We want our lives to be a song of praise.
Banners we will wave
to proclaim that 'he is good,
for his love endures for ever'.

*Come on, all us dancers, dance
that Jesus Christ is Lord.
Come on, all us dancers, dance
that Jesus Christ is Lord.
(Repeat)*

Help us, Lord, to realise
that our lips were made for praising you,
not for bringing others down,
but for boasting of your love.
Show us, Lord, that when we meet,
we have our feet on holy ground.
Come and purify our lives,
forgive us for the wrong we've done.
We desire to see your face
but teach us first to fear the Lord.
Let us not presume your grace
for the sin we bring is our disgrace.
In your mercy send your pow'r,
demons go in Jesus' name.
Heal the sick and save the lost,
reveal the power of the cross.

Continued overleaf

Open up the heavens, Lord,
open up the heavens, Lord.
Open up the heavens, Lord,
let us sing the song that Jesus saves us.

75 Patricia Morgan and Dave Bankhead

Come on and celebrate
his gift of love, we will celebrate
the Son of God who loved us
and gave us life.
We'll shout your praise, O King,
you give us joy nothing else can bring,
we'll give to you our offering
in celebration praise.

Come on and celebrate, celebrate,
celebrate and sing,
celebrate and sing to the King.
Come on and celebrate, celebrate,
celebrate and sing,
celebrate and sing to the King.

76 Elizabeth Bourbourze

Come, Spirit, come.
Come, holy wind,
blow through the temple of my life.
O come, Spirit, come,
all-pow'rful wind,
all-loving breeze and breath of life.
Breathe upon me, breathe upon me, Spirit.
Breathe upon me, blow, O wind of Spirit.
Breathe upon me, blow, O wind of God.

Come, Spirit, come.
Come, holy rain,
fall on the dry ground of my life.
O come, Spirit, come,
O mighty flood,
O loving stream and source of life.
Flow over me, flow over me, Spirit.
Flow over me, flow over me, Spirit.
Flow over me, flow, O rain of God.

Come, Spirit, come.
Come, holy fire,
consume the offering of my life.
O come, Spirit, come,
O blazing fire,
O burning love and flame of life.
Burn in my heart, burn in my heart, Spirit.
Burn in my heart, burn in my heart, Spirit.
Burn in my heart, burn, O fire of God.

77 Matthew Bridges

Crown him with many crowns,
the Lamb upon his throne;
hark, how the heav'nly anthem drowns
all music but its own:
awake, my soul, and sing
of him who died for thee,
and hail him as thy matchless King
through all eternity.

Crown him the Lord of life,
who triumphed o'er the grave,
and rose victorious in the strife
for those he came to save.
His glories now we sing,
who died and rose on high;
who died eternal life to bring,
and lives that death may die.

Crown him the Lord of love;
behold his hands and side,
rich wounds, yet visible above,
in beauty glorified:
no angel in the sky
can fully bear that sight,
but downward bends each burning eye
at mysteries so bright.

Crown him the Lord of peace,
whose pow'r a sceptre sways
from pole to pole, that wars may cease,
and all be prayer and praise:
his reign shall know no end,
and round his piercèd feet
fair flow'rs of paradise extend
their fragrance ever sweet.

Crown him the Lord of years,
the Potentate of time,
Creator of the rolling spheres,
ineffably sublime.
All hail, Redeemer, hail!
for thou hast died for me;
thy praise shall never, never fail
throughout eternity.

78 David Fellingham

Day of favour, day of grace;
this is the day of jubilee.
The Spirit of the sovereign Lord
is falling now on me.
Let the oil of heaven flow
from the presence of the King.
Jesus, let your power flow
as we worship, as we sing.
Set us free to make you known
to a world that's full of shame.
Jesus, let your glory fall,
give us pow'r to speak your name.

Day of favour, day of grace;
this is the day of jubilee.
The Spirit of the sovereign Lord
is falling now on me.
Open wide the prison doors,
where Satan's held the key.
Bring deliverance to the bound,
and set the captives free.
Bring the good news to the poor,
and cause the blind to see.
The Spirit of the Lord
is falling now on me.

79 John Greenleaf Whittier

Dear Lord and Father of mankind,
forgive our foolish ways!
Reclothe us in our rightful mind,
in purer lives thy service find,
in deeper reverence praise,
in deeper reverence praise.

In simple trust like theirs who heard,
beside the Syrian sea,
the gracious calling of the Lord,
let us, like them, without a word,
rise up and follow thee,
rise up and follow thee.

O Sabbath rest by Galilee!
O calm of hills above,
where Jesus knelt to share with thee
the silence of eternity,
interpreted by love,
interpreted by love!

Drop thy still dews of quietness,
till all our strivings cease;
take from our souls the strain and stress,
and let our ordered lives confess
the beauty of thy peace,
the beauty of thy peace.

Breathe through the heats of our desire
thy coolness and thy balm;
let sense be dumb, let flesh retire;
speak through the earthquake, wind and fire,
O still small voice of calm,
O still small voice of calm!

80 Martin Smith

Did you feel the mountains tremble?
Did you hear the oceans roar,
when the people rose to sing of
Jesus Christ, the risen one?

Did you feel the people tremble?
Did you hear the singers roar,
when the lost began to sing of
Jesus Christ, the saving one?

And we can see that God, you're moving,
a mighty river through the nations.
And young and old will turn to Jesus.
Fling wide, you heavenly gates,
prepare the way of the risen Lord.

Continued overleaf

Open up the doors and let the music play;
let the streets resound with singing.
Songs that bring your hope,
songs that bring your joy,
dancers who dance upon injustice.

Do you feel the darkness tremble,
when all the saints join in one song,
and all the streams flow as one river,
to wash away our brokenness?

And we can see that God, you're moving,
a time of jubilee is coming,
when young and old will turn to Jesus.
Fling wide, you heavenly gates,
prepare the way of the risen Lord.

81   Brian Doerksen

Don't let my love grow cold,
I'm calling out,
light the fire again.
Don't let my vision die,
I'm calling out,
light the fire again.

You know my heart, my deeds,
I'm calling out,
light the fire again.
I need your discipline,
I'm calling out,
light the fire again.

I am here to buy gold,
refined in the fire;
naked and poor,
wretched and blind,
I come.
Clothe me in white,
so I won't be ashamed:
Lord, light the fire again.

82   Chris Bowater

Do something new, Lord,
in my heart, make a start;
do something new, Lord,
do something new.

I open up my heart,
as much as can be known;
I open up my will
to conform to yours alone.

I lay before your feet
all my hopes and desires;
unreservedly submit
to what your Spirit may require.

I only want to live
for your pleasure now;
I long to please you, Father –
will you show me how?

83   Andy Park

Down the mountain the river flows,
and it brings refreshing wherever it goes.
Through the valleys and over the fields,
the river is rushing and the river is here.

> *The river of God sets our feet a-dancing,*
> *the river of God fills our hearts with cheer;*
> *the river of God fills our mouths with laughter,*
> *and we rejoice for the river is here.*

The river of God is teeming with life,
and all who touch it can be revived.
And those who linger on this river's shore
will come back thirsting for more of the Lord.

Up to the mountain we love to go
to find the presence of the Lord.
Along the banks of the river we run,
we dance with laughter, giving praise to
the Son.

84 Stuart Devane and Glenn Gore

Draw me closer, Lord;
draw me closer, dear Lord,
so that I might touch you,
so that I might touch you,
Lord, I want to touch you.

Touch my eyes, Lord;
touch my eyes, dear Lord,
so that I might see you,
so that I might see you,
Lord, I want to see you.

Your glory and your love,
your glory and your love,
your glory and your love,
and your majesty.

© Mercy/Vineyard Publishing/Music Services/CopyCare

85 Graham Kendrick

Earth lies spellbound in darkness,
sin's oppressive night;
yet in Bethlehem hope is burning bright.
Mysteries are unfolding,
but the only sign is a manger bed
where a baby cries.

Wake up, wake up, it's Christmas morning,
Christ's eternal day is dawning.
Angels sing in exultation,
fill the streets with celebration.
Now to God on high be glory,
to the earth proclaim the story.
Ring the bells in jubilation,
tell the news to every nation:
Christ has come! Christ has come!

Crowding stairways of starlight,
choirs of angels sing:
'Glory, glory to God in the highest heav'n.'
Peace is stilling the violence,
hope is rising high, God is watching us now
through a baby's eyes.

Weakness shatters the pow'rful,
meekness shames the proud,
vain imaginings come tumbling down.
Ancient mercies remembered,
hungry satisfied, lowly, humble hearts
are lifted high.

© 1994 Make Way Music

86 Russell Fragar

Every nation, pow'r and tongue
will bow down to your name;
every eye will see, every ear will hear
your name proclaimed.
This is gonna be our cry
until you come again.
Jesus is the only name
by which man can be saved.

All over the world people just like us
are calling your name,
living in your love;
all over the world people just like us
are calling on Jesus.
All over the world people just like us
are calling your name,
living in your love;
all over the world people just like us
are following Jesus.

(Last time)
We're worshipping Jesus,
we're following Jesus,
we're worshipping Jesus,
we're calling on Jesus.

Makes you wanna dance,
makes you wanna sing,
makes you wanna shout all about it,
shout all about it, shout it
that Jesus is King.

© Russell Fragar/Hillsongs Australia/Kingsway's Thankyou Music

87 Mike and Claire McIntosh

Exalt the Lord
who is clothed in majesty,
holy is he.
Exalt the Lord
who has girded himself with strength,
holy is he.
(Repeat)

Rise up, O soul,
and praise him joyfully,
rise up, O heart,
and praise his name.
(Repeat)

88 Chris Bowater

Faithful God, faithful God,
all-sufficient one, I worship you.
Shalom my peace,
my strong deliverer,
I lift you up,
faithful God.

89 Brian Doerksen

Faithful One, so unchanging,
Ageless One, you're my rock of peace.
Lord of all, I depend on you,
I call out to you again and again,
I call out to you again and again.

You are my rock in times of trouble,
you lift me up when I fall down.
All through the storm your love is the anchor,
my hope is in you alone.

90 Graham Kendrick

Far and near hear the call,
worship him, Lord of all;
families of nations, come,
celebrate what God has done.

Deep and wide is the love
heaven sent from above;
God's own Son, for sinners died,
rose again – he is alive.

Say it loud, say it strong,
tell the world what God has done;
say it loud, praise his name,
let the earth rejoice –
for the Lord reigns.

At his name, let praise begin;
oceans roar, nature sing,
for he comes to judge the earth
in righteousness and in his truth.

91 Ian Smale

Father God, I wonder
how I managed to exist
without the knowledge of your parenthood
and your loving care.
But now I am your child,
I am adopted in your family
and I can never be alone
'cause, Father God, you're there beside me.

I will sing your praises,
I will sing your praises,
I will sing your praises,
for evermore.
I will sing your praises,
I will sing your praises,
I will sing your praises,
for evermore.

92 Graham Kendrick

Father God, we worship you,
make us part of all you do.
As you move among us now,
we worship you.

Jesus King, we worship you,
help us listen now to you.
As you move among us now,
we worship you.

Spirit pure, we worship you,
with your fire our zeal renew.
As you move among us now,
we worship you.

93 Andy Piercy

Father, hear our prayer,
that our lives may be
consecrated only unto you.
Cleanse us with your fire,
fill us with your pow'r,
that the world may glorify your name.

Lord, have mercy on us.
Christ, have mercy on us.
Lord, have mercy on us.

94 Danny Daniels

Father, here I am again,
in need of mercy, hurt from sin,
so by the blood of Jesus' love,
let forgiveness flow.

In my heart and in my mind,
in word and deed I've been so blind,
so by the blood of Jesus' love,
let forgiveness flow.

To me, from me,
so my heart will know;
fully and sweetly,
let forgiveness flow.

95 John Barnett

Father, I come to you,
lifting up my hands
in the name of Jesus,
by your grace I stand.
Just because you love me
and I love your Son,
I know your favour,
unending love.

> *Unending love,*
> *your unending love.*

I receive your favour,
your unending love,
not because I've earned it,
not for what I've done,
just because you love me
and I love your Son,
I know your favour,
unending love.

It's the presence of your kingdom
as your glory fills this place,
and I see how much you love me
as I look into your face.
Nothing could be better,
there's nothing I would trade
for your favour,
unending love.

96 Bob Fitts

Father in heaven, how we love you,
we lift your name in all the earth.
May your kingdom be established in our
    praises
as your people declare your mighty works.
Blessèd be the Lord God Almighty,
who was and is and is to come.
Blessèd be the Lord God Almighty,
who reigns for evermore.

97 Jenny Hewer

Father, I place into your hands
the things I cannot do.
Father, I place into your hands
the things that I've been through.
Father, I place into your hands
the way that I should go,
for I know I always can trust you.

Father, I place into your hands
my friends and family.
Father, I place into your hands
the things that trouble me.
Father, I place into your hands
the person I would be,
for I know I always can trust you.

Father, we love to see your face,
we love to hear your voice.
Father, we love to sing your praise
and in your name rejoice.
Father, we love to walk with you
and in your presence rest,
for we know we always can trust you.

Father, I want to be with you
and do the things you do.
Father, I want to speak the words
that you are speaking too.
Father, I want to love the ones
that you will draw to you,
for I know that I am one with you.

98 Brian Doerksen

Father, I want you to hold me,
I want to rest in your arms today.
Father, I want you to show me,
how much you care for me
in every way.
I bring all my cares
and I lay them at your feet.
You are always there,
and you love me as I am,
yes, you love me as I am.

Father, I know you will hold me,
I know I am your child, your own.
Father, I know you will show me,
I feel your arms holding me,
I'm not alone.
I bring all my fears
and I lay them at your feet.
You are always here,
and you love me as I am,
yes, you love me as I am.

99 David Ruis

Father of creation,
unfold your sovereign plan.
Raise up a chosen generation
that will march through the land.
All of creation is longing
for your unveiling of pow'r.
Would you release your anointing,
O God, let this be the hour.

> Let your glory fall in this room,
> let it go forth from here to the nations.
> Let your fragrance rest in this place,
> as we gather to seek your face.

Ruler of the nations,
the world has yet to see
the full release of your promise,
the church in victory.
Turn to us, Lord, and touch us,
make us strong in your might.
Overcome our weakness,
that we could stand up and fight.

Men	Let your kingdom come.
Women	Let your kingdom come.
Men	Let your will be done.
Women	Let your will be done.
Men	Let us see on earth,
Women	let us see on earth
All	the glory of your Son.

100 Darlene Zschech

Father of life, draw me closer,
Lord, my heart is set on you;
let me run the race of time
with your life enfolding mine
and let the peace of God, let it reign.

O Holy Spirit, Lord, my comfort,
strengthen me, hold my head up high;
and I'll stand upon your truth,
bringing glory unto you,
and let the peace of God, let it reign.

O Lord, I hunger for more of you,
rise up within me,
let me know your truth.
O Holy Spirit, saturate my soul,
and let the life of God
fill me now, let your healing pow'r
bring life and make me whole
and let the peace of God, let it reign

101 Philip Lawson Johnston

Father, we adore you,
we are your children gathered here;
to be with you is our delight,
a feast beyond compare.

Father, in your presence
there is such freedom to enjoy.
We find in you a lasting peace
that nothing can destroy.

You are the fountain of life,
you are the fountain of life,
and as we drink,
we are more than satisfied by you,
O Fountain of Life.

102 Carl Tuttle

Father, we adore you,
you've drawn us to this place.
We bow down before you,
humbly on our face.

All the earth shall worship
at the throne of the King.
Of his great and awesome pow'r
we shall sing!
(Repeat)

Jesus, we love you,
because you first loved us,
you reached out and healed us
with your mighty touch.

Spirit, we need you,
to lift us from this mire,
consumer and empower us
with your holy fire.

Holy is he;
blessed is he;
worthy is he;
gracious is he;
faithful is he;
awesome is he;
Saviour is he;
Master is he;
mighty is he.
Have mercy on me.

103 Donna Adkins

Father, we love you,
we worship and adore you,
glorify your name in all the earth.
Glorify your name,
glorify your name,
glorify your name in all the earth.

Jesus, we love you . . .

Spirit, we love you . . .

104 Andy Park

Father, you are my portion in this life,
and you are my hope and my delight,
and I love you, yes, I love you.
Lord, I love you, my delight.

Jesus, you are my treasure in this life,
and you are so pure and so kind,
and I love you, yes, I love you,
Lord, I love you, my delight.

© Mercy/Vineyard Publishing/Music Services/CopyCare

105 Noel and Tricia Richards

Filled with compassion for all creation,
Jesus came into a world that was lost.
There was but one way that he could save us,
only through suffering death on a cross.

God, you are waiting, your heart is breaking
for all the people who live on the earth.
Stir us to action, filled with your passion
for all the people who live on the earth.

Great is your passion for all the people
living and dying without knowing you.
Having no saviour, they're lost for ever,
if we don't speak out and lead them to you.

From every nation we shall be gathered,
millions redeemed shall be Jesus' reward.
Then he will turn and say to his Father:
'Truly my suffering was worth it all.'

© 1994 Kingsway's Thankyou Music

106 Paul Oakley

Fire, there's a fire,
sweet fire burning in my heart.
(Repeat)

And I will run
with all of the passion you've put in me.
I will spread
the seed of the gospel everywhere.

And I can feel
the power of your hand upon me.
Now I know
I'll never be the same again.
For as long as you will give me breath,
my heart is so resolved,
O, to lay my life before you, Lord.
Let everything I do
be to your praise.

Let me feel your tongues of fire
resting upon me,
let me hear the sound
of your mighty rushing wind.
Let my life be like an offering of worship,
let me be a living sacrifice of praise.

© 1995 Kingsway's Thankyou Music

107 Ian Smale

5 0 0 0 + hungry folk,
5 0 0 0 + hungry folk,
5 0 0 0 + hungry folk
came 4 2 listen 2 Jesus.

The 6 x 2 said 0 0 0,
the 6 x 2 said 0 0 0,
the 6 x 2 said 0 0 0,
where can I get some food from?

Just 1 had 1 2 3 4 5,
just 1 had 1 2 3 4 5,
just 1 had 1 2 3 4 5
loaves and 1 2 fishes.

When Jesus blessed the 5 + 2,
when Jesus blessed the 5 + 2,
when Jesus blessed the 5 + 2
they were increased many x over.

5 0 0 0 + 8 it up,
5 0 0 0 + 8 it up,
5 0 0 0 + 8 it up,
with 1 2 3 4 5 6 7 8 9 10 11 12
basketfuls left over.

© 1985 Kingsway's Thankyou Music

108 Dennis Jernigan

For all that you've done
I will thank you.
For all that you're going to do.
For all that you've promised,
and all that you are
is all that has carried me through.
Jesus, I thank you.
And I thank you, thank you, Lord.
Thank you, thank you, Lord.

Thank you for loving and setting me free.
Thank you for giving your life just for me.
How I thank you.
Jesus, I thank you, gratefully thank you,
thank you.

109 Dave Richards

For I'm building a people of power
and I'm making a people of praise,
that will move through this land by my Spirit,
and will glorify my precious name.
Build your church, Lord,
make us strong, Lord,
join our hearts, Lord,
through your Son.
Make us one, Lord, in your body,
in the kingdom of your Son.

110 Graham Kendrick

For the joys and for the sorrows,
the best and worst of times,
for this moment, for tomorrow,
for all that lies behind;
fears that crowd around me,
for the failure of my plans,
for the dreams of all I hope to be,
the truth of what I am:

For this I have Jesus,
for this I have Jesus,
for this I have Jesus,
I have Jesus.

For the tears that flow in secret,
in the broken times,
for the moments of elation,
or the troubled mind;
for all the disappointments,
or the sting of old regrets,
all my prayers and longings,
that seem unanswered yet:

For the weakness of my body,
the burdens of each day,
for the nights of doubt and worry
when sleep has fled away;
needing reassurance
and the will to start again,
a steely-eyed endurance,
the strength to fight and win:

111 Graham Kendrick

For this purpose Christ was revealed
to destroy all the works of the evil one.
Christ in us has overcome,
so with gladness we sing
and welcome his kingdom in.

Over sin he has conquered,
hallelujah, he has conquered.
Over death victorious,
hallelujah, victorious.
Over sickness he has triumphed,
hallelujah, he has triumphed,
Jesus reigns over all!

In the name of Jesus we stand,
by the power of his blood we now claim
     this ground.
Satan has no authority here,
powers of darkness must flee,
for Christ has the victory.

112 Pete Sanchez Jnr

For thou, O Lord,
art high above all the earth.
Thou art exalted far above all gods.
For thou, O Lord,
art high above all the earth.
Thou art exalted far above all gods.

I exalt thee, I exalt thee,
I exalt thee, O Lord.
I exalt thee, I exalt thee,
I exalt thee, O Lord.

© 1977 Pete Sanchez Jnr/Gabriel Music Inc.

113 David Hadden

For unto us a child is born,
unto us a son is giv'n,
and the government shall be upon his shoulders.
(Repeat)

> And he will be called wonderful,
> wonderful Counsellor, mighty God,
> the everlasting Father,
> Prince of Peace, mighty God.

And there shall be no end
to the increase of his rule,
to the increase of his government and peace.
For he shall sit on David's throne
upholding righteousness.
Our God shall accomplish this.

For he is the mighty God,
he is the Prince of Peace,
the King of kings and Lord of lords.
All honour to the King,
all glory to his name,
for now and evermore.

© 1984 Restoration Music/Sovereign Music UK

114 Graham Kendrick

From heav'n you came, helpless babe,
entered our world, your glory veiled;
not to be served but to serve,
and give your life that we might live.

This is our God, the Servant King,
he calls us now to follow him,
to bring our lives as a daily offering
of worship to the Servant King.

There in the garden of tears,
my heavy load he chose to bear;
his heart with sorrow was torn.
'Yet not my will but yours,' he said.

Come, see his hands and his feet,
the scars that speak of sacrifice,
hands that flung stars into space,
to cruel nails surrendered.

So let us learn how to serve,
and in our lives enthrone him;
each other's needs to prefer,
for it is Christ we're serving.

© 1983 Kingsway's Thankyou Music

115 Don Harris and Gary Sadler

From the ends of the earth
(from the ends of the earth),
from the depths of the sea
(from the depths of the sea),
from the heights of the heavens
(from the heights of the heavens)
your name be praised;
from the hearts of the weak
(from the hearts of the weak),
from the shouts of the strong
(from the shouts of the strong),
from the lips of all people
(from the lips of all people),
this song we raise, Lord.

> *Throughout the endless ages*
> *you will be crowned with praises,*
> *Lord most high;*
> *exalted in every nation,*
> *sovereign of all creation,*
> *Lord most high, be magnified.*

© 1996 Integrity's Hosanna! Music/Kingsway's Thankyou Music

116 Graham Kendrick

From the sun's rising
unto the sun's setting,
Jesus our Lord
shall be great in the earth;
and all earth's kingdoms
shall be his dominion,
all of creation
shall sing of his worth.

Let every heart, every voice,
every tongue join with spirits ablaze;
one in his love, we will circle the world
with the song of his praise.
O, let all his people rejoice,
and let all the earth hear his voice!

To every tongue, tribe
and nation he sends us,
to make disciples
to teach and baptise.
For all authority
to him is given;
now as his witnesses
we shall arise.

Come, let us join with
the church from all nations,
cross every border,
throw wide every door;
workers with him
as he gathers his harvest,
till earth's far corners
our Saviour adore.

© 1988 Make Way Music

117 Graham Kendrick

From where the sun rises,
even to the place it goes down –
we're giving you praise,
giving you praise.
From sun-kissed islands
and even where the cold wind blows –
we're giving you praise,
giving you praise.

Even in the night when the sun goes down,
we're giving you praise;
passing it along as the world goes round,
we're giving you praise.

We're lifting our faces,
looking at the One we all love –
we're giving you praise,
giving you praise.
All colours and races
joining with the angels above –
we're giving you praise,
giving you praise.

© 1996 Make Way Music

118 Henry Smith

Give thanks with a grateful heart.
Give thanks to the Holy One.
Give thanks because he's given
Jesus Christ, his Son.
Give thanks with a grateful heart.
Give thanks to the Holy One.
Give thanks because he's given
Jesus Christ, his Son.

And now let the weak say, 'I am strong',
let the poor say, 'I am rich',
because of what the Lord has done for us.
And now let the weak say, 'I am strong',
let the poor say, 'I am rich',
because of what the Lord has done for us.

© 1978 Integrity's Hosannal Music/Kingsway's Thankyou Music

119 Taizé Community

Gloria, gloria in excelsis Deo!
Gloria, gloria, alleluia, alleluia.

© Ateliers et Presses de Taizé

120 Danny Daniels

Glory, glory in the highest;
glory to the Almighty;
glory to the Lamb of God,
and glory to the living Word;
glory to the Lamb!
(Repeat)

Continued overleaf

I give glory (glory),
glory (glory),
glory, glory to the Lamb!
I give glory (glory),
glory (glory),
glory, glory to the Lamb!
I give glory to the Lamb!

121 Geoff Bullock

Glory to the King of kings!
Majesty, pow'r and strength
to the Lord of lords!
(Repeat)

Holy One, all creation crowns you
King of kings.
Holy One, King of kings,
Lord of lords, Holy One.

Jesus, Lord, with eyes unveiled
we will see your throne.
Jesus, Prince of Peace,
Son of God, Emmanuel.

122 Graham Kendrick

God, be gracious and bless us
and make your face shine on us:
let your ways be known,
your salvation shown
all over the earth;
let your ways be known,
your salvation shown
all over the earth.

May the peoples praise you, O God,
may all the peoples praise you;
may the nations be glad and sing for joy,
for you come to rule them justly.
May the peoples praise you, O God,
for you guide the nations of the earth;
may the peoples praise you, O God,
the nations be glad and sing for joy.

123 Carol Owens

God forgave my sin in Jesus' name,
I've been born again in Jesus' name;
and in Jesus' name I come to you
to share his love as he told me to.

He said, 'Freely, freely you have received,
freely, freely give;
go in my name and because you believe
others will know that I live.'

All power is given in Jesus' name,
in earth and heaven in Jesus' name;
and in Jesus' name I come to you
to share his power as he told me to.

124 Graham Kendrick

God is good, we sing and shout it,
God is good, we celebrate.
God is good, no more we doubt it,
God is good, we know it's true.

And when I think of his love for me,
my heart fills with praise
and I feel like dancing.
For in his heart there is room for me
and I run with arms opened wide.

125 Don Moen and Paul Overstreet

God is good all the time!
He put a song of praise in this heart of mine;
God is good all the time!
Through the darkest night
his light will shine:
God is good, God is good all the time.

If you're walking
through the valley
and there are shadows all around,
do not fear,
he will guide you,

he will keep you safe and sound
'cause he has promised
to never leave you
nor forsake you,
and his word is true.

We were sinners,
so unworthy,
still for us he chose to die:
filled us with
his Holy Spirit,
now we can stand and testify
that his love
is everlasting
and his mercies
they will never end.

Though I may not understand
all the plans you have for me,
my life is in your hands,
and through the eyes of faith
I can clearly see:

© 1995 Integrity's Hosanna! Music/Scarlet Moon Music/Kingsway's
Thankyou Music

126 Graham Kendrick and Steve Thompson

God is great, amazing!
Come, let his praises ring.
God is great, astounding!
the whole creation sings.

His clothing is splendour and majesty bright,
for he wraps himself in a garment of light.
He spreads out the heavens, his palace of
    stars,
and rides on the wings of the wind.

What marvellous wisdom the Maker displays,
the sea vast and spacious, the dolphins and
    whales.
The earth full of creatures, the great and the
    small,
he watches and cares for them all.

The rain forest canopies darken the skies,
cathedrals of mist that resound with the choirs
of creatures discordant, outrageous, ablaze
in colourful pageants of praise.

Above his creation the Father presides.
The pulse of the planets, the rhythm of tides.
The moon marks the seasons, the day follows
    night,
yet he knows every beat of my heart.

Let cannons of thunder salute their acclaim,
the sunsets fly glorious banners of flame,
the angels shout 'holy' again and again
as they soar in the arch of the heavens.

© 1993 Make Way Music

127 Ian Smale

God is here, God is present,
God is moving by his Spirit.
Can you hear what he is saying,
are you willing to respond?
God is here, God is present,
God is moving by his Spirit.
Lord, I open up my life to you,
please do just what you will.

Lord, I won't stop loving you,
you mean more to me
than anyone else.
(Repeat)

© 1987 Kingsway's Thankyou Music

128 Arthur Campbell Ainger,
adapted by Michael Forster

God is working his purpose out
as year succeeds to year.
God is working his purpose out,
and the day is drawing near.
Nearer and nearer draws the time,
the time that shall surely be,
when the earth shall be filled
with the glory of God
as the waters cover the sea.

Continued overleaf

From the east to the utmost west
wherever foot has trod,
through the mouths of his messengers
echoes forth the voice of God:
'Listen to me, ye continents,
ye islands, give ear to me,
that the earth shall be filled
with the glory of God
as the waters cover the sea.'

March we forth in the strength of God,
his banner is unfurled;
let the light of the gospel shine
in the darkness of the world:
strengthen the weary, heal the sick
and set every captive free,
that the earth shall be filled
with the glory of God
as the waters cover the sea.

All our efforts are nothing worth
unless God bless the deed;
vain our hopes for the harvest tide
till he brings to life the seed.
Yet ever nearer draws the time,
the time that shall surely be,
when the earth shall be filled
with the glory of God
as the waters cover the sea.

129   John Wimber

God of all comfort,
God of all grace,
oh, we have come to seek you,
we have come to seek your face.
Because you have called us
we're gathered in this place,
oh, we have come to seek you,
we have come to seek your face.

130   David Fellingham

God of glory, we exalt your name,
you who reign in majesty.
We lift our hearts to you
and we will worship, praise and magnify
your holy name.

In pow'r resplendent (in pow'r resplendent)
you reign in glory (you reign in glory),
eternal King (eternal King),
you reign for ever.
Your word is mighty (your word is mighty),
releasing captives (releasing captives),
your love is gracious (your love is gracious),
you are my God.

131   Simon and Tina Triffitt

God of glory, you are worthy,
you ride above the heavens,
you are Lord,
God of fire, my desire
is to be a vessel in this end time move.

Fire of God's glory, fall on me,
burn away the chaff of self
and set me free;
make me pure and holy,
a light for all to see;
fire of God's glory, fall on me.

132   Chris Bowater

God of grace, I turn my face to you,
I cannot hide;
my nakedness, my shame, my guilt,
are all before your eyes.
Strivings and all anguished dreams
in rags lie at my feet;
and only grace provides the way
for me to stand complete.

And your grace
clothes me in righteousness,
and your mercy
covers me in love.
Your life adorns and beautifies,
I stand complete in you.

133 Unknown

God's not dead. No! He is alive.
God's not dead. No! He is alive.
God's not dead. No! He is alive.
Praise him with my mouth.
Praise him with my feet.
Praise him with my hands.
Love him in my life.
Jesus is alive in me.

134 Don Moen

God will make a way
where there seems to be no way.
He works in ways we cannot see.
He will make a way for me.
He will be my guide,
hold me closely to his side,
with love and strength for each new day.
He will make a way,
he will make a way.

By a roadway in the wilderness he'll lead me,
and rivers in the desert will I see;
heaven and earth will fade
but his Word will still remain,
he will do something new today.

135 Todd Pettygrove

Great and mighty is he,
great and mighty is he;
clothed in glory, arrayed in splendour,
great and mighty is he.
(Repeat)

Let us lift his name up high,
celebrate his grace;
for he has redeemed our lives
and he reigns on high.

136 Noel Richards and Gerald Coates

Great is the darkness that covers the earth,
oppression, injustice and pain.
Nations are slipping in hopeless despair,
though many have come in your name.
Watching while sanity dies,
touched by the madness and lies.

Come, Lord Jesus,
come, Lord Jesus,
pour out your Spirit, we pray.
Come, Lord Jesus,
come, Lord Jesus,
pour out your Spirit on us today.

May now your church rise with power and love,
this glorious gospel proclaim.
In every nation salvation will come
to those who believe in your name.
Help us bring light to this world
that we might speed your return.

Great celebrations on that final day
when out of the heavens you come.
Darkness will vanish, all sorrow will end,
and rulers will bow at your throne.
Our great commission complete,
then face to face we shall meet.

137 Steve McEwan

Great is the Lord and most worthy of praise,
the city of God, the holy place,
the joy of the whole earth.
Great is the Lord in whom we have the victory.
He aids us against the enemy,
we bow down on our knees.

Continued overleaf

And, Lord, we want to lift your name on high,
and, Lord, we want to thank you
for the works you've done in our lives;
and, Lord, we trust in your unfailing love,
for you alone are God eternal,
throughout earth and heaven above.

138   Thomas O. Chisholm

Great is thy faithfulness,
O God my Father,
there is no shadow
of turning with thee;
thou changest not,
thy compassions they fail not;
as thou hast been
thou for ever wilt be.

Great is thy faithfulness!
Great is thy faithfulness!
Morning by morning
new mercies I see;
all I have needed
thy hand has provided,
great is thy faithfulness,
Lord, unto me!

Summer and winter,
and springtime and harvest,
sun, moon and stars
in their courses above,
join with all nature
in manifold witness
to thy great faithfulness,
mercy and love.

Pardon for sin
and a peace that endureth,
thine own dear presence
to cheer and to guide;
strength for today
and bright hope for tomorrow,
blessings all mine,
with ten thousand beside!

139   Jarrod Cooper

Great is your name,
great are your deeds, O Lord.
Day after day
your mercies displayed to all.
There is none like you,
who loves the way you do, Jehovah.

Only you deserve the glory,
only you deserve the praise,
only you deserve the honour,
so great are your ways.
(Repeat)

Faithful and true
in all you do, O Lord.
Saviour and King,
my everything, my all.
There is none like you,
who loves the way you do, Jehovah.

140   Joseph Vogels

Leader	Hail, Jesus, you're my King.
All	Hail, Jesus, you're my King.
Leader	Your life frees me to sing.
All	Your life frees me to sing.
Leader	I will praise you all my days.
All	I will praise you all my days.
Leader	You're perfect in all your ways.
All	You're perfect in all your ways.
Leader	Hail, Jesus, you're my Lord.
All	Hail, Jesus, you're my Lord.
Leader	I will obey your word.
All	I will obey your word.
Leader	I want to see your kingdom come.
All	I want to see your kingdom come.
Leader	Not my will, but yours be done.
All	Not my will, but yours be done.
Leader	Glory, glory to the Lamb.
All	Glory, glory to the Lamb.
Leader	You take me into the land.
All	You take me into the land.

Leader	We will conquer in your name.
All	We will conquer in your name.
Leader	And proclaim that Jesus reigns!
All	And proclaim that Jesus reigns!
Leader	Hail, hail, Lion of Judah!
All	Hail, hail, Lion of Judah!
Leader	How powerful you are!
All	How powerful you are!
Leader	Hail, hail, Lion of Judah!
All	Hail, hail, Lion of Judah!
Leader	How wonderful you are!
All	How wonderful you are!
Leader	How wonderful you are!
All	How wonderful you are!
	How wonderful you are!

© 1985 Scripture in Song/Integrity's Hosanna! Music/Kingsway's
Thankyou Music

141 Terry Butler

Hallelujah, hallelujah,
hallelujah, the Lord reigns.
Hallelujah, hallelujah,
hallelujah, the Lord Almighty reigns.

He has showed his awesome power,
he has triumphed mightily,
he has triumphed over darkness and the grave.
He has broken chains that bound us,
he has set the prisoner free,
by his own great mercy we are saved.

© 1995 Mercy/Vineyard Publishing/Music Services/CopyCare

142 Ron Kenoly

Hallelujah! Jesus is alive,
death has lost its victory
and the grave has been denied;
Jesus lives for ever,
he's alive, he's alive!

He's the Alpha and Omega,
the first and last is he,
the curse of sin is broken

and we have perfect liberty,
the Lamb of God has risen,
he's alive, he's alive!

(Last time)
Hallelujah! Jesus is alive!

© 1987 Integrity's Hosanna! Music/Kingsway's Thankyou Music

143 Tim Cullen

Hallelujah, my Father,
for giving us your Son;
sending him into the world
to be given up for all.
Knowing we would bruise him
and smite him from the earth,
Hallelujah, my Father,
in his death is my birth;
hallelujah, my Father,
in his life is my life.

© 1975 Celebration/Kingsway's Thankyou Music

144 Charles Wesley, George Whitefield, Martin Madan and others

Hark, the herald-angels sing
glory to the new-born King;
peace on earth and mercy mild,
God and sinners reconciled:
joyful, all ye nations rise,
join the triumph of the skies,
with the angelic host proclaim,
'Christ is born in Bethlehem.'

Hark, the herald-angels sing
glory to the new-born King.

Christ, by highest heav'n adored,
Christ, the everlasting Lord,
late in time behold him come,
offspring of a virgin's womb!
Veiled in flesh the Godhead see,
hail the incarnate Deity!
Pleased as man with us to dwell,
Jesus, our Emmanuel.

Continued overleaf

Hail, the heav'n-born Prince of Peace!
Hail, the Sun of Righteousness!
Light and life to all he brings,
ris'n with healing in his wings;
mild he lays his glory by,
born that we no more may die,
born to raise us from the earth,
born to give us second birth.

Hark, the herald-angels sing
glory to the new-born King.

145 Mick Gisbey

Have you got an appetite?
Do you eat what is right?
Are you feeding on the word of God?
Are you fat or are you thin?
Are you really full within?
Do you find your strength in him
or are you starving?

You and me,
all should be
exercising regularly,
standing strong
all day long,
giving God the glory.
Feeding on the living Bread,
not eating crumbs but loaves instead;
standing stronger,
living longer,
giving God the glory.

If it's milk or meat you need,
why not have a slap-up feed,
and stop looking like a weed and start to grow?
Take the full of fitness food,
taste and see that God is good,
come on, feed on what you should
and be healthy.

© 1985 Kingsway's Thankyou Music

146 Stuart Garrard

Have you heard the good news,
have you heard the good news?
We can live in hope
because of what the Lord has done.
(Repeat)

There is a way when there seems no other way,
there is a light in the darkness;
there is a hope, an everlasting hope,
there is a God who can help us.

A hope for justice and a hope for peace,
a hope for those in desperation:
we have a future if only we believe
he works in every situation.

© 1995 Curious? Music/Kingsway's Thankyou Music

147 Matt Redman

Have you not said
as we pass through water,
you will be with us?
And you have said
as we walk through fire,
we will not be burned.
We are not afraid,
for you are with us;
we will testify
to the honour of your name.
We are witnesses,
you have shown us,
you are the one who can save.

Fill us up and send us out
in the power of your name.
Fill us up and send us out
in the power of your name.

Bring them from the west,
sons and daughters,
call them for your praise.
Gather from the east
all your children,
coming home again.
Bring them from afar,
all the nations,
from the north and south,
drawing all the peoples in.
Corners of the earth,
come to see
there's only one Saviour and King.

© 1995 Kingsway's Thankyou Music

148

Graham Kendrick

Hear, O Lord, our cry:
revive us, revive us again.
For the sake of your glory,
revive us, revive us again.
Lord, hear our cry.
Lord, hear our cry.

Hear, O Lord, our cry:
revive us, revive us again.
For the sake of the children
revive us, revive us again.
Lord, hear our cry.
Lord, hear our cry.

© 1989 Make Way Music

149

Graham Kendrick

Women   Hear our cry, O hear our cry:
Men   'Jesus, come!'
Women   Hear our cry, O hear our cry:
Men   'Jesus, come!'

The tide of prayer is rising,
a deeper passion burning –

Women   *Hear our cry, O hear our cry:*
Men   *'Jesus, come!'*
Women   *Hear our cry, O hear our cry:*
Men   *'Jesus, come!'*
Women   *Whoever is thirsty, come now*
               and drink the waters of life;
Men   *whoever is thirsty, come now*
               and drink the waters of life.
Women   *Hear our cry, O hear our cry:*
Men   *'Jesus, come!'*
Women   *Hear our cry, O hear our cry:*
Men   *'Jesus, come!'*

We lift our eyes with longing
to see your kingdom coming –

The streets of teeming cities
cry out for healing rivers –

Refresh them with your presence,
give grace for deep repentance –

Tear back the shroud of shadows
that covers all the peoples –

Revealing your salvation
in every tribe and nation –

© 1996 Make Way Music

150

Graham Kendrick

Heaven invites you to a party,
to celebrate the birth of a Son;
angels rejoicing in the starlight,
singing, 'Christ your Saviour has come.'
(Repeat)

And it's for you (and it's for you)
and it's for me (and it's for me),
for all your friends (for all your friends)
and family (and family).

Now heaven's door (now heaven's door)
is open wide (is open wide),
so come on in (so come on in),
come, step inside (come, step inside).

Angels from the realms of glory,
wing your flight o'er all the earth;
you who sang creation's story,
now proclaim Messiah's birth.

And it's for you . . .

Let trumpets blast (let trumpets blast),
let music play (let music play),
let people shout (let people shout),
let banners wave (let banners wave).

Come, all you people (come, all you people),
join hands together (join hands together),
bring all your neighbours
(bring all your neighbours),
everybody! (everybody!)

Send invitations (send invitations)
to every nation (to every nation),
come and adore him (come and adore him),
everybody! (everybody!)
everybody! (everybody!)

Continued overleaf

Heaven invites you to a party,
to celebrate the birth of a Son;
angels rejoicing in the starlight,
singing, 'Christ your Saviour has come.'

And it's for you (and it's for you)
and it's for me (and it's for me),
for all your friends (for all your friends)
and family (and family).

Let trumpets blast (let trumpets blast),
let music play (let music play),
let people shout (let people shout),
let banners wave (let banners wave).

© 1988 Make Way Music

151   John L. Bell and Graham Maule

Heav'n shall not wait
for the poor to lose their patience,
the scorned to smile,
the despised to find a friend:
Jesus is Lord;
he has championed the unwanted;
in him injustice
confronts its timely end.

Heav'n shall not wait
for the rich to share their fortunes,
the proud to fall,
the élite to tend the least:
Jesus is Lord;
he has shown his master's privilege –
to kneel and wash
servants' feet before they feast.

Heav'n shall not wait
for the dawn of great ideas,
thoughts of compassion
divorced from cries of pain:
Jesus is Lord;
he has married word and action;
his cross and company
make his purpose plain.

Heav'n shall not wait
for our legalised obedience,
defined by statute,
to strict conventions bound:
Jesus is Lord;
he has hallmarked true allegiance –
goodness appears
where his grace is sought and found.

Heav'n shall not wait
for triumphant hallelujahs,
when earth has passed
and we reach another shore:
Jesus is Lord
in our present imperfection;
his pow'r and love
are for now and then for evermore.

© 1987 WGRG

152   Kevin Prosch

He brought me to his banqueting table
(he brought me to his banqueting table),
he brought me to his banqueting table
(he brought me to his banqueting table),
and his banner over me is love.

I am my beloved's and he is mine
(I am my beloved's and he is mine),
I am my beloved's and he is mine
(I am my beloved's and he is mine),
and his banner over me is love.
Yes, his banner over me is love.

And we can feel the love of God in this place,
we believe your goodness, we receive your grace.
We delight ourselves at your table, O God,
you do all things well, just look at our lives.

© 1991 Mercy/Vineyard Publishing/Music Services/CopyCare

153   Steve and Vicki Cook

He has clothed us with his righteousness,
covered us with his great love.
He has showered us with mercy,
and we delight to know the glorious favour,
wondrous favour of God.

We rejoice in the grace of God
poured upon our lives,
loving kindness has come to us
because of Jesus Christ.
We rejoice in the grace of God,
our hearts overflow.
What a joy to know the grace of God.

He's brought us into his family,
made us heirs with his own Son.
All good things he freely gives us
and we cannot conceive what God's preparing,
God's preparing for us.

154 Andy Park

He has fire in his eyes
and a sword in his hand
and he's riding a white horse
across this land.
He has fire in his eyes
and a sword in his hand,
he's riding a white horse
all across this land.
And he's calling out to you and me,
'Will you ride with me?'

He has fire in his eyes
and a sword in his hand
and he's riding a white horse
across this land.
And he's calling out to you and me,
'Will you ride with me?'
and we say, 'Yes, yes, Lord,
we will ride with you.'

And we say, 'Yes, Lord,
we will ride with you.
We will stand up and fight.
We will ride with the armies of heaven,
we'll be dressed in white
(we'll be dressed in white).'
And we say, 'Yes, yes, Lord, we will ride.'

He has a crown on his head,
he carries a sceptre in his hand
and he's leading the armies
across this land.
And he's calling out to you and me,
'Will you ride with me?'
and we say, 'Yes, yes, Lord,
we will ride with you.'

And that fire in his eyes
is his love for his bride,
and he's longing that she be with him,
right by his side.
That fire in his eyes
is his burning desire
that his bride be with him,
right by his side.
And he's calling out to us right now,
'Will you ride with me?'

155 Gerald Coates, Noel Richards and Tricia Richards

He has risen, he has risen,
he has risen, Jesus is alive.

When the life flowed from his body,
seemed like Jesus' mission failed.
But his sacrifice accomplished,
victory over sin and hell.

In the grave God did not leave him,
for his body to decay;
raised to life, the great awakening,
Satan's pow'r he overcame.

If there were no resurrection,
we ourselves could not be raised;
but the Son of God is living,
so our hope is not in vain.

When the Lord rides out of heaven,
mighty angels at his side,
they will sound the final trumpet,
from the grave we shall arise.

Continued overleaf

He has given life immortal,
we shall see him face to face;
through eternity we'll praise him,
Christ the champion of our faith.

He has risen, he has risen,
he has risen, Jesus is alive.

© 1993 Kingsway's Thankyou Music

156 Twila Paris

He is exalted,
the King is exalted on high,
I will praise him.
He is exalted, for ever exalted,
and I will praise his name.

He is the Lord,
for ever his truth shall reign.
Heaven and earth
rejoice in his holy name.
He is exalted,
the King is exalted on high.

© 1985 Straightway/Mountain Spring/Universal Songs/CopyCare

157 Graham Kendrick

He is here,
and we have come to worship him,
in his presence opening
the treasures of our hearts.
He is here,
the centre of our longings,
all our restless journeyings
are ended in his peace.

And God is here with us,
our Saviour, Jesus;
his mercy covers us.
Immanuel is here,
so tender, so near.
We welcome you, Immanuel,
adore you more than words can tell,
we worship you.
Immanuel is here,
he is here.

He is here,
and we have come to worship him,
in his presence opening
the treasures of our hearts.
He is here,
the One for whom the angels sing.
Heav'n and earth are touching,
this is a holy place.

© 1994 Make Way Music

158 Unknown

He is Lord, he is Lord,
he is risen from the dead
and he is Lord.
Every knee shall bow,
every tongue confess
that Jesus Christ is Lord.

159 Kevin Prosch

He is the Lord, and he reigns on high;
he is the Lord.
Spoke into the darkness, created the light.
He is the Lord.
Who is like unto him, never ending in days;
he is the Lord.
And he comes in power when we call on his
    name.
He is the Lord.

Show your power,
O Lord our God,
show your power,
O Lord our God, our God.

Your gospel, O Lord, is the hope for our nation;
you are the Lord.
It's the power of God for our salvation.
You are the Lord.
We ask not for riches, but look to the cross;
you are the Lord.
And for our inheritance give us the lost.
You are the Lord.

Send your power.
O Lord our God,
send your power,
O Lord our God, our God.

160 Carol Owen

He is the mighty God,
he is the risen King,
he is the Lord of lords.
He is the first and last,
he is holy, he is true,
he is the Lord of lords.

And we know he is coming back again
in pow'r and glory.
He is coming back again
to claim his people;
he is coming back again
to bring his children home with him,
home with him.

He is the One who gave
his life for all the world,
he is the Lord of lords,
who rose up from the grave,
defeated death and hell;
he is the Lord of lords.

He's coming in the clouds
and every eye shall see
he is the Lord of lords;
then every knee shall bow
and every tongue proclaim
he is the Lord of lords.

161 Chris Bowater

Here I am, wholly available.
As for me, I will serve the Lord.
Here I am, wholly available.
As for me, I will serve the Lord.

The fields are white unto harvest,
but O, the labourers are so few,
so, Lord, I give myself to help the reaping,
to gather precious souls unto you.

The time is right in the nation
for works of power and authority;
God's looking for a people who are willing
to be counted in his glorious victory.

As salt are we ready to savour,
in darkness are we ready to be light?
God's seeking out a very special people
to manifest his truth and his might.

162 Don Moen

Here in your presence,
beholding your glory,
bowing in reverence
we worship you only.

Standing before you,
we love and adore you, O Lord,
there is none like you.

Name above all names,
beholding your glory,
to Jesus, our Saviour
our lives we surrender.

Worthy of glory,
worthy of honour,
we give you blessing,
glory and power.

163 Graham Kendrick

Here is bread, here is wine,
Christ is with us, he is with us.
Break the bread, taste the wine,
Christ is with us here.

Continued overleaf

Here is grace, here is peace,
Christ is with us, he is with us;
know his grace, find his peace,
feast on Jesus here.

In this bread there is healing,
in this cup is life for ever.
In this moment, by the Spirit,
Christ is with us here.

Here we are, joined in one,
Christ is with us, he is with us;
we'll proclaim till he comes
Jesus crucified.

© 1993 Make Way Music

164 William Rees

Here is love vast as the ocean,
loving kindness as the flood.
When the Prince of Life, our ransom,
shed for us his precious blood.
Who his love will not remember?
Who can cease to sing his praise?
He can never be forgotten,
throughout heav'n's eternal days.

On the mount of crucifixion
fountains opened deep and wide;
through the floodgates of God's mercy
flowed a vast and gracious tide.
Grace and love, like mighty rivers,
poured incessant from above,
and heaven's peace and perfect justice
kissed a guilty world in love.

165 C. Groves and A. Piercy

Here we stand
in total surrender,
lifting our voices,
abandoned to your cause;
here we stand,
praying in the glory
of the one and only
Jesus Christ, the Lord.

This time revival;
Lord, come and heal our land,
bring to completion
the work that you've begun.
This time revival;
stir up your church again,
pour out your Spirit
on your daughters and your sons.

Here we stand
in need of your mercy,
Father, forgive us
for the fire that we have lost.
Once again
make us an army
to conquer this nation
with the message of the cross.

© 1995 IQ Music

166 David Hadden

He's given me a garment of praise
instead of a spirit of despair.
He's given me a garment of praise
instead of a spirit of despair.
(Repeat)

A crown of beauty,
instead of ashes.
The oil of gladness,
instead of mourning.
My soul rejoices
as I delight myself in God.
He's given me a garment of praise
instead of a spirit of despair

© 1994 Restoration Music/Sovereign Music UK

167 Graham Kendrick

He that is in us is greater
than he that is in the world.
He that is in us is greater
than he that is in the world.

Therefore I will sing and I will rejoice
for his Spirit lives in me.
Christ the living one has overcome
and we share in his victory.

All the powers of death and hell and sin
lie crushed beneath his feet.
Jesus owns the name above all names,
crowned with honour and majesty.

© 1986 Kingsway's Thankyou Music

168 Graham Kendrick

He walked where I walk
(he walked where I walk).
He stood where I stand
(he stood where I stand).
He felt what I feel
(he felt what I feel).
He understands
(he understands).
He knows my frailty
(he knows my frailty),
shared my humanity
(shared my humanity),
tempted in every way
(tempted in every way),
yet without sin
(yet without sin).

God with us, so close to us,
God with us, Immanuel.

One of a hated race
(one of a hated race),
stung by the prejudice
(stung by the prejudice),
suffering injustice
(suffering injustice),
yet he forgives
(yet he forgives).
Wept for my wasted years
(wept for my wasted years),
paid for my wickedness
(paid for my wickedness),

he died in my place
(he died in my place),
that I might live
(that I might live).

© 1988 Make Way Music

169 Maggi Dawn

He was pierced for our transgressions,
and bruised for our iniquities;
and to bring us peace he was punished,
and by his stripes we are healed.

He was led like a lamb to the slaughter,
although he was innocent of crime;
and cut off from the land of the living,
he paid for the guilt that was mine.

We like sheep have gone astray,
turned each one to his own way,
and the Lord has laid on him
the iniquity of us all.

© 1987 Kingsway's Thankyou Music

170 Unknown

Higher, higher, higher, higher, higher,
higher, higher, lift up Jesus higher.
Higher, higher, higher, higher, higher,
higher, higher, lift up Jesus higher.

Lower, lower, lower, lower, lower,
lower, lower, lower Satan lower.
Lower, lower, lower, lower, lower,
lower, lower, lower Satan lower.

Cast your burdens on to Jesus,
he cares for you.
Cast your burdens on to Jesus,
he cares for you.

© 1990 Integrity's Hosanna! Music/Kingsway's Thankyou Music

171 David Ruis

His love is higher
than the highest of mountains.
His love goes deeper
than the deepest of seas.
His love, it stretches
to the farthest horizon,
and his love, it reaches to me.

His love is stronger
than the angels and demons.
His love, it keeps me
in my life's darkest hour.
His love secures me
on the pathway to heaven,
and his love is my strength and power.

His love is sweeter
than the sweetest of honey.
His love is better
than the choicest of wine.
His love, it satisfies
the deepest of hunger,
and his love, in Jesus it's mine.

Your love . . .

© 1992 Mercy/Vineyard Publishing/Music Services/CopyCare

172 Noel and Tricia Richards

Hold me closer to you each day;
may my love for you never fade.
Keep my focus on all that's true;
may I never lose sight of you.

In my failure, in my success,
if in sadness or happiness,
be the hope I am clinging to,
for my heart belongs to you.

You are only a breath away,
watching over me every day;
in my heart I am filled with peace
when I hear you speak to me.

No one loves me in the way you do,
no one cares for me like you do.
Feels like heaven has broken through;
God, you know how I love you.

© 1996 Kingsway's Thankyou Music

173 Danny Daniels

Hold me, Lord (hold me, Lord),
in your arms (in your arms).
Fill me, Lord (fill me, Lord),
with your Spirit.
Touch my heart (touch my heart),
with your love (with your love).
Let my life (let my life)
glorify your name.

Singing alleluia, singing alleluia,
singing alleluia, singing alleluia.
Alleluia (alleluia),
allelu (allelu),
alleluia (alleluia),
allelu (allelu).

© 1982 Mercy/Vineyard Publishing/Music Services/CopyCare

174 Brian Doerksen

Holiness is your life in me,
making me clean through your blood.
Holiness is your fire in me,
purging my heart like a flood.
I know you are perfect in holiness.
Your life in me, setting me free,
making me holy.

Only the blood of Jesus covers all of my sin.
Only the life of Jesus renews me from within.
Your blood is enough, your mercy complete,
your work of atonement paid for my debts,
making me holy.
Only the blood of Jesus.

© 1990 Mercy/Vineyard Publishing/Music Services/CopyCare

175 Danny Daniels

Holiness unto the Lord,
unto the King.
Holiness unto your name
I will sing.

Holiness unto Jesus,
holiness unto you, Lord.
Holiness unto Jesus,
holiness unto you, Lord.

I love you, I love your ways,
I love your name.
I love you, and all my days
I'll proclaim:

176 Reginald Heber

Holy, holy, holy!
Lord God Almighty!
Early in the morning
our song shall rise to thee;
holy, holy, holy!
merciful and mighty!
God in three persons,
blessed Trinity!

Holy, holy, holy!
all the saints adore thee,
casting down their golden crowns
around the glassy sea;
cherubim and seraphim
falling down before thee,
which wert, and art,
and evermore shall be.

Holy, holy, holy!
though the darkness hide thee,
though the eye made blind by sin
thy glory may not see,
only thou art holy,
there is none beside thee,
perfect in pow'r,
in love, and purity.

Holy, holy, holy!
Lord God Almighty!
All thy works shall praise thy name,
in earth, and sky, and sea;
holy, holy, holy!
merciful and mighty!
God in three persons,
blessèd Trinity!

177 Richard Lewis

Holy, holy, Lord God Almighty,
who was and who is and is to come.
Holy, holy, Lord God Almighty,
who was and who is and is to come.
All the angels cry, 'Holy',
all the angels cry, 'Holy',
all the angels cry, 'Holy is your name.'
Holy is your name. Holy is your name.
Holy is your name. Holy is your name.

178 Ron Kenoly and Louis Smith

Holy, holy, Lord, you're worthy
and I'm honoured to sing your praise.
King of glory, God Almighty,
hallowed be your name.

All creation, every nation,
has its being by your word;
as your will is done up in heaven,
let it be done here on earth,
let it be done on earth.

Hallowed be your name,
hallowed be your name,
hallowed be your name,
Lord and Majesty,
divine Authority.
hallowed be your name.

Holy, holy, Lord, you're worthy
and I'm honoured to sing your praise.
King of glory, God Almighty,
hallowed be your name,
hallowed be your name.

179 Geoff Bullock

Holy One of God,
the Son of Righteousness,
risen Lamb of God,
Prince of Peace.
Rejected and despised,
suffered, crucified.
This risen Lamb of God,
Jesus Christ,
suffered hell and death
in the pow'r of righteousness;
death is swallowed up in victory.
He's risen from the grave,
salvation has been made.
Worthy is the Lamb that was slain.

180 Geoff Bullock

Holy Spirit, come,
Holy Spirit, come.
Heal our hearts, our lives,
cleanse our thoughts, our minds.
Holy Spirit, come,
O come to us.

Holy Spirit, fall,
Holy Spirit, fall.
drench us with your love,
fill our lives with peace.
Holy Spirit, fall,
O fall on us.

Holy Spirit, flow,
Holy Spirit, flow.
Lead us in your will,
empowered to proclaim.
Holy Spirit, flow,
O flow through us.

181 Chris Bowater

Holy Spirit, we welcome you.
Holy Spirit, we welcome you.
Move among us with holy fire,
as we lay aside all earthly desires,
hands reach out and our hearts aspire.
Holy Spirit, Holy Spirit,
Holy Spirit, we welcome you.

Holy Spirit, we welcome you.
Holy Spirit, we welcome you.
Let the breeze of your presence blow,
that your children here might truly know
how to move in the Spirit's flow.
Holy Spirit, Holy Spirit,
Holy Spirit, we welcome you.

Holy Spirit, we welcome you.
Holy Spirit, we welcome you.
Please accomplish in me today
some new work of loving grace, I pray;
unreservedly have your way.
Holy Spirit, Holy Spirit,
Holy Spirit, we welcome you.

182 Carl Tuttle

Hosanna, hosanna, hosanna in the highest!
Hosanna, hosanna, hosanna in the highest!
Lord, we lift up your name,
with hearts full of praise;
be exalted, O Lord, my God!
Hosanna in the highest!

Glory, glory, glory to the King of kings!
Glory, glory, glory to the King of kings!
Lord, we lift up your name,
with hearts full of praise;
be exalted, O Lord, my God!
Glory to the King of kings!

183
Graham Kendrick and Steve Thompson

How can I be free from sin?
lead me to the cross of Jesus,
from the guilt, the pow'r, the pain,
lead me to the cross of Jesus.

There's no other way,
no price that I could pay,
simply to the cross I cling.
This is all I need,
this is all I plead,
that his blood was shed for me.

How can I know peace within?
lead me to the cross of Jesus,
sing a song of joy again,
lead me to the cross of Jesus.

Flowing from above,
all-forgiving love,
from the Father's heart to me.
What a gift of grace,
his own righteousness,
clothing me in purity.

How can I live day by day?
lead me to the cross of Jesus,
following his narrow way,
lead me to the cross of Jesus.

© 1991 Make Way Music

184
Wes Sutton

How can I not love you
when I see all that you've given me?
How can I not love you,
Jesus, my Lord?

I love you, first and last,
in your love I've come to rest.
I will dwell before your throne.
you are my eternal home.

How can I not serve you,
when I see all that you've done for me?
How can I not serve you,
Jesus, my Lord.

I draw near by your grace,
I desire to seek your face.
In your presence there is light,
you are my eternal life.

© 1997 Sovereign Lifestyle Music

185
Stuart Townend

How deep the Father's love for us,
how vast beyond all measure,
that he should give his only Son
to make a wretch his treasure.
How great the pain of searing loss,
the Father turns his face away,
as wounds which mar the Chosen One
bring many sons to glory.

Behold the man upon a cross,
my sin upon his shoulders;
ashamed, I hear my mocking voice
call out among the scoffers.
It was my sin that held him there
until it was accomplished;
his dying breath has brought me life –
I know that it is finished.

I will not boast in anything,
no gifts, no pow'r, no wisdom;
but I will boast in Jesus Christ,
his death and resurrection.
Why should I gain from his reward?
I cannot give an answer,
but this I know with all my heart,
his wounds have paid my ransom.

© 1995 Kingsway's Thankyou Music

186
Richard Keen

How firm a foundation,
you saints of the Lord,
is laid for your faith
in his excellent word;
what more can he say
than to you he has said,
you who unto Jesus
for refuge have fled?

Continued overleaf

Fear not, I am with you,
O be not dismayed;
for I am your God,
and will still give you aid;
I'll strengthen you, help you,
and cause you to stand,
upheld by my righteous,
omnipotent hand.

In every condition,
in sickness, in health,
in poverty's vale,
or abounding in wealth;
at home and abroad,
on the land, on the sea,
as your days may demand
shall your strength ever be.

When through the deep waters
I call you to go,
the rivers of grief
shall not you overflow;
for I will be with you
in trouble to bless,
and sanctify to you
your deepest distress.

When through fiery trials
your pathway shall lie,
my grace all-sufficient
shall be your supply;
the flame shall not hurt you,
my only design
your dross to consume
and your gold to refine.

The soul that on Jesus
has leaned for repose
I will not, I cannot,
desert to its foes;
that soul, though all hell
should endeavour to shake,
I never will leave,
I will never forsake.

187 Graham Kendrick

How good and how pleasant it is
when we all live in unity,
refreshing as dew at the dawn,
like rare anointing oil upon the head.

It's so good, so good
when we live together
in peace and harmony;
it's so good, so good
when we live together
in his love.

How deep are the rivers that run
when we are one in Jesus
and share with the Father and Son
the blessings of his everlasting life.

© 1995 Make Way Music

188 Matt Redman

How lovely is your dwelling place,
O Lord Almighty.
My soul longs and even faints for you.
For here my heart is satisfied,
within your presence.
I sing beneath the shadow of your wings.

Better is one day in your courts,
better is one day in your house,
better is one day in your courts
than thousands elsewhere.
(Repeat)

One thing I ask and I would seek;
to see your beauty:
to find you in the place your glory dwells.

My heart and flesh cry out
for you, the living God.
Your Spirit's water for my soul.
I've tasted and I've seen,
come once again to me;
I will draw near to you,
I will draw near to you.

© 1995 Kingsway's Thankyou Music

189 Leonard E. Smith Jnr

How lovely on the mountains
are the feet of him
who brings good news, good news,
proclaiming peace,
announcing news of happiness:
our God reigns, our God reigns,
our God reigns, our God reigns,
our God reigns, our God reigns!

You watchmen, lift your voices
joyfully as one,
shout for your King, your King.
See eye to eye
the Lord restoring Zion:
your God reigns, your God reigns!

Waste places of Jerusalem,
break forth with joy,
we are redeemed, redeemed.
The Lord has saved
and comforted his people:
your God reigns, your God reigns!

Ends of the earth,
see the salvation of your God,
Jesus is Lord, is Lord.
Before the nations
he has bared his holy arm:
your God reigns, your God reigns!

© 1974 Kingsway's Thankyou Music

190 John Newton

How sweet the name of Jesus sounds
in a believer's ear!
It soothes our sorrows, heals our wounds,
and drives away our fear.

It makes the wounded spirit whole,
and calms the troubled breast;
'tis manna to the hungry soul,
and to the weary rest.

Dear name! the rock on which I build,
my shield and hiding-place,
my never-failing treasury filled
with boundless stores of grace.

Jesus! my Shepherd, Saviour, Friend,
my Prophet, Priest and King,
my Lord, my life, my way, my end,
accept the praise I bring.

Weak is the effort of my heart,
and cold my warmest thought;
but when I see thee as thou art,
I'll praise thee as I ought.

Till then I would thy love proclaim
with every fleeting breath;
and may the music of thy name
refresh my soul in death.

191 Dave Bilbrough

I am a new creation,
no more in condemnation,
here in the grace of God I stand.
My heart is overflowing,
my love just keeps on growing,
here in the grace of God I stand.

And I will praise you, Lord,
yes, I will praise you, Lord,
and I will sing of all that you have done.

A joy that knows no limit,
a lightness in my spirit,
here in the grace of God I stand.

© 1983 Kingsway's Thankyou Music

192 Loren Bieg

I am so thankful
for the fullness of your love.
I am so thankful
for the shedding of your blood.
I am so thankful
you died in my place
Oh, Lord, I'm thankful for your love.

Continued overleaf

I am so thankful
that you came into my life.
I am so thankful
that you love me like a child.
I am so thankful
I'll be with you for all time.
Oh, Lord, I'm thankful for your love.

193 Andy Park

I am standing beneath your wings,
I am resting in your shelter,
your great faithfulness has been my shield
and it makes me want to sing.

> *Blessed be the name of the Lord,*
> *blessed be the name of the Lord.*
> *I will bless your holy name*
> *for all my days;*
> *blessed be the name of the Lord.*

I sing praises to your name, O Lord,
for you daily bear my burdens.
Your great faithfulness is my reward
and it makes me want to sing.

194 Don Moen

I am the God that healeth thee,
I am the Lord, your healer;
I sent my word and healed your disease,
I am the Lord, your healer.

You are the God that healeth me,
you are the Lord, my healer;
you sent your word and healed my disease,
you are the Lord, my healer.

195 Marc Nelson

> *I believe in Jesus;*
> *I believe he is the Son of God.*
> *I believe he died and rose again,*
> *I believe he paid for us all.*

And I believe he's here now
(I believe that he's here),
standing in our midst;
here with the power to heal now
(with the power to heal),
and the grace to forgive.

> *I believe in you, Lord;*
> *I believe you are the Son of God.*
> *I believe you died and rose again,*
> *I believe you paid for us all.*

And I believe you're here now
(I believe that you're here),
standing in our midst;
here with the power to heal now
(with the power to heal),
and the grace to forgive.

196 Russell Fragar

I believe the promise
about the visions and the dreams
that the Holy Spirit will be poured out
and his power will be seen.
Well, the time is now
and the place is here
and his people have come in faith;
there's a mighty sound and a touch of fire
when we're gathered in once place.

> *I believe that the presence of God is here;*
> *there's not one thing that can't be changed*
> *when the Spirit of God is near.*
> *I believe that the presence of God is here;*
> *when two or three are gathered,*
> *when people rise in faith,*
> *I believe God answers*
> *and his presence is in this place.*

Nothing in earth or heaven
can stop the power of God;
into our hands is given
the call to take it on;

no ocean can contain it,
no star can rise above;
into our hearts is given
the power of his love.

197 Bonnie Deuschle

I bow my knee before your throne,
I know my life is not my own;
I offer up a song of praise
to bring you pleasure, Lord.

I seek the giver, not the gift,
my heart's desire is to lift you
high above all earthly kings;
to bring you pleasure, Lord.

Hallelujah, hallelujah,
hallelujah, glory to the King.
Hallelujah, hallelujah,
hallelujah, glory to the King.

198 Debbie and Rob Eastwood

I bow my knee,
I give myself
as a living sacrifice for you.
I lay me down
before your throne.
Take my past; I will stand for you.
Let your blood wash over me,
let your blood wash over me;
you have cleansed my heart
and set my spirit free.

You are my Lord,
I'll love you more,
I'll follow you,
no matter when,
no matter where.

199 William Young Fullerton

I cannot tell
how he whom angels worship
should stoop to love
the peoples of the earth,
or why as shepherd
he should seek the wanderer
with his mysterious promise
of new birth.
But this I know,
that he was born of Mary,
when Bethlehem's manger
was his only home,
and that he lived at
Nazareth and laboured,
and so the Saviour,
Saviour of the world, is come.

I cannot tell
how silently he suffered,
as with his peace
he graced this place of tears,
or how his heart
upon the cross was broken,
the crown of pain
to three and thirty years.
But this I know,
he heals the broken-hearted,
and stays our sin,
and calms our lurking fear,
and lifts the burden
from the heavy laden,
for yet the Saviour,
Saviour of the world, is here.

I cannot tell
how he will win the nations,
how he will claim
his earthly heritage,
how satisfy
the needs and aspirations
of east and west,
of sinner and of sage.
But this I know,
all flesh shall see his glory,

Continued overleaf

and he shall reap
the harvest he has sown,
and some glad day
his sun shall shine in splendour
when he the Saviour,
Saviour of the world, is known.

I cannot tell
how all the lands shall worship,
when, at his bidding,
every storm is stilled,
or who can say
how great the jubilation
when every heart
with perfect love is filled.
But this I know,
the skies will thrill with rapture,
and myriad, myriad
human voices sing,
and earth to heav'n,
and heav'n to earth, will answer:
'At last the Saviour,
Saviour of the world, is King!'

200 Martin Smith

O, I could sing unending songs
of how you saved my soul.
Well, I could dance a thousand miles
because of your great love.

My heart is bursting, Lord,
to tell of all you've done.
Of how you changed my life
and wiped away the past.
I wanna shout it out,
from every roof-top sing.
For now I know that God
is for me, not against me.

Everybody's singing now,
'cos we're so happy!
Everybody's dancing now,
'cos we're so happy!

If only we could see your face
and see you smiling over us
and unseen angels celebrate,
for joy is in this place.

201 Craig Musseau

I cry out for your hand of mercy to heal me.
I am weak, I need your love to free me.
Oh, Lord, my rock, my strength in weakness,
come rescue me, oh, Lord.

You are my hope, your promise never fails me.
And my desire is to follow you for ever.

For you are good, for you are good,
for you are good to me.
For you are good, for you are good,
for you are good to me.

202 Graham Kendrick

If you are encouraged
in our union with Christ,
finding consolation in his love,
compassion, warmth and friendship
in the Spirit's flow of life;
this is how you make my joy complete:

By being of the same mind,
and loving with the same love,
united in the Spirit,
with the same goal in sight.
By being of the same mind,
and loving with the same love,
united in the Spirit
to the glory of Christ.

Be sure you do nothing
out of selfishness or pride,
never seeing past your own concerns;
but humbly keep the interests
of each other in your hearts,
seeing them as better than yourselves:

203 Carl Tuttle

I give you all the honour
and praise that's due your name,
for you are the King of Glory,
the Creator of all things.

And I worship you,
I give my life to you,
I fall down on my knees.
Yes, I worship you,
I give my life to you,
I fall down on my knees.

As your Spirit moves upon me now,
you meet my deepest need,
and I lift my hands up to your throne,
your mercy I've received.

You have broken chains that bound me,
you've set this captive free,
I will lift my voice to praise your name
for all eternity.

© 1982 Mercy/Vineyard Publishing/Music Services/CopyCare

204 Matt Redman

I have come to love you,
I have come to love you today.
(Repeat)

And today and for evermore
I'll love your name.
Lord, today and for evermore
I'll love your name.

I have come to worship,
I have come to worship today.
(Repeat)

I have come to thank you,
I have come to thank you today.
(Repeat)

© 1995 Kingsway's Thankyou Music

205 Lynn DeShazo

I have made you too small in my eyes,
O Lord, forgive me;
and I have believed in a lie
that you were unable to help me,
but now, O Lord, I see my wrong:
heal my heart and show yourself strong,
and in my eyes and with my song,
O Lord, be magnified,
O Lord, be magnified.

Be magnified, O Lord,
you are highly exalted;
and there is nothing you can't do,
O Lord, my eyes are on you.
Be magnified,
O Lord, be magnified.

I have leaned on the wisdom of men,
O Lord, forgive me;
and I have responded to them
instead of your light and your mercy.
But now, O Lord, I see my wrong:
heal my heart and show yourself strong,
and in my eyes and with my song,
O Lord, be magnified,
O Lord, be magnified.

© 1992 Integrity's Hosanna! Music/Kingsway's Thankyou Music

206 Horatius Bonar

I heard the voice of Jesus say,
'Come unto me and rest;
lay down, thou weary one,
lay down thy head upon my breast.'
I came to Jesus as I was,
so weary, worn and sad;
I found in him a resting-place,
and he has made me glad.

I heard the voice of Jesus say,
'Behold, I freely give
the living water, thirsty one;
stoop down and drink and live.'
I came to Jesus, and I drank
of that life-giving stream;
my thirst was quenched, my soul revived,
and now I live in him.

Continued overleaf

I heard the voice of Jesus say,
'I am this dark world's light;
look unto me, thy morn shall rise,
and all thy day be bright.'
I looked to Jesus, and I found
in him my star, my sun;
and in that light of life I'll walk
till travelling days are done.

207 Don Moen

I just want to be where you are,
dwelling daily in your presence;
I don't want to worship from afar:
draw me near to where you are.
I just want to be where you are,
in your dwelling-place for ever;
take me to the place where you are:
I just want to be with you.

I want to be where you are,
dwelling in your presence,
feasting at your table,
surrounded by your glory,
in your presence,
that's where I always want to be:
I just want to be,
I just want to be with you.

I just want to be where you are,
to enter boldly in your presence;
I don't want to worship from afar,
draw me near to where you are.

O my God, you are my strength and my song
and when I'm in your presence,
though I'm weak, you're always strong.
I just want to be where you are,
in your dwelling-place for ever.
Take me to the place where you are:
I just want to be,
I just want to be with you;
I just want to be,
I just want to be with you.

208 Arthur Tannous

I just want to praise you,
lift my hands and say, 'I love you.'
You are everything to me
and I exalt your holy name on high.
I just want to praise you,
lift my hands and say, 'I love you.'
You are everything to me
and I exalt your holy name,
I exalt your holy name,
I exalt your holy name on high.

209 Randy and Terry Butler

I know a place, a wonderful place,
where accused and condemned
find mercy and grace,
where the wrongs we have done
and the wrongs done to us
were nailed there with him,
there on the cross.

At the cross (at the cross),
he died for our sin.
At the cross (at the cross),
he gave us life again.

210 Darlene Zschech

I know it, I know it,
his blood has set me free,
I've been delivered, forgiven,
fear has got no hold on me.
I'm set apart,
not living life my own way,
no holding back
till I see him face to face
because I know it,
oh yes, I know it,
I know it,
the blood of Jesus has set me free!

There is healing in the name of Jesus,
salvation in the name of Jesus,
forgiveness in the name of Jesus.
I've never known it like I know it today;
there is power in the name of Jesus,
fullness of joy I've found in Jesus,
strength in the name of Jesus.
I know it, I know it,
oh, I've got to tell you that
I know it . . .

211 Brian Doerksen

I lift my eyes up to the mountains,
where does my help come from?
My help comes from you,
maker of heaven, creator of the earth.

> O how I need you, Lord,
> you are my only hope;
> you're my only prayer.
> So I will wait for you
> to come and rescue me,
> come and give me life.

212 Andre Kempen

I lift my hands to the coming King,
to the great 'I Am',
to you I sing,
for you're the One
who reigns within my heart.

> And I will serve no foreign god,
> or any other treasure;
> you are my heart's desire,
> Spirit without measure.
> Unto your name
> I would bring my sacrifice.

213 Paul Baloche and Ed Kerr

> I love to be in your presence
> with your people singing praises;
> I love to stand and rejoice,
> lift my hands and raise my voice.
> (Repeat)

You set my feet to dancing,
you fill my heart with song,
you give me reason to rejoice, rejoice.

(Last time)
Lift my hands, lift my hands,
lift my hands and raise my voice.

214 Laurie Klein

I love you, Lord,
and I lift my voice to worship you,
O my soul rejoice.
Take joy, my King, in what you hear.
May it be a sweet, sweet sound in your ear.

215 Mike Day and Dave Bell

I love you, Lord, with all of my heart.
I love you, Lord, with all of my soul.
Let all that is within me
cry, 'Holy is your name.'
Let all that is within me
cry, 'Holy is your name.'

I love you, Lord, with all of my mind.
I love you, Lord, with all of my strength.
Let all that is within me
cry, 'Holy is your name.'
Let all that is within me
cry, 'Holy is your name.'

> And we cry, 'Holy, holy is your name.'
> We sing, 'Glory to the Lamb that was slain.'
> We cry, 'Holy, holy is your name,
> holy is your name,
> holy is your name.'

216 Fabienne Pons trans. Judith Robertson

I love your presence, Jesus;
I love your presence, beloved Lord.
I love your presence, Jesus;
I love your presence, beloved Lord.

I know your love is here, powerful and real;
yes, your love is here, with the grace to heal.
I know your love is here, flowing from Calvary;
yes, your love is here, stirring faith in me.

Your Holy Spirit's here, mighty Counsellor;
yes, your Spirit's here, with releasing pow'r.
Your Holy Spirit's here, poured out from above;
yes, your Spirit's here, showing Father's love.

217 Rob Hayward

I'm accepted, I'm forgiven,
I am fathered by the true and living God.
I'm accepted, no condemnation,
I am loved by the true and living God.
There's no guilt or fear as I draw near
to the Saviour and Creator of the world.
There is joy and peace as I release
my worship to you, O Lord.

218 Capt. Alan J. Price

I'm gonna click, click, click,
I'm gonna clap, clap, clap,
I'm gonna click, I'm gonna clap
and praise the Lord!
Because of all he's done
I'm gonna make him 'number one',
I'm gonna click, I'm gonna clap
and praise the Lord!

I'm gonna zoom, zoom, zoom,
around the room, room, room,
I'm gonna zoom around the room
and praise the Lord!

Because of all he's done,
I'm gonna make him 'number one',
I'm gonna zoom around the room
and praise the Lord!

I'm gonna sing, sing, sing,
I'm gonna shout, shout, shout,
I'm gonna sing, I'm gonna shout
and praise the Lord!
Because of all he's done,
I'm gonna make him 'number one',
I'm gonna sing, I'm gonna shout
and praise the Lord!

I'm gonna click, click, click,
I'm gonna clap, clap, clap,
I'm gonna zoom around the room
and praise the Lord!
Because of all he's done,
I'm gonna make him 'number one',
I'm gonna sing, I'm gonna shout
and praise the Lord!

219 Graham Kendrick

Immanuel, O Immanuel,
bowed in awe I worship at your feet,
and sing Immanuel,
God is with us,
sharing my humanness, my shame,
feeling my weaknesses, my pain,
taking the punishment, the blame,
Immanuel.
And now my words cannot explain,
all that my heart cannot contain,
how great are the glories of your name,
Immanuel.

Immanuel, O Immanuel,
bowed in awe I worship at your feet,
and sing Immanuel . . .

220 Walter Chalmers Smith

Immortal, invisible,
God only wise,
in light inaccessible
hid from our eyes,
most blessed, most glorious,
the Ancient of Days,
almighty, victorious,
thy great name we praise.

Unresting, unhasting,
and silent as light,
nor wanting, nor wasting,
thou rulest in might;
thy justice like mountains
high soaring above
thy clouds which are fountains
of goodness and love.

To all life thou givest,
to both great and small;
in all life thou livest,
the true life of all;
we blossom and flourish
as leaves on the tree,
and wither and perish;
but naught changeth thee.

Great Father of glory,
pure Father of light,
thine angels adore thee,
all veiling their sight;
all laud we would render,
O help us to see,
'tis only the splendour
of light hideth thee.

Immortal, invisible,
God only wise,
in light inaccessible
hid from our eyes,
most blessed, most glorious,
the Ancient of Days,
almighty, victorious,
thy great name we praise.

221 Reuben Morgan

I'm so secure,
you're here with me;
you stay the same,
your love remains
here in my heart.

So close I believe
you're holding me now,
in your hands I belong.
You'll never let me go.
So close I believe
you're holding me now,
in your hands I belong.
You'll never let me go.

You gave your life
in your endless love;
you set me free
and showed the way:
now I am found.

All along, you were beside me,
even when I couldn't tell.
Through the years you showed me
more of you, more of you.

222 Graham Kendrick

I'm special because God has loved me,
for he gave the best thing that he had
      to save me;
his own Son, Jesus,
crucified to take the blame,
for all the bad things I have done.
Thank you, Jesus,
thank you, Lord,
for loving me so much.
I know I don't deserve anything;
help me feel your love right now
to know deep in my heart
that I'm your special friend.

223 Kevin Prosch

I'm standing here to testify
(O, the Lord is good),
to sing of how he changed my heart
(O, the Lord is good).
I was bound by hate and pride
(O, the Lord is good),
never knowing of his light
(O, the Lord is good).
I did not think I could have peace,
(O, the Lord is good)
trapped inside by fear and shame
(O, the Lord is good).
He wiped away all of my grief
(O, the Lord is good)
when I believed upon his name.

Come to the light,
come as you are;
you can be a friend of God.
Humble yourself,
give him your heart,
he will meet you where you are.
Come to the light,
just as you are;
fall on the Rock for the wasted years.
He will restore
all that was lost,
surrender now, his power is here.

Clap your hands, O God.
Clap your hands, O God.
Clap your hands, O God.
Clap your hands, O God.

224 Richard Hubbard

I'm your child and you are my God.
I thank you, Father, for your loving care.
I'm your child and you are my God.
You've made me special and you're always there.

I'm your child and you are my God.
I love you, Jesus, you're close to me.
I'm your child and you are my God.
I give you worship, I bow the knee.

I'm your child and you are my God.
Holy Spirit, flow out to me.
I'm your child and you are my God.
You give me power and authority.

225 Shawn Craig and Don Koch

In Christ alone I place my trust,
and find my glory in the power of the cross;
in every victory let it be said of me
my source of strength, my source of hope
is Christ alone.

226 Lindell Cooley and Bruce Haynes

I need you more,
more than yesterday,
I need you more,
more than words can say.
I need you more
than ever before,
I need you, Lord,
I need you, Lord.

More than the air I breathe,
more than the song I sing,
more than the next heartbeat,
more than anything.
And, Lord, as time goes by,
I'll be by your side
'cause I never want to go
back to my old life.

Right here in your presence
is where I belong;
this old broken heart
has finally found a home
and I'll never be alone.

227 David Fellingham

In every circumstance of life
you are with me, glorious Father.
And I have put my trust in you,
that I may know the glorious hope
to which I'm called.

And by the pow'r that works in me,
you've raised me up and set me free;
and now in every circumstance
I'll prove your love without a doubt;
your joy shall be my strength,
your joy shall be my strength.

© 1994 Kingsway's Thankyou Music

228 Jamie Owens-Collins

In heav'nly armour we'll enter the land,
the battle belongs to the Lord.
No weapon that's fashioned against us will
    stand,
the battle belongs to the Lord.

And we sing glory, honour,
power and strength to the Lord.
We sing glory, honour,
power and strength to the Lord.

When the power of darkness comes like a
    flood,
the battle belongs to the Lord.
He'll raise up a standard, the power of his
    blood,
the battle belongs to the Lord.

When your enemy presses in hard,
    do not fear,
the battle belongs to the Lord.
Take courage, my friend, your redemption
    is near,
the battle belongs to the Lord.

© 1984 Fairhill Music/CopyCare

229 David Graham

In moments like these
I sing out a song,
I sing out a love song to Jesus.
In moments like these
I lift up my hands,
I lift up my hands to the Lord.

Singing, 'I love you, Lord',
singing, 'I love you, Lord';
singing, 'I love you, Lord,
I love you.'

© 1980 CA Music/Word Music/CopyCare

230 Bob Kilpatrick

In my life, Lord,
be glorified, be glorified.
In my life, Lord,
be glorified today.

In your church, Lord,
be glorified, be glorified.
In your church, Lord,
be glorified, today.

© 1978 Bob Kilpatrick Music

231 Andy Park

In the morning when I rise
expectantly I lift my eyes
and I see you (and I see you).
Gazing on your heav'nly throne,
in your presence I'm at home,
here with you (here with you).
And all I want
is more and more of you.

Earthly cares and passions pale
when you take away the veil
and I see you (and I see you).
When you open heaven's door
all I want is to have more,
more of you (more of you).
And all I want
is more and more of you.

Continued overleaf

The earth and all its glory will fade,
but the word of our God will stand.
The earth and all its glory will fade,
but the kingdom of God I will seek.

Nothing in the world compares
to the love that I can share
alone with you (alone with you).
There is nothing else so real
as the things that you reveal
when I'm with you (when I'm with you).
And all I want
is more and more of you.

232 Mark Altrogge

In the presence of a holy God
there's new meaning now to grace;
you took all my sins upon yourself,
I can only stand amazed.

And I cry holy, holy, holy God,
how awesome is your name.
Holy, holy, holy God,
how majestic is your name,
and I am changed
in the presence of a holy God.

In the presence of your infinite might,
I'm so small and frail and weak;
when I see your pow'r and wisdom, Lord,
I have no words left to speak.

In the presence of your glory
all my crowns lie in the dust.
You are righteous in your judgements, Lord,
you are faithful, true and just.

233 Andy Park

In the secret, in the quiet place,
in the stillness you are there.
In the secret, in the quiet hour I wait
only for you
'cause I want to know you more.

I want to know you,
I want to hear your voice,
I want to know you more.
I want to see you,
I want to see your face,
I want to know you more.

I am reaching for the highest goal,
that I might receive the prize.
Pressing onward, pushing every hindrance aside,
out of my way,
'cause I want to know you more.

234 Graham Kendrick

In the tomb so cold they laid him,
death its victim claimed.
Pow'rs of hell, they could not hold him;
back to life he came!

Christ is risen!
(Christ is risen!)
Death has been conquered.
(Death has been conquered.)
Christ is risen!
(Christ is risen!)
He shall reign for ever.

Hell had spent its fury on him,
left him crucified.
Yet, by blood, he boldly conquered,
sin and death defied.

Now the fear of death is broken,
love has won the crown.
Prisoners of the darkness listen,
walls are tumbling down.

Raised from death to heav'n ascending,
love's exalted King.
Let his song of joy, unending,
through the nations ring!

235 Judy Bailey

I reach up high, I touch the ground,
I stomp my feet and turn around.
I've got to (woo woo) praise the Lord.
I jump and dance with all my might,
I might look funny, but that's all right,
I've got to (woo woo) praise the Lord.

I'll do anything just for my God
'cos he's done everything for me.
It doesn't matter who is looking on,
Jesus is the person that I want to please.

May my whole life be a song of praise
to worship God in every way.
In this song the actions praise his name,
I want my actions every day to do the same.

236 Paul Armstrong

I receive your love,
I receive your love,
in my heart I receive your love, O Lord.
I receive your love
by your Spirit within me,
I receive, I receive your love.

I confess your love,
I confess your love,
from my heart I confess your love, O Lord.
I confess your love
by your Spirit within me,
I confess, I confess your love.

237 Graham Kendrick

Is anyone thirsty? – (yes!) – anyone?
Is anyone thirsty? (Yes!)
Is anyone thirsty? – (yes!) – anyone?
Is anyone thirsty? (Yes!)
Jesus said, 'Let them come to me and drink,
let them come to me.'

O let the living waters flow,
O let the living waters flow,
let the river of your Spirit flow through me;
O let the living waters flow,
O let the living waters flow,
let the river of your Spirit flow through me.

(Last time)
Flow through me.
Flow through me.

Let the living waters flow,
let the living waters flow.
Let the living waters flow,
let the living waters flow.

238 Chris Falson

I see the Lord
seated on the throne, exalted;
and the train of his robe
fills the temple with glory:
the whole earth is filled,
the whole earth is filled,
the whole earth is filled
with your glory.

Holy, holy, holy, holy,
yes, holy is the Lord;
holy, holy, holy, holy,
yes, holy is the Lord of lords.

239 Craig Musseau

I sing a simple song of love
to my Saviour, to my Jesus.
I'm grateful for the things you've done,
my loving Saviour, O precious Jesus.
My heart is glad
that you've called me your own;
there's no place I'd rather be than

in your arms of love,
in your arms of love,
holding me still,
holding me near,
in your arms of love.

(Last time)
Holding me still,
holding me near,
holding me still,
holding me near
in your arms of love.

240 Terry MacAlmon

I sing praises to your name, O Lord,
praises to your name, O Lord,
for your name is great
and greatly to be praised.
(Repeat)

I give glory to your name, O Lord,
glory to your name, O Lord,
for your name is great
and greatly to be praised.
(Repeat)

241 Martin Smith

Is it true today
that when people pray
cloudless skies will break,
kings and queens will shake?
Yes, it's true and I believe it,
I'm living for you.

Well, it's true today
that when people pray
we'll see dead men rise
and the blind set free.
Yes, it's true and I believe it,
I'm living for you.

I'm going to be a history maker
in this land.
I'm going to be a speaker of truth
to all mankind.
I'm going to stand,
I'm going to run into your arms,
into your arms again,
into your arms, into your arms again.

Well, it's true today
that when people stand
with the fire of God
and the truth in hand,
we'll see miracles,
we'll see angels sing,
we'll see broken hearts
making history.
Yes it's true and I believe it,
I'm living for you.

242 John Wimber

Isn't he beautiful, beautiful, isn't he?
Prince of Peace, Son of God, isn't he?
Isn't he wonderful, wonderful, isn't he?
Counsellor, Almighty God, isn't he,
isn't he, isn't he?

Yes, you are beautiful, beautiful, yes, you are.
Prince of Peace, Son of God, yes, you are.
Yes, you are wonderful, wonderful, yes, you are.
Counsellor, Almighty God, yes, you are,
yes, you are, yes, you are.

243 Charles H. Gabriel

I stand amazed in the presence
of Jesus the Nazarene,
and wonder how he could love me,
a sinner, condemned, unclean.

O, how marvellous! O, how wonderful,
and my song shall ever be:
O, how marvellous! O, how wonderful!
is my Saviour's love for me.

For me it was in the garden
he prayed – 'Not my will, but thine';
he had no tears for his own griefs,
but sweat drops of blood for mine.

In pity angels beheld him,
and came from the world of light,
to comfort him in the sorrows
he bore for my soul that night.

He took my sins and my sorrows,
he made them his very own;
he bore the burden to Calvary,
and suffered, and died alone.

When with the ransomed in glory
his face I at last shall see,
'twill be my joy through the ages
to sing of his love for me.

244 Mavis Ford

I stand before the presence
of the Lord God of hosts,
a child of my Father
and an heir of his grace,
for Jesus paid the debt for me,
the veil was torn in two,
and the Holy of Holies
has become my dwelling-place.

245 Matthew Ling

I stand before your throne,
the beauty of your holiness amazes me.
From you and you alone
comes the word of life
and pow'r that changes me.
You are bounteous in mercy,
abundant in your grace.
You make your face to shine upon me.

I will seek your face,
draw me closer to embrace your glory.
I will seek your face,
I run into your secret place
with all my heart and all my strength.
I will seek your face.

In adoration now,
my spirit soars upon the breeze of mercy.
The rapture of my heart
poured out in songs of love
for you are worthy;
worth the price of sacrifice,
surrendering my all,
changed from glory into glory.

246 Dan Schutte

I, the Lord of sea and sky,
I have heard my people cry.
All who dwell in dark and sin
my hand will save.
I who made the stars of night,
I will make their darkness bright.
Who will bear my light to them?
Whom shall I send?

Here I am, Lord.
Is it I, Lord?
I have heard you calling in the night.
I will go, Lord,
if you lead me.
I will hold your people in my heart.

Continued overleaf

I, the Lord of snow and rain,
I have borne my people's pain.
I have wept for love of them.
They turn away.
I will break their hearts of stone,
give them hearts for love alone.
I will speak my word to them.
Whom shall I send?

Here I am, Lord.
Is it I, Lord?
I have heard you calling in the night.
I will go, Lord,
if you lead me.
I will hold your people in my heart.

I, the Lord of wind and flame,
I will tend the poor and lame.
I will set a feast for them.
My hand will save.
Finest bread I will provide
till their hearts be satisfied.
I will give my life to them.
Whom shall I send?

© 1981 Daniel L. Schutte/New Dawn Music

247 Duke Kerr

It is to you I give the glory,
it is to you I give the praise,
because you have done so much for me,
I will magnify your name.
It is to you, Holy Father,
no one else but you,
and I will praise your name,
praise your name,
and I will praise your name
for evermore.

© Duke Kerr and Remission Music UK

248 David Ruis

It's our confession, Lord,
that we are weak,
so very weak,
but you are strong.

And though we've nothing, Lord,
to lay at your feet,
we come to your feet
and say, 'Help us along'.

A broken heart and a contrite spirit
you have yet to deny.
Your heart of mercy beats
with love's strong current;
let the river flow by your Spirit now,
Lord, we cry:

Let your mercies fall from heaven,
sweet mercies flow from heaven,
new mercies for today,
O shower them down, Lord, as we pray.
(Repeat)

© 1995 Mercy/Vineyard Publishing/Music Services/CopyCare

249 Matt Redman and Martin Smith

It's rising up from coast to coast,
from north to south, and east to west;
the cry of hearts that love your name,
which with one voice we will proclaim.

The former things have taken place.
Can this be the new day of praise?
A heav'nly song that comes to birth,
and reaches out to all the earth.
O let the cry to nations ring,
that all may come and all may sing:

Holy is the Lord.
Holy is the Lord.
Holy is the Lord.
Holy is the Lord.

And we have heard the lion's roar,
that speaks of heaven's love and pow'r.
Is this the time, is this the call
that ushers in your kingdom rule?
O let the cry to nations ring,
that all may come and all may sing:

Jesus is alive!
Jesus is alive!
Jesus is alive!
Jesus is alive!

© 1995 Kingsway's Thankyou Music

250 Michael Christ

It's your blood that cleanses me,
it's your blood that gives me life,
it's your blood that took my place
in redeeming sacrifice,
and washes me whiter than the snow,
than the snow.
My Jesus, God's precious sacrifice.

251 Russell Fragar

I've found a friend, O such a friend,
he made my heart his home.
God himself is with me
and I know I'm never alone.
I know all my tomorrows
will be better than all my hopes;
we've got love! grace! peace and pow'r and
joy in the Holy Ghost.

My God is never wrong
and he makes time for me.
It blew apart my chains
and set this sinner free.
It's like a river
and you'll never run it dry.
We've got power over fear and death
and hearts filled up with joy.

The Holy Spirit fills me up
and I need him every day
for fire, faith and confidence
and knowing what to say.
I gave my heart and all I am
to the one who loves me most;
we've got love! grace! peace and pow'r and
joy in the Holy Ghost.

252 Matt Redman

I've got a love song in my heart.
(I've got a love song in my heart.)
It is for you, Lord, my God.
(It is for you, Lord, my God.)
(Repeat)

I've got a passion in my heart.
(I've got a passion in my heart.)
It is for you, Lord, my God.
(It is for you, Lord, my God.)
(Repeat)

La la la, la la, la la,
la la la, la la, la la,
la la la, la la, la la
(Repeat)

I've got rejoicing in my heart.
(I've got rejoicing in my heart.)
It is for you, Lord, my God.
(It is for you, Lord, my God.)
(Repeat)

And there is dancing in my heart.
(And there is dancing in my heart.)
It is for you, Lord, my God.
(It is for you, Lord, my God.)
(Repeat)

La la la, la la, la la . . .

I've never known a love like this.
(I've never known a love like this.)
I've never known a love like this.
(I've never known a love like this.)
(Repeat)

253 Chris Falson

I walk by faith, each step by faith,
to live by faith, I put my trust in you.
I walk by faith, each step by faith,
to live by faith, I put my trust in you.

Every step I take is a step of faith;
no weapon formed against me shall prosper.
And every prayer I make is a prayer of faith;
and if my God is for me,
then who can be against me?

254 Doug Horley

I want to be a tree that's bearing fruit,
that God has pruned and caused to shoot,
O, up in the sky, so very, very high.
I want to be, I want to be a blooming tree.

God has promised his Holy Spirit
will water our roots and help us grow.
Listen and obey, and before you know it
your fruit will start to grow, grow, grow, grow,
   grow.

You'll be a tree that's bearing fruit,
with a very, very, very strong root,
bright colours like daisies, more fruit than
   Sainsbury's,
you'll be a blooming tree.

255 Doug Horley and Noel Richards

I want to be out of my depth in your love,
feeling your arms so strong around me.
Out of my depth in your love,
out of my depth in you.
(Repeat)

Learning to let you lead,
putting all trust in you;
deeper into your arms,
surrounded by you.
Things I have held so tight,
made my security;
give me the strength I need
to simply let go.

256 Mark Altrogge

I want to serve the purpose of God
in my generation.
I want to serve the purpose of God
while I am alive.
I want to give my life for something
that'll last for ever,
oh, I delight, I delight to do your will.

What is on your heart?
Show me what to do.
Let me know your will
and I will follow you.
(Repeat)

I want to build with silver and gold
in my generation . . .

I want to see the kingdom of God
in my generation . . .

I want to see the Lord come again
in my generation . . .

257 Richard Black

I went to the enemy's camp
and I took back what he stole from me,
I took back what he stole from me,
I took back what he stole from me.
I went to the enemy's camp
and I took back what he stole from me.
He's under my feet, he's under my feet,
he's under my feet, he's under my feet,
he's under my feet, he's under my feet,
Satan is under my feet.

258 Brian Doerksen

I will be yours, you will be mine,
together in eternity.
Our hearts of love will be entwined,
together in eternity,
for ever in eternity.
(Repeat)

No more tears of pain in our eyes;
no more fear or shame,
for we will be with you,
for we will be with you.

259 Graham Kendrick

Men	I will build my church
Women	I will build my church
Men	and the gates of hell
Women	and the gates of hell
Men	shall not prevail
Women	shall not prevail
All	against it.

(Repeat)

So you pow'rs in the heavens above,
bow down!
And you pow'rs on the earth below,
bow down!
And acknowledge that Jesus, Jesus,
Jesus is Lord, is Lord.

© 1988 Make Way Music

260 D. J. Butler

I will change your name,
you shall no longer be called
wounded outcast,
lonely or afraid.
I will change your name,
your new name shall be
confidence, joyfulness,
overcoming one.
Faithfulness,
friend of God,
one who seeks my face.

© 1987 Mercy/Vineyard Publishing/Music Services/CopyCare

261 Matt Redman

I will dance, I will sing,
to be mad for my King.
Nothing, Lord, is hindering
the passion in my soul.
(Repeat)

And I'll become
even more undignified than this.
I'll become
even more undignified than this.

Na, na, na, na, na, na! Hey!
Na, na, na, na, na, na! Hey!
(Repeat)

© 1995 Kingsway's Thankyou Music

262 Leona von Brethorst

I will enter his gates with thanksgiving in my
    heart,
I will enter his courts with praise,
I will say this is the day that the Lord has
    made,
I will rejoice for he has made me glad.
He has made me glad,
he has made me glad,
I will rejoice for he has made me glad.
He has made me glad,
he has made me glad,
I will rejoice for he has made me glad.

© 1976 Maranatha! Music/CopyCare

263 Geoff Bullock

I will lift my voice to the King of kings
as an offering to him.
I will lift my heart to the King of kings
as an offering to him.

Jesus, how I love you,
I will worship you alone.
Jesus, precious Jesus,
I will serve you, you alone.

I will lift my hands to the Lord of lords
as an offering to him.
I will lift my life to the Lord of lords
as an offering to him.

© 1988 Word Music Inc./CopyCare

264 Geoff Bullock

I will never be the same again,
I can never return,
I've closed the door.
I will walk the path,
I'll run the race
and I will never be the same again.

Continued overleaf

Fall like fire, soak like rain,
flow like mighty waters again and again:
sweep away the darkness,
burn away the chaff
and let a flame burn
to glorify your name.

There are higher heights,
there are deeper seas:
whatever you need to do,
Lord, do in me;
the glory of God fills my life
and I will never be the same again,
and I will never be the same again.

265 Matt Redman

I will offer up my life
in spirit and truth,
pouring out the oil of love
as my worship to you.
In surrender I must give
my every part;
Lord, receive the sacrifice
of a broken heart.

Jesus, what can I give,
what can I bring
to so faithful a friend,
to so loving a King?
Saviour, what can be said,
what can be sung
as a praise of your name
for the things you have done?
O my words could not tell,
not even in part,
of the debt of love that is owed
by this thankful heart.

You deserve my every breath
for you've paid the great cost;
giving up your life to death,
even death on a cross.
You took all my shame away,
there defeated my sin,
opened up the gates of heav'n,
and have beckoned me in.

266 Mark Altrogge

I will praise you all my life;
I will sing to you with my whole heart.
I will trust in you, my hope and my help,
my Maker and my faithful God.

O faithful God, O faithful God,
you lift me up and you uphold my cause;
you give me life, you dry my eyes,
you're always near, you're a faithful God.

267 Matthew Lockwood

I will seek you with all of my heart,
I will trust you with all of my life,
I will hope in all that you say,
for you are my Lord.
I will give you my hopes and my dreams,
I will fix my thoughts on your word,
I will speak of all you have done for me,
for you are my Lord.

For you are the rock on which I stand,
and you are the friend who holds my hand,
and you are the bright morning star,
the light in my darkest hour.

268 Noel and Tricia Richards

I will seek your face, O Lord;
I will seek your face, O Lord;
I will seek your face, O Lord;
I will seek your face, O Lord.

Lord, how awesome is your presence.
Who can stand in your light?
Those who by your grace and mercy
are made holy in your sight.

I will dwell in your presence
all the days of my life;
there to gaze upon your glory,
and to worship only you.

269 Ian Smale

I will wave my hands
in praise and adoration,
I will wave my hands
in praise and adoration,
I will wave my hands
in praise and adoration,
praise and adoration to the living God.

For he's given me hands
that just love clapping:
one, two, one, two, three,
and he's given me a voice
that just loves shouting:
'hallelujah!'
He's given me feet
that just love dancing:
one, two, one, two, three,
and he's put me in a being
that has no trouble seeing
that whatever I am feeling
he is worthy to be praised.

270 David Ruis

I will worship (I will worship)
with all of my heart (with all of my heart).
I will praise you (I will praise you)
with all of my strength (all my strength).
I will seek you (I will seek you)
all of my days (all of my days).
I will follow (I will follow)
all of your ways (all your ways).

I will give you all my worship,
I will give you all my praise.
You alone I long to worship,
you alone are worthy of my praise.

I will bow down (I will bow down),
hail you as King (hail you as King).
I will serve you (I will serve you),
give you everything (give you everything).

I will lift up (I will lift up)
my eyes to your throne (my eyes to your
   throne).
I will trust you (I will trust you),
I will trust you alone (trust in you alone).

271 Sondra Corbett

I worship you, Almighty God,
there is none like you.
I worship you, O Prince of Peace,
that is what I love to do.
I give you praise,
for you are my righteousness.
I worship you, Almighty God,
there is none like you.

272 Graham Kendrick

I worship you (I worship you),
O Lamb of God,
who takes away (who takes away)
the sin of the world.
(Repeat)

Alleluia, alleluia,
alleluia, alleluia.

I kneel before (I kneel before)
the Lamb of God,
who takes away (who takes away)
the sin of the world.
(Repeat)

273 Chris Bowater

Jesus, at your name we bow the knee.
Jesus, at your name we bow the knee.
Jesus, at your name we bow the knee,
and acknowledge you as Lord.
(Repeat)

Continued overleaf

You are the Christ, you are the Lord.
Through your Spirit in our lives
we know who you are.
(Repeat)

274 Matt Redman

Jesus Christ, I think upon your sacrifice;
you became nothing, poured out to death.
Many times I've wondered at your gift of life,
and I'm in that place once again,
I'm in that place once again.

> *And once again I look upon*
> *the cross where you died.*
> *I'm humbled by your mercy*
> *and I'm broken inside.*
> *Once again I thank you,*
> *once again I pour out my life.*

Now you are exalted to the highest place,
King of the heavens, where one day I'll bow.
But for now I marvel at this saving grace,
and I'm full of praise once again,
I'm full of praise once again.

Thank you for the cross, thank you for the cross,
thank you for the cross, my friend.
Thank you for the cross, thank you for the cross,
thank you for the cross, my friend.

275 Graham Kendrick

Jesus Christ is Lord of all
(Jesus Christ is Lord of all),
King of kings and Lord of lords
(King of kings and Lord of lords),
he will reign for evermore
(he will reign for evermore),
from East to West and shore to shore
(from East to West and shore to shore).

Jesus (Jesus),
King of kings (King of kings),
Jesus (Jesus),
Lord of all (Lord of all),
Jesus (Jesus),
King of kings (King of kings),
Jesus (Jesus),
Lord of all,
(Lord of all, Lord of all,
Lord of all).

Jesus is our battle cry
(Jesus is our battle cry),
King of justice, peace and joy
(King of justice, peace and joy).
We want Jesus more and more
(we want Jesus more and more).
He's the one we're marching for
(he's the one we're marching for).

276 From *Lyra Davidica*

Jesus Christ is ris'n today, alleluia!
our triumphant holy day, alleluia!
who did once, upon the cross, alleluia!
suffer to redeem our loss, alleluia!

Hymns of praise then let us sing, alleluia!
unto Christ, our heav'nly King, alleluia!
who endured the cross and grave, alleluia!
sinners to redeem and save, alleluia!

But the pains that he endured, alleluia!
our salvation have procured; alleluia!
now above the sky he's King, alleluia!
where the angels ever sing, alleluia!

277 Steve Israel and Gerrit Gustafson

> *Jesus Christ is the Lord of all,*
> *Lord of all the earth.*
> *Jesus Christ is the Lord of all,*
> *Lord of all the earth.*
> *(Repeat)*

Only one God,
over the nations,
only one Lord of all;
in no other name
is there salvation,
Jesus is Lord of all.

Jesus Christ is Lord of all,
Jesus Christ is Lord of all.
Jesus Christ is Lord of all,
Jesus Christ is Lord of all.

278 Geoff Bullock

Jesus, God's righteousness revealed,
the Son of Man, the Son of God,
his kingdom comes.
Jesus, redemption's sacrifice,
now glorified, now justified,
his kingdom comes.

And his kingdom will know no end,
and its glory shall know no bounds,
for the majesty and power
of this kingdom's King has come,
and this kingdom's reign,
and this kingdom's rule,
and this kingdom's power and authority,
Jesus, God's righteousness revealed.

Jesus, the expression of God's love,
the grace of God, the word of God,
revealed to us;
Jesus, God's holiness displayed,
now glorified, now justified,
his kingdom comes.

279 Dave Bolton

Jesus, how lovely you are,
you are so gentle, so pure and kind.
You shine as the morning star,
Jesus, how lovely you are.

Hallelujah, Jesus is my Lord and King;
hallelujah, Jesus is my everything.

Hallelujah, Jesus died and rose again;
hallelujah, Jesus forgave all my sin.

Hallelujah, Jesus is meek and lowly;
hallelujah, Jesus is pure and holy.

Hallelujah, Jesus is the Bridegroom;
hallelujah, Jesus will take his bride soon.

280 Jean Sophia Pigott

Jesus! I am resting, resting
in the joy of what thou art;
I am finding out the greatness
of thy loving heart.
Thou hast bid me gaze upon thee,
and thy beauty fills my soul,
for, by thy transforming power,
thou hast made me whole.

O how great thy loving kindness,
vaster, broader than the sea!
O how marvellous thy goodness,
lavished all on me!
Yes, I rest in thee, beloved,
know what wealth of grace is thine,
know thy certainty of promise,
and have made it mine.

Simply trusting thee, Lord Jesus,
I behold thee as thou art,
and thy love so pure, so changeless,
satisfies my heart,
satisfies its deepest longings,
meets, supplies its every need,
compasses me round with blessings;
thine is love indeed!

Ever lift thy face upon me,
as I work and wait for thee;
resting 'neath thy smile, Lord Jesus,
earth's dark shadows flee.
Brightness of my Father's glory,
sunshine of my Father's face,
keep me ever trusting, resting,
fill me with thy grace.

281 Don Harris and Martin J. Nystrom

Jesus, I am thirsty,
won't you come and fill me?
Earthly things have left me dry,
only you can satisfy,
all I want is more of you.

All I want is more of you,
all I want is more of you;
nothing I desire, Lord,
but more of you.
(Repeat)

© 1993 Integrity's Hosanna! Music/Kingsway's Thankyou Music

282 Gill Hutchinson

Jesus is greater than the greatest heroes,
Jesus is closer than the closest friends.
He came from heaven and he died to save us,
to show us love that never ends.
(Repeat)

Son of God, and the Lord of glory,
he's the light, follow in his way.
He's the truth that we can believe in,
and he's the life, he's living today.
(Repeat)

© 1992 Sea Dream Music

283 Wendy Churchill

Jesus is King and I will extol him,
give him the glory and honour his name.
He reigns on high, enthroned in the heavens,
Word of the Father, exalted for us.

We have a hope that is steadfast and certain,
gone through the curtain and touching the
    throne.
We have a Priest who is there interceding,
pouring his grace on our lives day by day.

We come to him, our Priest and Apostle,
clothed in his glory and bearing his name,
laying our lives with gladness before him;
filled with his Spirit we worship the King.

O holy One, our hearts do adore you;
thrilled with your goodness we give you our
    praise.
Angels in light with worship surround him,
Jesus, our Saviour, for ever the same.

© 1982 Springtide/Word Music/CopyCare

284 David Mansell

Jesus is Lord! creation's voice proclaims it,
for by his pow'r each tree and flow'r
was planned and made.
Jesus is Lord! the universe declares it,
sun, moon and stars in heaven
cry, 'Jesus is Lord!'

Jesus is Lord! Jesus is Lord!
Praise him with hallelujahs
for Jesus is Lord!

Jesus is Lord! yet from his throne eternal
in flesh he came to die in pain
on Calvary's tree.
Jesus is Lord! from him all life proceeding,
yet gave his life a ransom
thus setting us free.

Jesus is Lord! o'er sin the mighty conqueror,
from death he rose, and all his foes
shall own his name.
Jesus is Lord! God sent his Holy Spirit
to show by works of power
that Jesus is Lord.

© 1982 Springtide/Word Music/CopyCare

285 Philip Lawson Johnston

Jesus is the name we honour;
Jesus is the name we praise.
Majestic Name above all other names,
the highest heav'n and earth proclaim
that Jesus is our God.

We will glorify,
we will lift him high,
we will give him honour and praise.
We will glorify,
we will lift him high,
we will give him honour and praise.

Jesus is the name we worship;
Jesus is the name we trust.
He is the King above all other kings,
let all creation stand and sing
that Jesus is our God.

Jesus is the Father's splendour;
Jesus is the Father's joy.
He will return to reign in majesty,
and every eye at last will see
that Jesus is our God.

286   John Barnett

Jesus, Jesus,
holy and anointed One, Jesus.
Jesus, Jesus,
risen and exalted One, Jesus.

Your name is like honey on my lips,
your Spirit like water to my soul.
Your word is a lamp unto my feet.
Jesus, I love you, I love you.

287   Chris Bowater

Jesus, Jesus, Jesus,
your love has melted my heart.
Jesus, Jesus, Jesus,
your love has melted my heart.

288   David Hadden

Jesus (Jesus), Jesus (Jesus).
You have the name
that's higher than all other names.
Jesus (Jesus), Jesus (Jesus).
You are the King,
the mighty God, the one who reigns.
Glorious in splendour and majesty,
clothed with the robe of authority.
Jesus, my King, you will always be
my deepest joy,
my one desire.
O Prince of Peace,
you set my heart on fire.

289   Graham Kendrick

Jesus' love has got under our skin,
Jesus' love has got under our skin.
Deeper than colour oh;
richer than culture oh;
stronger than emotion oh;
wider than the ocean oh.
Don't you want to celebrate
and congratulate somebody,
talk about a family!
It's under our skin, under our skin.

Leader	Everybody say love:
All	love.
Leader	Everybody say love:
All	love,
Leader	love,
All	love.

Isn't it good to be
living in harmony.
Jesus in you and me;
he's under our skin,
under our skin,
he's under our skin,
under our skin.

290 John Ezzy, Daniel Grul and Stephen McPherson

Jesus, lover of my soul,
Jesus, I will never let you go;
you've taken me from the miry clay,
you've set my feet upon the rock
and now I know

I love you, I need you,
though my world will fall,
I'll never let you go.
My Saviour, my closest friend,
I will worship you until the very end.

291 Naida Hearn

Jesus, name above all names,
beautiful Saviour, glorious Lord;
Emmanuel, God is with us,
blessed Redeemer, Living Word.

292 Graham Kendrick

Jesus put this song into our hearts,
Jesus put this song into our hearts,
it's a song of joy no one can take away,
Jesus put this song into our hearts.

Jesus taught us how to live in harmony,
Jesus taught us how to live in harmony,
different faces, different races, he made us one,
Jesus taught us how to live in harmony.

Jesus taught us how to be a family,
Jesus taught us how to be a family,
loving one another with the love that he gives,
Jesus taught us how to be a family.

Jesus turned our sorrow into dancing,
Jesus turned our sorrow into dancing,
changed our tears of sadness into rivers of joy,
Jesus turned our sorrow into a dance.

293 Colin Owen

Jesus reigns over sin,
Jesus reigns deep within,
Jesus is the King of kings.
Jesus brings life and breath,
Jesus rules over death
Jesus is the King of kings.

Jesus, holy Lamb of God,
who triumphed over sin;
gentle, humble Lamb of God
with a lion's heart within,
you are Messiah
and you're coming back again.

Jesus, mighty living Lord,
whose face shines like the sun;
awesome in your majesty,
you are God's Holy One,
you are Messiah
and you're coming back again.

Jesus, Name above all names,
the most exalted One;
you are the Way, the Truth, the Life,
God's precious living Son,
you are Messiah
and you're coming back again.

294 Taizé Community

Jesus, remember me
when you come into your kingdom.
Jesus, remember me
when you come into your kingdom.

295 Graham Kendrick

Jesus, restore to us again
the gospel of your holy name,
that comes with pow'r, not words alone,
owned, signed and sealed from heaven's throne.
Spirit and word in one agree;
the promise to the power wed.

The word is near,
here in our mouths
and in our hearts,
the word of faith;
proclaim it on the Spirit's breath:
Jesus.

Your word, O Lord, eternal stands,
fixed and unchanging in the heav'ns.
The Word made flesh, to earth came down
to heal our world with nail-pierced hands.
Among us here you lived and breathed,
you are the message we received.

Spirit of truth, lead us, we pray,
into all truth as we obey.
And as God's will we gladly choose,
your ancient pow'r again will prove
Christ's teaching truly comes from God,
he is indeed the living Word.

Upon the heights of this dark land
with Moses and Elijah stand.
Reveal your glory once again,
show us your face, declare your name.
Prophets and law, in you, complete
where promises and power meet.

Grant us in this decisive hour
to know the Scriptures and the pow'r;
the knowledge in experience proved,
the pow'r that moves and works by love.
May words and works join hands as one,
the word go forth, the Spirit come.

© 1992 Make Way Music

296   Chris Bowater

Jesus shall take the highest honour,
Jesus shall take the highest praise;
let all earth join heav'n in exalting
the Name which is above all other names.
Let's bow the knee in humble adoration,
for at his name every knee must bow.
Let every tongue confess
he is Christ, God's only Son,
Sovereign Lord, we give you glory now.

For all honour and blessing and power
belongs to you, belongs to you.
All honour and blessing and power
belongs to you, belongs to you,
Lord Jesus Christ, Son of the living God.

© 1988 Sovereign Lifestyle Music

297   Dave Bryant

Jesus, take me as I am,
I can come no other way.
Take me deeper into you,
make my flesh life die away.
Make me like a precious stone,
crystal clear and finely honed.
Life of Jesus shining through,
giving glory back to you.

© 1978 Kingsway's Thankyou Music

298   Charles Wesley

Jesus! The name high over all,
in hell, or earth, or sky;
Angels and mortals prostrate fall
and devils fear and fly.

Jesus, the name to sinners dear,
the name to sinners giv'n;
it scatters all their guilty fear,
it turns their hell to heav'n.

Jesus, the prisoner's fetters breaks,
and bruises Satan's head;
pow'r into strengthless souls he speaks,
and life into the dead,
and life into the dead.

O, that the world might taste and see
the riches of his grace!
The arms of love that compass me,
hold all the human race.

His only righteousness I show,
his saving grace proclaim:
'tis all my business here below
to cry: 'Behold the Lamb!'

Happy, if with my latest breath
I may but gasp his name:
preach him to all, and cry in death:
'Behold, behold the Lamb!'

299 John Gibson

Jesus, we celebrate your victory;
Jesus, we revel in your love.
Jesus, we rejoice you've set us free;
Jesus, your death has brought us life.

It was for freedom that Christ has set us free,
no longer to be subject to a yoke of slavery;
so we're rejoicing in God's victory,
our hearts responding to his love.

His Spirit in us releases us from fear,
the way to him is open, with boldness we
    draw near.
And in his presence our problems disappear;
our hearts responding to his love.

© 1987 Kingsway's Thankyou Music

300 Paul Kyle

Jesus, we enthrone you,
we proclaim you our King,
standing here in the midst of us,
we raise you up with our praise.
And as we worship, build a throne,
and as we worship, build a throne,
and as we worship, build a throne;
come, Lord Jesus, and take your place.

© 1980 Kingsway's Thankyou Music

301 Tanya Riches

Jesus, what a beautiful name.
Son of God, Son of Man,
Lamb that was slain.
Joy and peace, strength and hope,
grace that blows all fear away.
Jesus, what a beautiful name.

Jesus, what a beautiful name.
Truth revealed, my future sealed,
healed my pain.
Love and freedom, life and warmth,
grace that blows all fear away.
Jesus, what a beautiful name.

Jesus, what a beautiful name.
Rescued my soul, my stronghold,
lifts me from shame.
Forgiveness, security, power and love,
grace that blows all fear away.
Jesus, what a beautiful name.

© 1995 Tanya Riches/Hillsongs Australia/Kingsway's Thankyou Music

302 Nancy Gordon and Jamie Harvill

Jesus, you're my firm foundation,
I know I can stand secure;
Jesus, you're my firm foundation,
I put my hope in your holy word,
I put my hope in your holy word.

I have a living hope
(I have a living hope),
I have a future
(I have a future);
God has a plan for me
(God has a plan for me),
of this I'm sure
(of this I'm sure).

Your word is faithful
(your word is faithful),
mighty in power
(mighty in power);
God will deliver me
(God will deliver me),
of this I'm sure
(of this I'm sure).

© 1994 Integrity's Hosanna! Music/Integrity's Praise! Music/Kingsway's
Thankyou Music

303 Reuben Morgan

Jesus, your loving kindness,
I'm so blessed by all that you've done,
this life that you give.
Jesus, your loving kindness
is life that's changing my heart,
drawing me near to you.

Your love is better than life,
I know it well
and I'll find all that I need in you, in you.
Your love is better than life,
I know it well
and I'll find all that I need in you.

304 Claire Cloninger

Jesus, your name is power,
Jesus, your name is might.
Jesus, your name will break every stronghold,
Jesus, your name is life.

Jesus, your name is healing,
Jesus, your name gives sight.
Jesus, your name will free every captive,
Jesus, your name is life.

Jesus, your name is holy,
Jesus, your name brings light.
Jesus, your name above every other,
Jesus, your name is life.

Jesus, your name is power,
Jesus, your name is might.
Jesus, your name will break every stronghold,
Jesus, your name is life.

305 Isaac Watts

Joy to the world! The Lord is come;
let earth receive her King;
let every heart prepare him room
and heav'n and nature sing,
and heav'n and nature sing,
and heav'n, and heav'n and nature sing.

Joy to the earth! The Saviour reigns;
let us our songs employ;
while fields and floods, rocks, hills and plains
repeat the sounding joy,
repeat the sounding joy,
repeat, repeat the sounding joy.

He rules the world with truth and grace,
and makes the nations prove
the glories of his righteousness,
and wonders of his love,
and wonders of his love,
and wonders, wonders of his love.

306 Charlotte Elliott

Just as I am, without one plea
but that thy blood was shed for me,
and that thou bid'st me come to thee,
O Lamb of God, I come.

Just as I am, though tossed about
with many a conflict, many a doubt,
fightings and fears within, without,
O Lamb of God, I come.

Just as I am, poor, wretched, blind;
sight, riches, healing of the mind,
yea, all I need, in thee to find,
O Lamb of God, I come.

Just as I am, thou wilt receive,
wilt welcome, pardon, cleanse, relieve:
because thy promise I believe,
O Lamb of God, I come.

Just as I am, thy love unknown
has broken every barrier down,
now to be thine, yea, thine alone,
O Lamb of God, I come.

Just as I am, of that free love
the breadth, length, depth and height to prove,
here for a season, then above,
O Lamb of God, I come.

307 Naomi Batya and Sophie Conty

King of kings and Lord of lords,
glory, hallelujah.
King of kings and Lord of lords,
glory, hallelujah.
Jesus, Prince of Peace,
glory, hallelujah.
Jesus, Prince of Peace,
glory, hallelujah.

308 Graham Kendrick

King of kings, Lord of lords,
Lion of Judah, Word of God.
King of kings, Lord of lords,
Lion of Judah, Word of God.
Word of God.
And here he comes,
the King of glory comes!
In righteousness he comes to judge the earth.
And here he comes,
the King of glory comes!
With justice he'll rule the earth.

(Shout)
Almighty God, you are the Rock;
all your works are perfect,
and all your ways are just.
You are a faithful God who does no wrong.
Yet we your people,
both church and nation,
are covered with shame
because of our unfaithfulness to you.
We have sinned so seriously against you,
and against one another –
therefore the foundations of our society crumble.
Have mercy, Lord,
forgive us, Lord,
restore us, Lord,
revive your church again;
let justice flow
like rivers,
and righteousness like a never-failing stream.

© 1988 Make Way Music

309 Jarrod Cooper

King of kings, majesty,
God of heaven living in me,
gentle Saviour, closest friend,
strong deliverer, beginning and end,
all within me falls at your throne.

Your majesty, I can but bow.
I lay my all before you now.
In royal robes I don't deserve
I live to serve your majesty.

Earth and heav'n worship you,
love eternal, faithful and true,
who bought the nations, ransomed souls,
brought this sinner near to your throne;
all within me cries out in praise.

© 1996 Jarrod Cooper

310 Chris Bowater

Lamb of God, Holy One,
Jesus Christ, Son of God,
lifted up willingly to die;
that I the guilty one may know
the blood once shed still freely flowing,
still cleansing, still healing.

I exalt you, Jesus, my sacrifice,
I exalt you, my Redeemer and my Lord.
I exalt you, worthy Lamb of God,
and in honour I bow down
before your throne.

© 1988 Sovereign Lifestyle Music Ltd.

311 James Edmeston

Lead us, heav'nly Father, lead us
o'er the world's tempestuous sea;
guard us, guide us, keep us, feed us,
for we have no help but thee;
yet possessing every blessing
if our God our Father be.

Saviour, breathe forgiveness o'er us:
all our weakness thou dost know;
thou didst tread this earth before us,
thou didst feel its keenest woe;
lone and dreary, faint and weary,
through the desert thou didst go.

Spirit of our God, descending,
fill our hearts with heav'nly joy,
love with every passion blending,
pleasure that can never cloy:
thus provided, pardoned, guided,
nothing can our peace destroy.

312 Graham Kendrick

Led like a lamb to the slaughter
in silence and shame,
there on your back you carried
a world of violence and pain.
Bleeding, dying, bleeding, dying.

You're alive, you're alive,
you have risen, alleluia!
And the pow'r and the glory is given,
alleluia! Jesus to you.

At break of dawn, poor Mary,
still weeping she came,
when through her grief she heard your voice
now speaking her name.
(Men) Mary, *(Women)* Master,
(Men) Mary, *(Women)* Master.

At the right hand of the Father
now seated on high
you have begun your eternal reign
of justice and joy.
Glory, glory, glory, glory.

© 1983 Kingsway's Thankyou Music

313 Graham Kendrick

Let it be to me
according to your word.
Let it be to me
according to your word.

I am your servant,
no rights shall I demand.
Let it be to me,
let it be to me,
let it be to me
according to your word.
(Repeat)

© 1988 Make Way Music

314 Joel Pott

Let it rain, let it rain, let it rain,
let it rain on every nation.
Let it rain, let it rain, let it rain,
let it rain on every nation.
(Repeat)

Take our hearts as fuel for the fire,
now is the time to see your power.
Take our prayers as abundant rain,
open up the floodgates of heaven.
Let the trumpet sound
and the rain come down.

Love rain down, down on me.
Love rain down, down on me.
Love rain down, down on me.
Love rain down on me.
(Repeat)

© 1995 Joel Pott

315 Daniel Gardner

Let me be a sacrifice,
holy and acceptable,
let me be a sacrifice,
consumed in your praise;
let me be a sacrifice,
holy and acceptable,
let me be a sacrifice,
worshipping your name.

© 1981 Integrity's Hosanna! Music/ Kingsway's Thankyou Music

316 Bryn Haworth

Let the righteous sing,
come, let the righteous dance,
rejoice before your God,
be happy and joyful.
Give him your praise.
We give you our praise.
Shout for joy to God
who rides upon the clouds;
how awesome are his deeds,
so great is his power.
Give him your praise.
We give you our praise.

He gives the desolate a home.
He leads the prisoners out with singing.
Father to the fatherless,
defender of the widow,
is God in his holy place.

© 1991 Kingsway's Thankyou Music

317 Dave Bilbrough

Let there be love shared among us,
let there be love in our eyes.
May now your love sweep this nation,
cause us, O Lord, to arise.
Give us a fresh understanding
of brotherly love that is real.
Let there be love shared among us,
let there be love.

318 John Watson

Let your living water flow over my soul.
Let your Holy Spirit come and take control
of every situation that has troubled my mind.
All my cares and burdens on to you I roll.

Jesus, Jesus, Jesus.
Father, Father, Father.
Spirit, Spirit, Spirit.

Come now, Holy Spirit, and take control.
Hold me in your loving arms and make me
    whole.
Wipe away all doubt and fear and take my pride.
Draw me to your love and keep me by your side.

Give your life to Jesus, let him fill your soul.
Let him take you in his arms and make you
    whole.
As you give your life to him, he'll set you free.
You will live and reign with him eternally.

Let your living water flow over my soul.
Let your Holy Spirit come and take control
of every situation that has troubled my mind.
All my cares and burdens on to you I roll.

319 Noel and Tricia Richards

Oh, oh, oh,
let your love come down.
(Repeat)

There is violence in the air.
Fear touches all our lives.
How much pain can people bear?
Are we reaping what we've sown,
voices silent for too long?
We are calling, let your love come down.

There is power in your love,
bringing laughter out of tears.
It can heal the wounded soul.
In the streets where anger reigns,
love will wash away the pain.
We are calling, heaven's love come down.

320 Robin Mark

Let your word go forth among the nations,
let your voice be heard among the people.
May they know our God, the only true God,
reigns on earth as you reign in heaven.

May your church be bold and speak with one
    voice,
may our hearts be strong and never failing.
May we know no fear
except a holy fear of you, my King.

321 Graham Kendrick

Lift up your heads, O you gates,
swing wide, you everlasting doors.
Lift up your heads, O you gates,
swing wide, you everlasting doors.

That the King of glory may come in,
that the King of glory may come in.
That the King of glory may come in,
that the King of glory may come in.

Up from the dead he ascends,
through every rank of heav'nly power.
Let heaven prepare the highest place,
throw wide the everlasting doors.

With trumpet blast and shouts of joy,
all heaven greets the risen King.
With angel choirs come line the way,
throw wide the gates and welcome him.

© 1991 Make Way Music

322 Graham Kendrick

Like a candle flame,
flick'ring small
in our darkness.
Uncreated light
shines through infant eyes.

God is with us,
alleluia,
come to save us,
alleluia,
alleluia!

Stars and angels sing,
yet the earth
sleeps in shadows;
can this tiny spark
set a world on fire?

Yet his light shall shine
from our lives,
spirit blazing,
as we touch the flame
or his holy fire.

© Copyright 1988 Make Way Music

323 David Hadden and Bob Silvester

Living under the shadow of his wing
we find security.
Standing in his presence we will bring
our worship, worship, worship to the King.

Bowed in adoration at his feet
we dwell in harmony.
Voices joined together that repeat,
worthy, worthy, worthy is the Lamb.

Heart to heart embracing in his love
reveals his purity.
Soaring in my spirit like a dove,
holy, holy, holy is the Lord.

© 1983 Restoration Music/Sovereign Music UK

324 Charles Wesley, John Cennick and Martin Madan

Lo, he comes with clouds descending,
once for mortal sinners slain;
thousand, thousand saints attending
swell the triumph of his train.
Alleluia! Alleluia! Alleluia!
Christ appears on earth to reign.

Every eye shall now behold him
robed in glorious majesty;
we who set at naught and sold him,
pierced and nailed him to the tree,
deeply wailing, deeply wailing, deeply wailing,
shall the true Messiah see.

Those dear tokens of his passion
still his dazzling body bears,
cause of endless exultation
to his ransomed worshippers:
with what rapture, with what rapture, with
    what rapture
gaze we on those glorious scars!

Yea, amen, let all adore thee,
high on thine eternal throne;
Saviour, take the pow'r and glory,
claim the kingdom for thine own.
Alleluia! Alleluia! Alleluia!
Thou shalt reign, and thou alone.

325 Graham Kendrick

Look what God has done for us,
over all the years we've shared,
ever since the day
he joined our flickering lights into one flame.
Look at all the lives he's changed,
by his grace we're not the same;
all the fruit that's grown,
all that's yet to come,
look what God has done.
And his love goes on and on for ever.

Continued overleaf

Look at all we've shared in him,
joy and laughter, tears and pain,
grace to carry on when darks were dark
and all our strength was gone.
Look at all the prayers he's heard,
all the times he's proved his word;
blessing on our homes,
children that have grown,
look what God has done.
And his love goes on and on for ever.

Freely we have all received,
freely we must also give,
thinking of the price he paid
that we might be his very own.
Born for such a time as this,
chosen for the harvest years,
we have just begun,
the best is yet to come,
look what God has done.
And his love goes on and on for ever.

© 1996 Make Way Music

326 Mark David Hanby

Look what the Lord has done,
look what the Lord has done,
he healed my body,
he touched my mind,
he saved me just in time.
Oh I'm gonna praise his name,
each day he's just the same.
Come on and praise him,
look what the Lord has done.

© 1974 Exaltation Music/Ministry Management Associates

327 Timothy Dudley-Smith

Lord, for the years
your love has kept and guided,
urged and inspired us,
cheered us on our way,
sought us and saved us,
pardoned and provided,
Lord of the years,
we bring our thanks today.

Lord, for that Word,
the Word of life which fires us,
speaks to our hearts
and sets our souls ablaze,
teaches and trains,
rebukes us and inspires us:
Lord of the Word,
receive your people's praise.

Lord, for our land,
in this our generation,
spirits oppressed by pleasure,
wealth and care;
for young and old,
for commonwealth and nation,
Lord of our land,
be pleased to hear our prayer.

Lord, for our world;
when we disown and doubt him,
loveless in strength,
and comfortless in pain,
hungry and helpless,
lost indeed without him:
Lord of the world,
we pray that Christ may reign.

Lord for ourselves;
in living pow'r remake us –
self on the cross
and Christ upon the throne,
past put behind us,
for the future take us:
Lord of our lives,
to live for Christ alone.

© Timothy Dudley-Smith

328 Graham Kendrick

Lord, have mercy on us,
come and heal our land.
Cleanse with your fire,
heal with your touch.
Humbly we bow
and call upon you now.
O Lord, have mercy on us,
O Lord, have mercy on us.

© 1991 Make Way Music

329 Geoff Bullock

Lord, I come to you,
let my heart be changed, renewed,
flowing from the grace
that I found in you.
And, Lord, I've come to know
the weaknesses I see in me
will be stripped away
by the pow'r of your love.

Hold me close,
let your love surround me,
bring me near,
draw me to your side;
and as I wait,
I'll rise up like an eagle,
and I will soar with you;
your Spirit leads me on
in the pow'r of your love.

Lord, unveil my eyes,
let me see you face to face,
the knowledge of your love
as you live in me.
Lord, renew my mind
as your will unfolds in my life,
in living every day
in the pow'r of your love.

© 1992 Word Music Inc./CopyCare

330 Rick Founds

Lord, I lift your name on high;
Lord, I love to sing your praises.
I'm so glad you're in my life;
I'm so glad you came to save us.
(Repeat)

You came from heaven to earth
to show the way,
from the earth to the cross,
my debt to pay,
from the cross to the grave,
from the grave to the sky,
Lord, I lift your name on high.

© 1989 Maranatha! Music/CopyCare

331 Darlene Zschech

Lord, my heart cries out,
glory to the King,
my greatest love in life.
I hand you everthing.
Glory, glory, I hear the angels sing.

Open my ears,
let me hear your voice
to know that sweet sound.
O, my soul, rejoice.
Glory, glory, I hear the angels sing.

You're the Father to the fatherless,
the answer to my dreams.
I see you crowned in righteousness.
We cry glory to the King.
Comforter to the lonely,
the lifter of my head,
I see you veiled in majesty,
we cry glory, glory,
we cry glory, to the King.
We cry glory, glory,
we cry glory, to the King.

© 1997 Darlene Zschech/Hillsongs Australia/Kingsway's Thankyou Music

332 Jessy Dixon, Randy Scruggs and John Thompson

Lord of lords, King of kings,
maker of heaven and earth
and all good things.
We give you glory.
Lord Jehovah, Son of Man,
precious Prince of Peace and the great 'I Am'.
We give you glory.

Glory to God! Glory to God!
Glory to God Almighty in the highest!

Lord, you're righteous in all your ways.
We bless your holy name
and we will give you praise.
We give you glory.
You reign for ever in majesty.
We praise you and lift you up for eternity.
We give you glory.

© 1983 Windswept Pacific Music

333 Lucy Fisher

Lord of the heavens and the earth,
my Saviour, Redeemer, risen Lord,
all honour and glory, pow'r and strength
to him upon the throne.
(Repeat)

Holy, holy, you are worthy,
praises to the Son of God.
Jesus, you alone are worthy,
crowned in righteousness and peace.
Glory, glory, hallelujah,
praises to the great 'I Am'.
Hosanna, join with angels singing,
worthy is the Lamb of God.

(Last time)
Worthy is the Lamb of God,
worthy is the Lamb of God,
worthy is the Lamb of God.

334 John Thompson and Randy Scruggs

Lord, prepare me
to be a sanctuary
pure and holy, tried and true,
with thanksgiving.
I'll be a living sanctuary
for you.

335 Graham Kendrick

Lord, the light of your love is shining,
in the midst of the darkness, shining;
Jesus, Light of the World, shine upon us,
set us free by the truth you now bring us.
Shine on me, shine on me.

Shine, Jesus, shine,
fill this land with the Father's glory;
blaze, Spirit, blaze,
set our hearts on fire.

Flow, river, flow,
flood the nations with grace and mercy;
send forth your word, Lord,
and let there be light.

Lord, I come to your awesome presence,
from the shadows into your radiance;
by the blood I may enter your brightness,
search me, try me, consume all my darkness.
Shine on me, shine on me.

As we gaze on your kingly brightness,
so our faces display your likeness,
ever changing from glory to glory;
mirrored here may our lives tell your story.
Shine on me, shine on me.

336 Judy Bailey

Lord, we lift you high
when we praise your name,
when we worship you
and our hands are raised,
that is how we lift you up.
Lord, we lift you high
when we tell the truth,
when we give our best
in everything we do,
that is how we lift you up.

By our voices be lifted, lifted,
by our actions, Lord, be lifted high.
By our love, Lord, be lifted, lifted,
by our lives, O Lord, be lifted high.

Lord, we lift you high
when we're good and kind,
when we turn from wrong
and we do what's right,
that is how we lift you up.
Lord, we lift you high
when we shine like stars,
when we tell our friends
just how good you are,
that is how we lift you up.

You are God, Jesus the Lord of all,
we place you above all else.
So shine through me
and keep drawing the world
to your heart.

Lord, we lift you high
when we praise your name,
when we worship you
and our hands are raised,
that is how we lift you up.
Lord, we lift you high
when we tell the truth,
when we give our best
in everything we do,
that is how we lift you up.

© Ice Music Ltd

337 Trish Morgan, Ray Goudie, Ian Townend and Dave Bankhead

Lord, we long for you to move in power.
There's a hunger deep within our hearts
to see healing in our nation.
Send your Spirit to revive us.

Heal our nation!
Heal our nation!
Heal our nation!
Pour out your Spirit on this land!

Lord, we hear your Spirit coming closer,
a mighty wave to break upon our land,
bringing justice and forgiveness.
God, we cry to you, 'Revive us!'

© 1986 Kingsway's Thankyou Music

338 Richard Lewis

Lord, we long to see your glory,
gaze upon your lovely face.
Holy Spirit, come among us,
lead us to that secret place.
Holy God, we long to see your glory,
to touch your holy majesty, O Lord.
Holy God, let us stay in your presence,
and worship at your feet for evermore.
Holy God. Holy God.

© 1997 Kingsway's Thankyou Music

339 Lynn DeShazo

Lord, you are more precious than silver,
Lord, you are more costly than gold.
Lord, you are more beautiful than diamonds,
and nothing I desire compares with you.

© 1982 Integrity's Hosanna! Music/Kingsway's Thankyou Music

340 Graham Kendrick

Lord, you are so precious to me,
Lord, you are so precious to me
and I love you, yes, I love you
because you first loved me.

Lord, you are so gracious to me . . .

Lord, you a father to me . . .

Lord, you are so faithful to me . . .

Lord, you are so loving to me . . .

© 1986 Kingsway's Thankyou Music

341 Martin Smith

Lord, you have my heart,
and I will search for yours;
Jesus, take my life and lead me on.
Lord, you have my heart,
and I will search for yours;
let me be to you a sacrifice.

And I will praise you, Lord
(I will praise you, Lord).
And I will sing of love come down
(I will sing of love come down).
And as you show your face
(show your face),
we'll see your glory here.

© 1992 Kingsway's Thankyou Music

342 Ian Smale

Lord, you put a tongue in my mouth
and I want to sing to you.
Lord, you put a tongue in my mouth
and I want to sing to you.
Lord, you put a tongue in my mouth
and I want to sing only to you.
Lord Jesus, free us in our praise;
Lord Jesus, free us in our praise.

Lord, you put some hands on my arms
which I want to raise to you . . .

Lord, you put some feet on my legs
and I want to dance to you . . .

© 1983 Kingsway's Thankyou Music

343 Charles Wesley

Love divine, all loves excelling,
joy of heav'n, to earth come down,
fix in us thy humble dwelling,
all thy faithful mercies crown.

Jesu, thou art all compassion,
pure unbounded love thou art;
visit us with thy salvation,
enter every trembling heart.

Breathe, O breathe thy loving Spirit
into every troubled breast;
let us all in thee inherit,
let us find thy promised rest.

Take away the love of sinning,
Alpha and Omega be;
end of faith, as its beginning,
set our hearts at liberty.

Come, almighty to deliver,
let us all thy grace receive;
suddenly return, and never,
never more thy temples leave.

Thee we would be always blessing,
serve thee as thy hosts above;
pray, and praise thee without ceasing,
glory in thy perfect love.

Finish then thy new creation,
pure and spotless let us be;
let us see thy great salvation
perfectly restored in thee.

Changed from glory into glory,
till in heav'n we take our place,
till we cast our crowns before thee,
lost in wonder, love, and praise.

344 Graham Kendrick

Love of Christ, come now,
like a mighty ocean.
Flow through here,
with mercy and grace;
love of Christ, come now.

© 1989 Make Way Music

345 Robert Lowry

Low in the grave he lay,
Jesus, my Saviour;
waiting the coming day,
Jesus, my Lord.

> *Up from the grave he arose,*
> *with a mighty triumph o'er his foes;*
> *he arose a victor from the dark domain,*
> *and he lives for ever with his saints to reign.*
> *He arose! He arose!*
> *Hallelujah! Christ arose!*

Vainly they watch his bed,
Jesus, my Saviour;
vainly they seal the dead,
Jesus, my Lord.

Death cannot keep its prey,
Jesus, my Saviour;
he tore the bars away,
Jesus, my Lord.

346 Jack W. Hayford

Majesty, worship his majesty,
unto Jesus be glory, honour and praise.
Majesty, kingdom authority
flows from his throne unto his own,
his anthem raise.
So exalt, lift up on high the name of Jesus;
magnify, come glorify Christ Jesus the King.
Majesty, worship his majesty,
Jesus who died, now glorified,
King of all kings.

347 Edwin Hawkins

Make a joyful noise, all ye people,
sing a song to the Lord
of his goodness and his mercy,
of his faithfulness and love.
(Repeat)

> *Worship the Lord,*
> *let's praise his holy name.*
> *Worship the Lord,*
> *let's magnify his name.*
> (Repeat)

348 Sebastian Temple

Make me a channel of your peace.
Where there is hatred, let me bring your love.
Where there is injury, your pardon, Lord,
and where there's doubt, true faith in you.

> *O Master, grant that I may never seek*
> *so much to be consoled as to console,*
> *to be understood, as to understand,*
> *to be loved, as to love with all my soul.*

Make me a channel of your peace.
Where there's despair in life, let me bring hope.
Where there is darkness, only light,
and where there's sadness, ever joy.

Make me a channel of your peace.
It is in pardoning that we are pardoned,
in giving of ourselves that we receive,
and in dying that we're born to eternal life.

349 Graham Kendrick

Make way, make way, for Christ the King
in splendour arrives;
fling wide the gates and welcome him
into your lives.

> *Make way (make way),*
> *make way (make way),*
> *for the King of kings*
> *(for the King of kings);*
> *make way (make way),*
> *make way (make way),*
> *and let his kingdom in!*

He comes the broken hearts to heal,
the prisoners to free;
the deaf shall hear, the lame shall dance,
the blind shall see.

And those who mourn with heavy hearts,
who weep and sigh,
with laughter, joy and royal crown
he'll beautify.

We call you now to worship him
as Lord of all,
to have no gods before him,
their thrones must fall.

350 Philipp Bliss

Man of sorrows! What a name
for the Son of God who came
ruined sinners to reclaim!
Alleluia! What a Saviour!

Bearing shame and scoffing rude,
in my place condemned he stood;
sealed my pardon with his blood:
Alleluia! What a Saviour!

Continued overleaf

Guilty, vile and helpless we;
spotless Lamb of God was he:
full atonement – can it be?
Alleluia! What a Saviour!

Lifted up was he to die:
'It is finished!' was his cry;
now in heav'n exalted high:
Alleluia! What a Saviour!

When he comes, our glorious King,
all his ransomed home to bring,
then anew this song we'll sing:
Alleluia! What a Saviour!

351 Chris Bowater

May our worship
be as fragrance,
may our worship
be as incense poured forth,
may our worship
be acceptable as a living sacrifice,
as a living sacrifice.

We are willing
to pay the price,
we are willing
to lay down our lives
as an offering of obedience,
as a living sacrifice,
as a living sacrifice.

© 1992 Sovereign Lifestyle Music

352 Graham Kendrick

May the fragrance of Jesus fill this place
(may the fragrance of Jesus fill this place).
May the fragrance of Jesus fill this place
(lovely fragrance of Jesus),
rising from the sacrifice
of lives laid down in adoration.

May the glory of Jesus fill his church
(may the glory of Jesus fill his church).
May the glory of Jesus fill his church
(radiant glory of Jesus),
shining from our faces
as we gaze in adoration.

May the beauty of Jesus fill my life
(may the beauty of Jesus fill my life).
May the beauty of Jesus fill my life
(perfect beauty of Jesus),
fill my thoughts, my words, my deeds;
may I give in adoration.
Fill my thoughts, my words, my deeds;
may I give in adoration.

© 1986 Kingsway's Thankyou Music

353 Graham Kendrick

Meekness and majesty,
manhood and deity,
in perfect harmony,
the Man who is God.
Lord of eternity
dwells in humanity,
kneels in humility
and washes our feet.

O what a mystery,
meekness and majesty.
Bow down and worship
for this is your God,
this is your God.

Father's pure radiance,
perfect in innocence,
yet learns obedience
to death on a cross.
Suffering to give us life,
conquering through sacrifice,
and as they crucify
prays: 'Father, forgive.'

Wisdom unsearchable,
God the invisible,
love indestructible
in frailty appears.
Lord of infinity,
stooping so tenderly,
lifts our humanity
to the heights of his throne.

© 1986 Kingsway's Thankyou Music

354 Martin Smith

Men of faith, rise up and sing
of the great and glorious King.
You are strong when you feel weak,
in your brokenness complete.

Shout to the north and the south,
sing to the east and the west.
Jesus is Saviour to all,
Lord of heaven and earth.

Rise up, women of the truth,
stand and sing to broken hearts.
Who can know the healing pow'r
of our awesome King of love.

We've been through fire,
we've been through rain,
we've been refined by the pow'r of his name.
We've fallen deeper in love with you,
you've burned the truth on our lips.

Rise up, church with broken wings,
fill this place with songs again
of our God who reigns on high,
by his grace again we'll fly.

© 1995 Curious? Music UK/Kingsway's Thankyou Music

355 David Ruis

Mercy is falling, is falling, is falling,
mercy it falls like the sweet spring rain.
Mercy is falling, is falling all over me.
(Repeat)

Hey O, I receive your mercy.
Hey O, I receive your grace.
Hey O, I will dance for evermore.
(Repeat)

© 1994 Mercy/Vineyard Publishing/Music Services/CopyCare

356 Mark Johnson, Helen Johnson and Chris Bowater

Mighty God,
everlasting Father,
wonderful Counsellor,
you're the Prince of Peace.
(Repeat)

You are Lord of heaven,
you are called Emmanuel;
God is now with us,
ever-present to deliver.
You are God eternal,
you are Lord of the all the earth;
love has come to us,
bringing us new birth.

A light to those in darkness,
and a guide to paths of peace;
love and mercy dawns,
grace, forgiveness and salvation.
Light for revelation,
glory to your people;
Son of the Most High,
God's love-gift to all.

© 1991 Sovereign Lifestyle Music

357 Eugene Greco, Gerrit Gustafson and Don Moen

Mighty is our God,
mighty is our King;
mighty is our Lord,
ruler of everything.
(Repeat)

His name is higher,
higher than any other name;
his pow'r is greater
for he has created everything.

Glory to our God,
glory to our King,
glory to our Lord,
ruler of everything.
(Repeat)

His name is higher . . .

Mighty is our God . . .

© 1989 Integrity's Hosanna! Music/Kingsway's Thankyou Music

358 E. E. Hewitt

More about Jesus would I know,
more of his grace to others show;
more of his saving fullness see,
more of his love who died for me.

More, more about Jesus,
more, more about Jesus;
more of his saving fullness see,
more of his love who died for me.

More about Jesus let me learn,
more of his holy will discern;
Spirit of God my teacher be,
showing the things of Christ to me.

More about Jesus; in his word,
holding communion with my Lord;
hearing his voice in every line,
making each faithful saying mine.

More about Jesus; on his throne,
riches in glory all his own;
more of his kingdom's sure increase;
more of his coming, Prince of Peace.

359 Jude del Hierro

More love (more love),
more power (more power),
more of you in my life.
(Repeat)

And I will worship you with all of my heart,
and I will worship you with all of my mind,
and I will worship you with all of my strength,
for you are my Lord.

And I will seek your face with all of my heart,
and I will seek your face with all of my mind,
and I will seek your face with all of my strength,
for you are my Lord.

(Last time)
For you are my Lord; you are my Lord.

© 1987 Mercy/Vineyard Publishing/Music Services/CopyCare

360 Lindell Cooley and Bruce Haynes

More of your glory,
more of your power,
more of your Spirit in me.
Speak to my heart
and change my life,
manifest yourself in me.

It's been a long time,
you have stayed on my mind.
There's a stirring in my soul
that causes me to know
how much I need you.

Send your glory
(send your glory),
send your power
(send your power),
send your Spirit
(send your Spirit),
come and change me
(come and change me).

© 1996 Integrity's Hosanna! Music/Kingsway's Thankyou Music/
Centergy Music/CopyCare

361 Brian Doerksen

More than oxygen
I need your love.
More than life-giving food
the hungry dream of.
More than an eloquent word
depends on the tongue.
More than a passionate song
needs to be sung.

More than a word could ever say,
more than a song could ever convey.
I need you more than all of these things.
Father, I need you more.

More than magnet and steel
are drawn to unite.
More than poets love words
to rhyme as they write.

More than the comforting warmth
of the sun in the spring.
More than the eagle loves wind
under its wings.

More than a blazing fire
on a winter's night.
More than the tall evergreens
reach for the light.
More than the pounding waves
long for the shore.
More than these gifts you give,
I love you more.

362 Stuart Townend

My first love is a blazing fire,
I feel his pow'rful love in me;
for he has kindled a flame of passion,
and I will let it grow in me.
And in the night I will sing your praise, my love.
And in the morning I'll seek your face, my love.

And like a child I will dance in your presence.
O let the joy of heaven pour down on me.
I still remember the first day I met you,
and I don't ever want to lose that fire,
my first love.

My first love is a rushing river,
a waterfall that will never cease;
and in the torrent of tears and laughter,
I feel a healing power released.
And I will draw from your well of life, my love.
And in your grace I'll be satisfied, my love.

Restore the years of the church's slumber,
revive the fire that has grown so dim;
renew the love of those first encounters,
that we may come alive again.
And we will rise like the dawn throughout
the earth,
until the trumpet announces your return.

363 Graham Kendrick

My heart is full of admiration
for you, my Lord, my God and King.
Your excellence, my inspiration,
your words of grace have made my spirit sing.

All the glory, honour and pow'r
belong to you, belong to you.
Jesus, Saviour, anointed One,
I worship you, I worship you.

You love what's right and hate what's evil,
therefore your God sets you on high,
and on your head pours oil of gladness,
while fragrance fills your royal palaces.

Your throne, O God, will last for ever,
justice will be your royal decree.
In majesty, ride out victorious,
for righteousness, truth and humility.

364 Robin Mark

My heart will sing to you because of your
great love,
a love so rich, so pure, a love beyond compare;
the wilderness, the barren place,
become a blessing in the warmth of your
embrace.

When earthly wisdom dims the light of
knowing you,
or if my search for understanding clouds
your way,
to you I fly, my hiding-place,
where revelation is beholding face to face.

May my heart sing your praise for ever,
may my voice lift your name, my God;
may my soul know no other treasure
than your love, than your love.

365 Edward Mote

My hope is built on nothing less
than Jesus' blood and righteousness.
I dare not trust the sweetest frame,
but wholly lean on Jesus' name.

On Christ the solid Rock I stand;
all other ground is sinking sand,
all other ground is sinking sand.

When darkness veils his lovely face,
I rest on his unchanging grace;
in every high and stormy gale
my anchor holds within the veil.

His oath, his covenant, his blood
support me in the 'whelming flood;
when all around my soul gives way,
he then is all my hope and stay.

When he shall come with trumpet sound,
O may I then in him be found;
dressed in his righteousness alone,
faultless to stand before the throne.

366 William R. Featherston and Adoniram J. Gordon

My Jesus, I love thee, I know thou art mine.
For thee all the follies of sin I resign.
My gracious Redeemer, my Saviour art thou.
If ever I loved thee, my Jesus, 'tis now.

I love thee because thou has first lovèd me,
and purchased my pardon on Calvary's tree.
I love thee for wearing the thorns on thy brow.
If ever I loved thee, my Jesus, 'tis now.

In mansions of glory and endless delight,
I'll ever adore thee in heaven so bright.
I'll sing with a glittering crown on my brow.
If ever I loved thee, my Jesus, 'tis now.

367 Darlene Zschech

My Jesus, my Saviour,
Lord, there is none like you.
All of my days
I want to praise
the wonders of your mighty love.

My comfort, my shelter,
tower of refuge and strength,
let every breath,
all that I am,
never cease to worship you.

Shout to the Lord,
all the earth, let us sing
power and majesty, praise to the King.
Mountains bow down and the seas will roar
at the sound of your name.
I sing for joy
at the work of your hands.
For ever I'll love you, for ever I'll stand.
Nothing compares to the promise
I have in you.

368 Daniel Gardner

My life is in you, Lord,
my strength is in you, Lord,
my hope is in you, Lord,
in you, it's in you.
(Repeat)

I will praise you with all of my life,
I will praise you with all of my strength,
with all of my life,
with all of my strength.
All of my hope is in you.

369 Noel and Tricia Richards

My lips shall praise you, my great Redeemer;
my heart will worship, Almighty Saviour.

You take all my guilt away,
turn the darkest night to brightest day;
you are the restorer of my soul.

Love that conquers every fear,
in the midst of trouble you draw near;
you are the restorer of my soul.

You're the source of happiness,
bringing peace when I am in distress;
you are the restorer of my soul.

370 Graham Kendrick

My Lord, what love is this,
that pays so dearly,
that I, the guilty one,
may go free!

Amazing love, O what sacrifice,
the Son of God, giv'n for me.
My debt he pays, and my death he dies,
that I might live,
that I might live.

And so they watched him die,
despised, rejected;
but O, the blood he shed
flowed for me!

And now this love of Christ
shall flow like rivers;
come, wash your guilt away,
live again!

© 1989 Make Way Music

371 Reuben Morgan

My spirit rests in you alone,
you're all I know.
Embrace and touch me
like a child,
I'm safe in you.

You're my shelter through it all,
you're my refuge and my strength,
Lord, I hide in the shadow of your wings.
(Repeat)

My Lord, you're faithful,
you supply all good things,
you know completely
all my thoughts,
my deepest needs.

© 1997 Reuben Morgan/Hillsongs Australia/Kingsway's Thankyou Music

372 Sarah Flower Adams

Nearer, my God, to thee,
nearer to thee!
And though it be
a cross that raises me:
still all my song would be,
'Nearer, my God, to thee.
Nearer, my God, to thee,
nearer to thee.'

Though, like the wanderer,
the sun gone down,
darkness be over me,
my rest a stone;
yet in my dreams I'd be
nearer, my God, to thee.
Nearer, my God, to thee,
nearer to thee!

There let the way appear,
steps unto heav'n;
all that thou sendest me
in mercy giv'n:
angels to beckon me
nearer, my God, to thee.
Nearer, my God, to thee,
nearer to thee!

Then, with my waking thoughts
bright with thy praise,
out of my stony griefs
Bethel I'll raise;
so by my woes to be
nearer, my God, to thee.
Nearer, my God, to thee,
nearer to thee.

Or if on joyful wing
cleaving the sky,
sun, moon and stars forgot,
upwards I fly,
still all my song shall be,
'Nearer, my God, to thee.
Nearer, my God, to thee,
nearer to thee.'

373 Andy Park

No one but you, Lord,
can satisfy the longing in my heart.
Nothing I do, Lord,
can take the place of drawing near to you.

Only you can fill my deepest longing,
only you can breathe in me new life;
only you can fill my heart with laughter,
only you can answer my heart's cry.

Father, I love you,
come satisfy the longing in my heart.
Fill me, overwhelm me,
until I know your love deep in my heart.

© 1988 Mercy/Vineyard Publishing/Music Services/CopyCare

374 Robert Gay

No other name but the name of Jesus,
no other name but the name of the Lord;
no other name but the name of Jesus
is worthy of glory,
and worthy of honour,
and worthy of power and all praise.
(Repeat)

His name is exalted far above the earth.
His name is high above the heavens;
his name is exalted far above the earth;
give glory and honour and praise unto his name.

© 1988 Integrity's Hosanna! Music/Kingsway's Thankyou Music

375 Graham Kendrick

No scenes of stately majesty
for the King of kings.
No nights aglow with candle flame
for the King of love.
No flags of empire hung in shame
for Calvary.
No flowers perfumed the lonely way
that led him to
a borrowed tomb for Easter Day.

No wreaths upon the ground were laid
for the King of kings.
Only a crown of thorns remained
where he gave his love.
A message scrawled in irony –
King of the Jews –
lay trampled where they turned away,
and no one knew
that it was the first Easter Day.

Yet nature's finest colours blaze
for the King of kings.
And stars in jewelled clusters say,
'Worship heaven's King.'
Two thousand springtimes more have bloomed –
is that enough?
Oh, how can I be satisfied
until he hears
the whole world sing of Easter love.

My prayers shall be a fragrance sweet
for the King of kings.
My love the flowers at his feet
for the King of love.
My vigil is to watch and pray
until he comes.
My highest tribute to obey
and live to know
the pow'r of that first Easter Day.

I long for scenes of majesty
for the risen King.
For nights aglow with candle flame
for the King of love.
A nation hushed upon its knees
at Calvary,
where all our sins and griefs were nailed
and hope was born
of everlasting Easter Day.

© 1997 Make Way Music

376 Robin Mark

No, not by might,
nor even power,
but by your Spirit, O Lord.
Healer of hearts, binder of wounds.

Lives that are lost, restored.
Flow through this land
till everyone praises your name
once more.

377 Noel and Tricia Richards

Nothing shall separate us
from the love of God.
Nothing shall separate us
from the love of God.

God did not spare his only Son,
gave him to save us all.
Sin's price was met by Jesus' death
and heaven's mercy falls.

Up from the grave Jesus was raised
to sit at God's right hand;
pleading our cause in heaven's courts,
forgiven we can stand.

Now by God's grace we have embraced
a life set free from sin;
we shall deny all that destroys
our union with him.

378 Joey Holder

Now unto the King eternal,
unto the King immortal,
unto the King invisible,
the only wise God,
the only wise God.
(Repeat)

Unto the King be glory and honour,
unto the King for ever.
Unto the King be glory and honour
for ever and ever, Amen. Amen.

379 Elizabeth Ann Porter Head

O Breath of Life, come sweeping through us,
revive your church with life and pow'r;
O Breath of Life, come cleanse, renew us,
and fit your church to meet this hour.

O Breath of Love, come breathe within us,
renewing thought and will and heart;
come, love of Christ, afresh to win us,
revive your church in every part!

O Wind of God, come bend us, break us,
till humbly we confess our need;
then, in your tenderness remake us,
revive, restore – for this we plead.

Revive us, Lord; is zeal abating
while harvest fields are vast and white?
Revive us, Lord, the world is waiting –
equip thy church to spread the light.

380 John Francis Wade, trans. Frederick Oakeley and others

O come, all ye faithful,
joyful and triumphant,
O come ye, O come ye to Bethlehem;
come and behold him,
born the king of angels:

> *O come, let us adore him,*
> *O come, let us adore him,*
> *O come, let us adore him,*
> *Christ the Lord.*

God of God,
Light of Light,
lo, he abhors not the Virgin's womb;
very God,
begotten not created:

See how the shepherds,
summoned to his cradle,
leaving their flocks, draw nigh with lowly fear;
we too will thither
bend our joyful footsteps:

Continued overleaf

Lo, star-led chieftains,
Magi, Christ adoring,
offer him incense, gold and myrrh;
we to the Christ-child
bring our hearts' oblations:

O come, let us adore him,
O come, let us adore him,
O come, let us adore him,
Christ the Lord.

Sing, choirs of angels,
sing in exultation,
sing, all ye citizens of heav'n above;
glory to God
in the highest:

Yea, Lord, we greet thee,
born this happy morning,
Jesu, to thee be glory giv'n;
Word of the Father,
now in flesh appearing:

381 Graham Kendrick

O come and join the dance
that all began so long ago,
when Christ the Lord was born in Bethlehem.
Through all the years of darkness
still the dance goes on and on,
oh, take my hand and come and join the song.

Rejoice! (Rejoice!)
Rejoice! (Rejoice!)
O lift your voice and sing,
and open up your heart to welcome him.
Rejoice! (Rejoice!)
Rejoice! (Rejoice!)
and welcome now your King,
for Christ the Lord was born in Bethlehem.

Come, shed your heavy load
and dance your worries all away,
for Christ the Lord was born in Bethlehem.
He came to break the pow'r of sin
and turn your night to day,
oh, take my hand and come and join the song.

Let laughter ring and angels sing
and joy be all around,
for Christ the Lord was born in Bethlehem.
And if you seek with all your heart
he surely can be found,
oh, take my hand and come and join the song.

© Copyright 1988 Make Way Music

382 Graham Kendrick

O Father of the fatherless,
in whom all families are blessed,
I love the way you father me.
You gave me life, forgave the past,
now in your arms I'm safe at last;
I love the way you father me.

Father me,
for ever you'll father me,
and in your embrace
I'll be for ever secure;
I love the way you father me.
I love the way you father me.

When bruised and broken I draw near,
you hold me close and dry my tears;
I love the way you father me.
At last my fearful heart is still,
surrendered to your perfect will;
I love the way you father me.

If in my foolishness I stray,
returning empty and ashamed,
I love the way you father me.
Exchanging for my wretchedness
your radiant robes of righteousness,
I love the way you father me.

And when I look into your eyes,
from deep within my spirit cries,
I love the way you father me.
Before such love I stand amazed
and ever will through endless days;
I love the way you father me.

© 1992 Make Way Music

383 Charles Wesley

O for a thousand tongues to sing
my dear Redeemer's praise,
my dear Redeemer's praise,
the glories of my God and King,
the triumphs of his grace.

Jesus! the name that charms our fears,
that bids our sorrows cease,
that bids our sorrows cease;
'tis music in the sinner's ears,
'tis life and health and peace.

He breaks the pow'r of cancelled sin,
he sets the prisoner free,
he sets the prisoner free;
his blood can make the foulest clean;
his blood availed for me.

He speaks; and listening to his voice,
new life the dead receive,
new life the dead receive,
the mournful broken hearts rejoice,
the humble poor believe.

Hear him, ye deaf; his praise, ye dumb,
your loosened tongues employ,
your loosened tongues employ;
ye blind, behold your Saviour come;
and leap, ye lame, for joy!

My gracious Master and my God,
assist me to proclaim,
assist me to proclaim,
and spread through all the earth abroad
the honours of thy name.

384 Graham Kendrick

O give thanks to the Lord,
for his love will never end.
O give thanks to the Lord,
for his love it never will end.
(Repeat)

Sing to him, sing your praise to him.
Tell the world of all he has done.
Fill the nations with celebrations,
to welcome him as he comes.

Give him thanks for the fruitful earth,
for the sun, the seasons, the rain.
For the joys of his good creation,
the life and breath he sustains.

Let the heavens rejoice before him,
the earth and all it contains.
All creation in jubilation,
join in the shout, 'The Lord reigns!'

Let the hearts of those who seek him
be happy now in his love.
Let their faces look up and gaze
at his gracious smile from above.

© 1991 Make Way Music

385 Jamie Owens-Collins

O God, Most High, Almighty King,
the champion of heaven, Lord of everything;
you've fought, you've won, death's lost its
    sting,
and standing in your victory we sing.

You have broken the chains
that held our captive souls.
You have broken the chains
and used them on your foes.
All your enemies are bound,
they tremble at the sound of your name;
Jesus, you have broken the chains.

The pow'r of hell has been undone,
captivity held captive by the risen One,
and in the name of God's great Son,
we claim the mighty victory you've won.

(Last time)
Jesus, you have broken the chains.
Jesus, you have broken the chains.

© 1992 Fairhill Music/CopyCare

386
William Booth

O God of burning, cleansing flame:
send the fire!
Your blood-bought gift today we claim:
send the fire today!
Look down and see this waiting host,
and send the promised Holy Ghost;
we need another Pentecost!
Send the fire today!
Send the fire today!

God of Elijah, hear our cry:
send the fire!
and make us fit to live or die:
send the fire today!
To burn up every trace of sin,
to bring the light and glory in,
the revolution now begin!
Send the fire today!
Send the fire today!

It's fire we want, for fire we plead:
send the fire!
The fire will meet our every need:
send the fire today!
For strength to always to do what's right,
for grace to conquer in the fight,
for pow'r to walk the world in white.
Send the fire today!
Send the fire today!

To make our weak heart strong and brave:
send the fire!
To live, a dying world to save:
send the fire today!
O, see us on your altar lay,
we give our lives to you today,
so crown the offering now we pray:
send the fire today!
Send the fire today!
Send the fire today!

© 1994 Kingsway's Thankyou Music

387
Philip Doddridge

O happy day! that fixed my choice
on thee, my Saviour and my God!
Well may this glowing heart rejoice,
and tell its raptures all abroad.

O happy day! O happy day!
when Jesus washed my sins away;
he taught me how to watch and pray,
and live rejoicing every day;
O happy day! O happy day!
when Jesus washed my sins away.

'Tis done, the work of grace is done!
I am the Lord's, and he is mine!
He drew me, and I followed on,
glad to confess the voice divine.

Now rest, my long-divided heart,
fixed on this blissful centre, rest;
nor ever from thy Lord depart,
with him of every good possessed.

High heav'n, that heard the solemn vow,
that vow renewed shall daily hear;
till in life's latest hour I bow,
and bless in death a bond so dear.

388
Graham Kendrick

O, heaven is in my heart.
O, heaven is in my heart.
(Repeat)

Leader	The kingdom of our God is here,
All	heaven is in my heart.
Leader	The presence of his majesty,
All	heaven is in my heart.
Leader	And in his presence joy abounds,
All	heaven is in my heart.
Leader	The light of holiness surrounds,
All	heaven is in my heart.
Leader	His precious life on me he spent,
All	heaven is in my heart.
Leader	To give me life without an end,
All	heaven is in my heart.
Leader	In Christ is all my confidence,
All	heaven is in my heart.
Leader	The hope of my inheritance,
All	heaven is in my heart.

Leader	We are a temple for his throne,
All	heaven is in my heart.
Leader	And Christ is the foundation stone,
All	heaven is in my heart.
Leader	He will return to take us home,
All	heaven is in my heart.
Leader	The Spirit and the Bride say, 'Come!',
All	heaven is in my heart.

© 1991 Make Way Music

389 Graham Kendrick

Oh, I was made for this,
to know your tender kiss,
to know a love divine,
to know this love is mine.
And I was made to laugh,
and I was made to sing,
given the gift of life,
you gave me everything.
(Repeat)

So I will celebrate
and drink your cup of joy,
I will give thanks each day and sing.
My joy is found in you
and you are all my joy.
Oh, I was made for this.

My feet were made to dance,
my spirit made to soar;
my life is not by chance,
you give me more and more.
For I was made for you,
and I have made my choice,
and all that stole my joy,
I left it at the cross.

When I was far away,
you ran to welcome me;
I felt your warm embrace,
I saw your smiling face.
And when you rescued me,
I saw my destiny:
to worship you, my Lord,
to be a friend of God.

I was made to love you, Jesus,
I was made for this.
I was made to love you, Jesus,
I was made for this.

© 1995 Make Way Music

390 Martin Smith

Oh, lead me
to the place where I can find you,
oh, lead me
to the place where you'll be.
Lead me to the cross
where we first met,
draw me to my knees
so we can talk;
let me feel your breath,
let me know you're here with me.

© 1994 Curious? Music UK/Kingsway's Thankyou Music

391 John Ernest Bode

O Jesus, I have promised
to serve thee to the end;
be thou for ever near me,
my Master and my friend:
I shall not fear the battle
if thou art by my side,
nor wander from the pathway
if thou wilt be my guide.

O let me feel thee near me:
the world is ever near;
I see the sights that dazzle,
the tempting sounds I hear;
my foes are ever near me,
around me and within;
but, Jesus, draw thou nearer,
and shield my soul from sin.

O let me hear thee speaking
in accents clear and still,
above the storms of passion,
the murmurs of self-will;
O speak to reassure me,
to hasten or control;
O speak and make me listen,
thou guardian of my soul.

Continued overleaf

O Jesus, thou hast promised
to all that follow thee,
that where thou art in glory
there shall thy servants be;
and, Jesus, I have promised
to serve thee to the end:
O give me grace to follow,
my Master and my friend.

O let me see thy footmarks,
and in them plant my own;
my hope to follow duly
is in thy strength alone:
O guide me, call me, draw me,
uphold me to the end;
and then in heav'n receive me,
my Saviour and my friend,
and then in heav'n receive me,
my Saviour and my friend.

392 John Wimber

O let the Son of God enfold you
with his Spirit and his love,
let him fill your heart and satisfy your soul.
O let him have the things that hold you,
and his Spirit like a dove
will descend upon your life and make you whole.

Jesus, O Jesus,
come and fill your lambs.
Jesus, O Jesus,
come and fill your lambs.

O come and sing this song with gladness
as your hearts are filled with joy,
lift your hands in sweet surrender to his name.
O give him all your tears and sadness,
give him all your years of pain,
and you'll enter into life in Jesus' name.

© 1979 Mercy/Vineyard Publishing/Music Services/CopyCare

393 Phillips Brooks

O little town of Bethlehem,
how still we see thee lie!
Above thy deep and dreamless sleep
the silent stars go by.

Yet in thy dark streets shineth
the everlasting light;
the hopes and fears of the all the years
are met in thee tonight.

O morning stars, together
proclaim the holy birth,
and praises sing to God the King,
and peace upon the earth.
For Christ is born of Mary;
and, gathered all above,
while mortals sleep, the angels keep
their watch of wondering love.

How silently, how silently,
the wondrous gift is giv'n!
So God imparts to human hearts
the blessings of his heav'n.
No ear may hear his coming;
but in this world of sin,
where meek souls will receive him, still
the dear Christ enters in.

O holy child of Bethlehem,
descend to us, we pray;
cast out our sin, and enter in,
be born in us today.
We hear the Christmas angels
the great glad tidings tell:
O come to us, abide with us,
our Lord Emmanuel.

394 Traditional

O Lord, hear my prayer,
O Lord, hear my prayer:
when I call, answer me.
O Lord, hear my prayer,
O Lord, hear my prayer.
Come and listen to me.

395 Ben Lindquist and Don Moen

O Lord, how majestic is your name,
O Lord, how majestic is your name,
you are high and lifted up
and your glory fills the temple,
you are high and lifted up
and we worship you.

You are high and lifted up
and your glory fills the temple.
We worship you in spirit and truth,
we worship you in spirit and truth.
(Repeat)

You are exalted on high,
you reign in wisdom,
in power and in might.

396 Karl Boberg trans. Stuart K. Hine

O Lord, my God, when I, in awesome wonder,
consider all the works thy hand has made,
I see the stars, I hear the rolling thunder,
thy pow'r throughout the universe displayed.

> *Then sings my soul, my Saviour God, to thee:*
> *how great thou art, how great thou art.*
> *Then sings my soul, my Saviour God, to thee:*
> *how great thou art, how great thou art.*

When through the woods and forest glades I
    wander,
and hear the birds sing sweetly in the trees;
when I look down from lofty mountain grandeur,
and hear the brook, and feel the gentle breeze.

And when I think that God, his Son not sparing,
sent him to die, I scarce can take it in
that on the cross, my burden gladly bearing,
he bled and died to take away my sin.

When Christ shall come with shout of
    acclamation,
and take me home, what joy shall fill my heart;
then I shall bow in humble adoration,
and there proclaim: my God, how great thou
    art.

397 Psalm 131

O Lord, my heart is not proud,
nor haughty my eyes.
I have not gone after things too great,
nor marvels beyond me.

Truly I have set my soul
in silence and peace;
at rest, as a child in its mother's arms,
so is my soul.

398 Philip Lawson Johnston

O Lord our God, how majestic is your name;
the earth is filled with your glory.
O Lord our God, you are robed in majesty;
you've set your glory above the heavens.

> *We will magnify, we will magnify*
> *the Lord enthroned in Zion.*
> *We will magnify, we will magnify*
> *the Lord enthroned in Zion.*

O Lord our God, you have established a throne,
you reign in righteousness and splendour.
O Lord our God, the skies are ringing with
    your praise;
soon those on earth will come to worship.

O Lord our God, the world was made at your
    command,
in you all things now hold together.
Now to him who sits on the throne and to the
    Lamb
be praise and glory and pow'r for ever.

399 Graham Kendrick

O Lord, the clouds are gathering,
the fire of judgement burns,
how we have fallen!
O Lord, you stand appalled
to see your laws of love so scorned
and lives so broken.

> *Have mercy, Lord (have mercy, Lord),*
> *forgive us, Lord (forgive us, Lord),*
> *restore us, Lord,*
> *revive your church again.*
> *Let justice flow (let justice flow)*
> *like rivers (like rivers)*
> *and righteousness like a never-failing stream.*

Continued overleaf

O Lord, over the nations now,
where is the dove of peace?
Her wings are broken.
O Lord, while precious children starve,
the tools of war increase;
their bread is stolen.

Have mercy, Lord (have mercy, Lord),
forgive us, Lord (forgive us, Lord),
restore us, Lord,
revive your church again.
Let justice flow (let justice flow)
like rivers (like rivers)
and righteousness like a never-failing stream.

O Lord, dark pow'rs are poised to flood
our streets with hate and fear;
we must awaken!
O Lord, let love reclaim the lives
that sin would sweep away,
and let your kingdom come.

Yet, O Lord, your glorious cross shall tower
triumphant in this land,
evil confounding.
Through the fire your suffering church displays
the glories of her Christ:
praises resounding.

© 1987 Make Way Music

400   Geoff Bullock

O Lord, you lead me
by the still waters,
quietly restoring my soul.
You speak words of wisdom,
the promise of glory,
the pow'r of the presence of God.

Have faith in God,
let your hope rest
on the faith he has placed in your heart.
Never give up,
never let go
of the faith he has placed in your heart.

O Lord, you guide me
through all the darkness,
turning my night into day;
you'll never leave me,
never forsake me
the pow'r of the presence of God.

© 1993 Word Music Inc./CopyCare

401   Keith Green

O Lord, you're beautiful,
your face is all I seek,
for when your eyes are on this child,
your grace abounds to me.

O Lord, please light the fire
that once burned bright and clear,
replace the lamp of my first love
that burns with holy fear!

I wanna take your word
and shine it all around,
but first help me just to live it, Lord!
And when I'm doing well,
help me to never seek a crown,
for my reward is giving glory to you.

O Lord, you're beautiful,
your face is all I seek,
for when your eyes are on this child,
your grace abounds to me.

© Birdwing Music/BMG Songs Inc./Universal Songs/CopyCare

402   Graham Kendrick

O Lord, your tenderness,
melting all my bitterness,
O Lord, I receive your love.
O Lord, your loveliness,
changing all my ugliness,
O Lord, I receive your love.
O Lord, I receive your love,
O Lord, I receive your love.

© 1986 Kingsway's Thankyou Music

403 George Bennard

On a hill far away,
stood an old rugged cross,
the emblem of suffering and shame;
and I loved that old cross
where the dearest and best
for a world of lost sinners was slain.

So I'll cherish the old rugged cross,
till my trophies at last I lay down;
I will cling to the old rugged cross
and exchange it some day for a crown.

O, that old rugged cross,
so despised by the world,
has a wondrous attraction for me:
for the dear Lamb of God
left his glory above
to bear it to dark Calvary.

In the old rugged cross,
stained with blood so divine,
a wondrous beauty I see.
For 'twas on that old cross
Jesus suffered and died
to pardon and sanctify me.

To the old rugged cross
I will ever be true,
its shame and reproach gladly bear.
Then he'll call me some day
to my home far away;
there his glory for ever I'll share.

404 Cecil Frances Alexander (v. 4: Michael Forster)

Once in royal David's city
stood a lowly cattle shed,
where a mother laid her baby
in a manger for his bed:
Mary was that mother mild,
Jesus Christ her little child.

He came down to earth from heaven,
who is God and Lord of all,
and his shelter was a stable,
and his cradle was a stall;
with the poor and meek and lowly,
lived on earth our Saviour holy.

And through all his wondrous childhood
day by day like us he grew;
he was little, weak and helpless,
tears and smiles like us he knew;
and he feeleth for our sadness,
and he shareth in our gladness.

Still among the poor and lowly
hope in Christ is brought to birth,
with the promise of salvation
for the nations of the earth;
still in him our life is found
and our hope of heav'n is crowned.

And our eyes at last shall see him
through his own redeeming love,
for that child so dear and gentle
is our Lord in heav'n above;
and he leads his children on
to the place where he is gone.

Not in that poor lowly stable,
with the oxen standing by,
we shall see him, but in heaven,
set at God's right hand on high;
when like stars his children crowned,
all in white shall wait around.

405 David Hadden

One heart, one voice, one mind.
One in Spirit, and one in love.
This will be the hope that we long for,
this will be the covenant we live,
one heart, one voice, one mind.

Heirs of God, and children of the kingdom.
Living proof that he's alive.
We're reconciled, sinners now forgiven.
One in heart, and one in voice and mind.

406 Graham Kendrick

One shall tell another,
and he shall tell his friend,
husbands, wives and children
shall come following on.
From house to house in families
shall more be gathered in,
and lights will shine in every street,
so warm and welcoming.

Come on in and taste the new wine,
the wine of the kingdom,
the wine of the kingdom of God.
Here is healing and forgiveness,
the wine of the kingdom,
the wine of the kingdom of God.

Compassion of the Father
is ready now to flow,
through acts of love and mercy
we must let it show.
He turns now from his anger
to show a smiling face,
and longs that all should stand beneath
the fountain of his grace.

He longs to do much more than
our faith has yet allowed,
to thrill us and surprise us
with his sovereign power.
Where darkness has been darkest
the brightest light will shine;
his invitation comes to us,
it's yours and it is mine.

407 Andy Park

One thing I ask, one thing I seek,
that I may dwell in your house, O Lord.
All of my days, all of my life,
that I may see you, Lord.

Hear me, O Lord, hear me when I cry;
Lord, do not hide your face from me.
You have been my strength,
you have been my shield,
and you will lift me up.

One thing I ask, one thing I desire,
is to see you, is to see you.

408 Gerrit Gustafson

Only by grace can we enter,
only by grace can we stand;
not by our human endeavour,
but by the blood of the Lamb.
Into your presence you call us,
you call us to come.
Into your presence you draw us,
and now by your grace we come,
now by your grace we come.

Lord, if you mark our transgressions,
who would stand?
Thanks to your grace we are cleansed
by the blood of the Lamb.
(Repeat)

409 Wes Sutton

On this day we now come
to stand before the Father,
enveloped in his love.
Humbly now offering all
to live for the glory of God.

It is so good to know,
Lord, you are faithful,
you love without end.
We pledge our heart and soul
to live for the glory of God.

On this day we now come
to kneel before the Saviour,
Jesus Christ the Lord.
With his word in our hearts
we will live for the glory of God.

On this day we now come
walking in the Spirit –
the holy fire of God.
Anointed with the living flame
we will live for the glory of God.

410 Graham Kendrick

On this day of happiness,
we have gathered here to bless
the union of two lives in holy love.
Love's blossoming is now expressed
in solemn vows and promises,
with flowers and golden rings, a wedding dress.
We look around with joy to see
the smiles of friends and family
as witness to this day.
But, best of all, a friend unseen
is here with us, and once again,
water turns to wine.

On this, their wedding day,
we ask you, Lord, to stay,
and by your Spirit join these hearts together.
And from this moment on,
teach them your lover's song,
that all the world may hear
a three-part harmony,
a three-part harmony.

Oh, may this song of love ring clear
though health or sickness, joy or tears,
for as long as both of them shall live.
May they harmonise with heaven above,
stay tuned into the key of love,
keep their eyes on Jesus day by day.
And may the music of their days
become a symphony of praise
in honour of their Lord.
And may the song become a dance
to celebrate the great romance
of Jesus and his bride.

© 1991 Make Way Music

411 Ian White

Open the doors of praise.
Open the doors of praise.
Open the doors of praise
and let the Lord come in.

In the spirit world
there's a battle going on,
and it rages endlessly.

But in the name of the Lord,
we can stand on his word,
for in him we have the victory.
Leader For he lives in the praises of his
people.
All For he lives in the praises of his
people.
Here among us to empow'r us!

And the demons will flee,
as he said it would be,
and the skies will ring
with shouts of praise.
And the Lord Jesus Christ
will be lifted high,
the Holy One who truly saves!
Leader For he lives in the praises of his
people.
All For he lives in the praises of his
people.
Here among us to empow'r us!

© 1997 Little Misty Music/Kingsway's Thankyou Music

412 Unknown

O the blood of Jesus,
O the blood of Jesus,
O the blood of Jesus,
it washes white as snow.

413 Colin Owen

O the blood of my Saviour,
O the blood of the Lamb,
O the blood of God's only Son
has paid the price for my sin.

It's the blood, it's the blood,
the blood that my Lord shed for me.
It's the blood, it's the blood,
the blood of my Lord set me free.

O the blood shed at Calvary,
O the blood spilled for me,
O the blood of God's only Son,
Jesus, your blood set me free.

Continued overleaf

O the blood from the nail prints,
O the blood from the thorns,
O the blood from the spear in his side
has given me life evermore.

It's the blood, it's the blood,
the blood that my Lord shed for me.
It's the blood, it's the blood,
the blood of my Lord set me free.

414 Samuel Trevor Francis

O the deep, deep love of Jesus!
Vast, unmeasured, boundless, free;
rolling as a mighty ocean
in its fullness over me.
Underneath me, all around me,
is the current of thy love;
leading onward, leading homeward,
to my glorious rest above.

O the deep, deep love of Jesus!
Spread his praise from shore to shore,
how he loveth, ever loveth,
changeth never, nevermore;
how he watches o'er his loved ones,
died to call them all his own;
how for them he intercedeth,
watcheth o'er them from the throne.

O the deep, deep love of Jesus!
Love of every love the best;
'tis an ocean vast of blessing,
'tis a haven sweet of rest.
O the deep, deep love of Jesus!
'Tis a heav'n of heav'ns to me;
and it lifts me up to glory,
for its lifts me up to thee.

415 Steven Fry

O the glory of your presence,
we, your temple, give you reverence.
So arise to your rest
and be blessed by our praise
as we glory in your embrace,
as your presence now fills this place.

416 Charles Wesley

O thou who camest from above
the pure celestial fire to impart,
kindle a flame of sacred love
on the mean altar of my heart.

There let it for thy glory burn
with inextinguishable blaze,
and trembling to its source return
in humble prayer and fervent praise.

Jesus, confirm my heart's desire
to work and speak and think for thee;
still let me guard the holy fire
and still stir up thy gift in me.

Ready for all thy perfect will,
my acts of faith and love repeat,
till death thy endless mercies seal,
and make the sacrifice complete.

417 Noel and Tricia Richards

Our confidence is in the Lord,
the source of our salvation.
Rest is found in him alone,
the Author of creation.
We will not fear the evil day,
because we have a refuge;
in every circumstance we say,
our hope is built on Jesus.

He is our fortress,
we will never be shaken.
He is our fortress,
we will never be shaken.
He is our fortress,
we will never be shaken.
He is our fortress,
we will never be shaken.
We will put our trust in God.
We will put our trust in God.

418 Rich Mullins

Our God is an awesome God,
he reigns from heaven above
with wisdom, pow'r and love.
Our God is an awesome God.
(Repeat)

419 Noel and Tricia Richards

Our God is awesome in power,
scatters his enemies;
our God is mighty in bringing
the powerful to their knees.
He has put on his armour,
he is prepared for war;
mercy and justice triumph
when the Lion of Judah roars.

> *The Lord is a warrior,*
> *we will march with him.*
> *The Lord is a warrior,*
> *leading us to win.*
> (Repeat)

Waken the warrior spirit,
army of God, arise;
challenge the powers of darkness,
there must be no compromise.
We shall attack their strongholds,
our hands are trained for war;
we shall advance the kingdom,
for the victory belongs to God.

420 Unknown

Our God is so great,
so strong and so mighty,
there's nothing that he cannot do.
(Repeat)

The rivers are his,
the mountains are his,
the stars are his handiwork too.

Our God is so great,
so strong and so mighty,
there's nothing that he cannot do.

421 Martin Smith

Over the mountains and the sea
your river runs with love for me,
and I will open up my heart
and let the Healer set me free.
I'm happy to be in the truth,
and I will daily lift my hands,
for I will always sing of
when your love came down.

> *I could sing of your love for ever,*
> *I could sing of your love for ever,*
> *I could sing of your love for ever,*
> *I could sing of your love for ever.*

O, I feel like dancing,
it's foolishness, I know;
but when the world has seen the light,
they will dance with joy
like we're dancing now.

422 Noel Richards

Overwhelmed by love,
deeper than oceans,
high as the heavens.
Ever-living God,
your love has rescued me.

All my sin was laid
on your dear Son,
your precious One.
All my debt he paid,
great is your love for me.

> *No one could ever earn your love,*
> *your grace and mercy is free.*
> *Lord, these words are true,*
> *so is my love for you.*

423

Steven Fry

O, we are more than conquerors,
O, we are more than conquerors,
and who can separate us from the love,
the love of God?
O yes, we are,
we are more than conquerors,
O, we are more than conquerors.

For he has promised to fulfil his will in us,
he said that he would guide us with his eye;
for he has blessed us with all gifts in Christ
and we are his delight.

For he's within to finish what's begun in me,
he opens doors that no one can deny,
he makes a way where there's no other way
and gives me wings to fly.

424

Graham Kendrick

O, what a morning, O, how glorious,
O, what a light has broken through!
Out of the tomb of death and dark despair,
angels in white announce incredible news.

Christ is risen!
He's alive, alleluia!
Yes, he's risen,
he's alive, alleluia!

Suddenly hope has filled our darkest night,
suddenly life has blossomed here;
suddenly joy has rushed like rivers,
he is alive and love has conquered our fear.

425

Robert Grant

O worship the King
all glorious above;
O gratefully sing
his pow'r and his love:
our shield and defender,
the Ancient of Days,
pavilioned in splendour,
and girded with praise.

O tell of his might,
O sing of his grace,
whose robe is the light,
whose canopy space;
his chariots of wrath
the deep thunder-clouds form,
and dark is his path
on the wings of the storm.

This earth with its store
of wonders untold,
almighty, thy pow'r
hath founded of old:
hath stablished it fast
by a changeless decree,
and round it hath cast,
like a mantle, the sea.

Thy bountiful care
what tongue can recite?
It breathes in the air,
it shines with the light;
it streams from the hills,
it descends to the plain,
and sweetly distils
in the dew and the rain.

Frail children of dust,
and feeble as frail,
in thee do we trust,
nor find thee to fail;
thy mercies how tender,
how firm to the end!
Our maker, defender,
redeemer, and friend.

O measureless might,
ineffable love,
while angels delight
to hymn thee above,
thy humbler creation,
though feeble their lays,
with true adoration
shall sing to thy praise.

426 John Samuel Bewley Monsell

O worship the Lord
in the beauty of holiness;
bow down before him,
his glory proclaim;
with gold of obedience,
and incense of lowliness,
kneel and adore him:
the Lord is his name.

Low at his feet lay
thy burden of carefulness:
high on his heart
he will bear it for thee,
comfort thy sorrows,
and answer thy prayerfulness,
guiding thy steps
as may best for thee be.

Fear not to enter
his courts in the slenderness
of the poor wealth
thou wouldst reckon as thine:
truth in its beauty,
and love in its tenderness,
these are the offerings
to lay on his shrine.

These, though we bring them
in trembling and fearfulness,
he will accept
for the name that is dear;
mornings of joy give
for evenings of tearfulness,
trust for our trembling
and hope for our fear.

O worship the Lord
in the beauty of holiness;
bow down before him,
his glory proclaim;
with gold of obedience,
and incense of lowliness,
kneel and adore him:
the Lord is his name.

427 Graham Kendrick

Peace be to these streets,
peace be to these streets,
Peace be to these streets
in the name of Jesus.

Walk here, Lord,
draw near, Lord,
pass through these streets today.
Bring healing, forgiveness;
here let your living waters flow.

Peace be to these streets . . .

Love come to these streets . . .

Joy come to these streets . . .

© 1996 Make Way Music

428 Graham Kendrick

Peace I give to you,
I give to you my peace.
Peace I give to you,
I give to you my peace.

Let it flow to one another,
let it flow, let it flow.
Let it flow to one another,
let it flow, let it flow.

Love I give to you . . .

Hope I give to you . . .

Joy I give to you . . .

Grace I give to you . . .

Pow'r I give to you . . .

© 1979 Kingsway's Thankyou Music

429 John Watson

Peace like a river,
love like a mountain,
the wind of your Spirit
is blowing everywhere.
Joy like a fountain,
healing spring of life;
come, Holy Spirit,
let your fire fall.

© 1989 Ampelos Music/CopyCare

430 Kevin Mayhew

Peace, perfect peace,
is the gift of Christ our Lord.
Peace, perfect peace,
is the gift of Christ our Lord.
Thus, says the Lord,
will the world know my friends.
Peace, perfect peace,
is the gift of Christ our Lord.

Love, perfect love . . .

Faith, perfect faith . . .

Hope, perfect hope . . .

Joy, perfect joy . . .

© 1976 Kevin Mayhew Ltd

431 Graham Kendrick

Peace to you.
We bless you now
in the name of the Lord.
Peace to you.
We bless you now
in the name of the Prince of Peace.
Peace to you.

© 1988 Make Way Music

432 Andy Piercy and Dave Clifton

Praise God, from whom all blessings flow,
praise him, all creatures here below.
Praise him above, you heav'nly host,
praise Father, Son and Holy Ghost.
(Repeat)

Give glory to the Father,
give glory to the Son,
give glory to the Spirit
while endless ages run.
'Worthy the Lamb,' all heaven cries,
'to be exalted thus.'
'Worthy the Lamb,' our hearts reply,
'for he was slain for us.'

Praise God, from whom all blessings flow.
Praise God, from whom all blessings flow.
Praise God, from whom all blessings flow.
Praise God, from whom all blessings flow.

© 1993 IQ Music Ltd

433 Henry Francis Lyte

Praise, my soul, the King of heaven!
To his feet thy tribute bring;
ransomed, healed, restored, forgiven,
who like me his praise should sing?
Praise him! Praise him!
Praise him! Praise him!
Praise the everlasting King!

Praise him for his grace and favour
to our fathers in distress;
praise him still the same as ever,
slow to chide and swift to bless.
Praise him! Praise him!
Praise him! Praise him!
Glorious in his faithfulness.

Father-like, he tends and spares us;
well our feeble frame he knows;
in his hands he gently bears us,
rescues us from all our foes.
Praise him! Praise him!
Praise him! Praise him!
Widely as his mercy flows.

Angels, help us to adore him;
ye behold him face to face;
sun and moon, bow down before him,
dwellers all in time and space.
Praise him! Praise him!
Praise him! Praise him!
Praise with us the God of grace!

434 Jeannie Hall and Carol Owen

Praise the Lord, O my soul,
praise his holy name.
Praise the Lord, O my soul,
praise his holy name.

All of my inmost being,
praise his holy name , . .

Forget not all his benefits,
praise his holy name . . .

He forgives me all my sins,
praise his holy name . . .

He heals all my diseases,
praise his holy name . . .

He redeems my life from the pit,
praise his holy name . . .

He crowns me with love and compassion,
praise his holy name . . .

He satisfies your desires with good things,
praise his holy name . . .

So my youth is renewed like the eagles',
praise his holy name . . .

© 1991 Kingsway's Thankyou Music

435   Roy Hicks

Praise the name of Jesus,
praise the name of Jesus,
he's my rock, he's my fortress,
he's my deliverer, in him will I trust.
Praise the name of Jesus.

© 1976 Latter Rain Music/CopyCare

436   Brian Doerksen

Purify my heart,
let me be as gold and precious silver.
Purify my heart,
let me be as gold, pure gold.

Refiner's fire,
my heart's one desire
is to be holy,
set apart for you, Lord.
I choose to be holy,
set apart for you, my master,
ready to do your will.

Purify my heart,
cleanse me from within and make me holy.
Purify my heart,
cleanse me from my sin, deep within.

© 1990 Mercy/Vineyard Publishing/Music Services/CopyCare

437   Chris Bowater

Reign in me, Sovereign Lord,
reign in me.
Reign in me, Sovereign Lord,
reign in me.

Captivate my heart,
let your kingdom come,
establish there your throne,
let your will be done.

© 1985 Sovereign Lifestyle Music

438   Graham Kendrick

Rejoice! Rejoice! Christ is in you,
the hope of glory in our hearts.
He lives! He lives! His breath is in you,
arise a mighty army, we arise.

Now is the time for us
to march upon the land,
into our hands
he will give the ground we claim.
He rides in majesty
to lead us into victory,
the world shall see that Christ is Lord!

God is at work in us
his purpose to perform,
building a kingdom
of power not of words,
where things impossible
by faith shall be made possible;
let's give the glory to him now.

Though we are weak, his grace
is everything we need;
we're made of clay
but this treasure is within.
He turns our weaknesses
into his opportunities,
so that the glory goes to him.

© 1983 Kingsway's Thankyou Music

439 Graham Kendrick and Chris Rolinson

Restore, O Lord,
the honour of your name,
in works of sovereign power
come shake the earth again,
that all may see,
and come with reverent fear
to the living God,
whose kingdom shall outlast the years.

Restore, O Lord,
in all the earth your fame,
and in our time revive
the church that bears your name.
And in your anger,
Lord, remember mercy,
O living God,
whose mercy shall outlast the years.

Bend us, O Lord,
where we are hard and cold,
in your refiner's fire:
come purify the gold.
Though suffering comes
and evil crouches near,
still our living God
is reigning, he is reigning here.

440 Helena Barrington

Righteousness, peace, joy in the Holy Ghost,
righteousness, peace, and joy in the Holy
*   Ghost:*
that's the kingdom of God.
(Repeat)

Don't you want to be a part of the kingdom,
don't you want to be a part of the kingdom,
don't you want to be a part of the kingdom?
Come on, everybody.
(Repeat)

There's love in the kingdom,
so much love in the kingdom;
there's love in the kingdom.
Come on, everybody!

There's peace in the kingdom . . .

There's joy in the kingdom . . .

I'm an heir of the kingdom,
I'm an heir of the kingdom,
I'm an heir of the kingdom.
Come on, everybody!

441 Dougie Brown

River, wash over me,
cleanse me and make me new.
Bathe me, refresh me and fill me anew.
River, wash over me.

Spirit, watch over me,
lead me to Jesus' feet.
Cause me to worship and fill me anew.
Spirit, watch over me.

Jesus, rule over me,
reign over all my heart.
Teach me to praise you and fill me anew.
Jesus, rule over me.

442 David Fellingham

Ruach, Ruach,
holy wind of God, blow on me.
Touch the fading embers,
breathe on me.
Fan into a flame
all that you've placed in me.
Let the fire burn more pow'rfully.
Ruach, Ruach,
holy wind of God,
holy wind of God, breathe on me.

443 Adrian Howard and Pat Turner

Salvation belongs to our God,
who sits on the throne,
and to the Lamb.
Praise and glory, wisdom and thanks,
honour and power and strength.

Be to our God for ever and ever,
be to our God for ever and ever,
be to our God for ever and ever. Amen.

And we, the redeemed, shall be strong
in purpose and unity,
declaring aloud,
praise and glory, wisdom and thanks,
honour and power and strength.

444 Graham Kendrick

Save the people, save the people now. (x4)
Lord, have mercy. Christ, have mercy.
Father, hear our prayer: save the people now.

Save the children, save the children now. (x4)
Lord, have mercy. Christ, have mercy.
Father, hear our prayer: save the children now.

Send your Spirit, send your Spirit now. (x4)
Lord, have mercy. Christ, have mercy.
Father, hear our prayer: send your Spirit now.

Send revival, send revival now. (x4)
Lord, have mercy. Christ, have mercy.
Father, hear our prayer: send revival now.

445 Stuart Townend

Say the word, I will be healed;
you are the great Physician,
you meet every need.
Say the word, I will be free;
where chains have held me captive,
come, sing your songs to me,
say the word.

Say the word, I will be filled;
my hands reach out to heaven,
where striving is stilled.
Say the word, I will be changed;
where I am dry and thirsty,
send cool, refreshing rain,
say the word.

His tears have fallen like rain on my life,
each drop a fresh revelation.
I will return to the place of the cross,
where grace and mercy pour from heaven's
    throne.

Say the word, I will be poor,
that I might know the riches
that you have in store.
Say the word, I will be weak;
your strength will be the power
that satisfies the meek,
say the word.

The Lord will see the travail of his soul,
and he and I will be satisfied.
Complete the work you have started in me:
O come, Lord Jesus, shake my life again.

446 Chris Bowater

See his glory, see his glory,
see his glory now appear.
See his glory, see his glory,
see his glory now appear.
God of light, holiness and truth,
pow'r and might,
see his glory, see it now appear.

Now we declare our God is good,
and his mercies endure for ever.
Now we declare our God is good,
and his mercies endure for ever.

447 Karen Lafferty

Seek ye first the kingdom of God
and his righteousness,
and all these things shall be added unto you,
hallelu, hallelujah!

Hallelujah! hallelujah!
Hallelujah! Hallelu, hallelujah!

You shall not live by bread alone,
but by every word
that proceeds from the mouth of God,
hallelu, hallelujah!

Ask and it shall be given unto you,
seek and you shall find.
Knock, and it shall be opened unto you,
hallelu, hallelujah.

If the Son shall set you free,
you shall be free indeed.
You shall know the truth and the truth shall
    set you free,
hallelu, hallelujah!

Let your light so shine before men
that they may see your good works
and glorify your Father in heaven,
hallelu, hallelujah!

Trust in the Lord with all your heart,
he shall direct your paths,
in all your ways acknowledge him,
hallelu, hallelujah!

© 1972 Maranatha! Music/CopyCare

448 Graham Kendrick

See, your Saviour comes;
see, your Saviour comes.

Desolate cities, desolate homes,
desolate lives on the streets,
angry and restless. When will you know
the things that would make for your peace?

Father of mercy, hear as we cry
for all who live in this place;
show here your glory, come satisfy
your longing that all should be saved.

Where lives are broken, let there be hope,
where there's division bring peace;
where there's oppression, judge and reprove,
and rescue the crushed and the weak.

Lord, let your glory dwell in this land,
in mercy restore us again:
pour out salvation, grant us your peace,
and strengthen the things that remain.

© 1996 Make Way Music

449 Dave Bilbrough

Shout for joy and sing,
let your praises ring;
see that God is building a kingdom for a King.
His dwelling-place with men,
the new Jerusalem;
where Jesus is Lord over all.

And we will worship, worship,
we will worship Jesus the Lord.
We will worship, worship,
we will worship Jesus the Lord.

A work so long concealed,
in time will be revealed,
as the sons of God shall rise and take their
    stand.
Clothed in his righteousness,
the church made manifest,
where Jesus is Lord over all.

Sovereign over all,
hail him risen Lord.
He alone is worthy of our praise.
Reigning in majesty,
ruling in victory,
Jesus is Lord over all.

© 1983 Kingsway's Thankyou Music

450 David Fellingham

Shout for joy and sing your praises to the King,
lift your voice and let your hallelujahs ring;
come before his throne to worship and adore,
enter joyfully now the presence of the Lord.

You are my Creator, you are my Deliverer,
you are my Redeemer, you are Lord,
and you are my Healer.
You are my Provider,
you are now my Shepherd, and my Guide,
Jesus, Lord and King, I worship you.

451 Dave Bell

Shout, shout for joy,
shout, shout for joy,
for the Lord has given you the victory.
Shout, shout for joy,
shout, shout for joy,
for the Lord has given you the victory.

No weapon formed against you shall prosper.
No kingdom raised against you shall stand.
For the Lord is the rock of our salvation,
and we have overcome by the blood of the
   Lamb.

452 Graham Kendrick

Shout! The Lord is risen!
His work on earth is done.
Shout! We are forgiven!
This is the day of his power,
(woa-oh) his power.

Shout together in the day of his power.
Sing together in the day of his power.
Walk together in the day of his power.
Serve together in the day of his power.
Pray together in the day of his power.

Work together in the day of his power.
Come together in the day of his power.
This is the day of his power,
(woa-oh) his power, (woa-oh) his power.
Shout!

Shout! He has ascended,
he reigns at God's right hand.
Shout! Till death is ended.
This is the day of his power,
(woa-oh) his power.

Shout! With fire from heaven,
he sends his Spirit down.
Shout! And gifts were given.
This is the day of his power,
(woa-oh) his power.

Shout! Proclaim the kingdom!
Announce the Jubilee.
Shout! The year of freedom!
This is the day of his power,
(woa-oh) his power.

Shout! A new generation
rises across this land.
Shout! A new demonstration.
This is the day of his power,
(woa-oh) his power.

Go! Tell every nation.
Our hearts are willing now.
Go! He is our passion.
This is the day of his power,
(woa-oh) his power.

Come! O come, Lord Jesus.
We cry, O Lord, how long?
Come! And end injustice.
This is the day of his power,
(woa-oh) his power.

Come! If you are thirsty,
while living waters flow.
Come! And taste his mercy.
This is the day of his power,
(woa-oh) his power.

Continued overleaf

Shout! In expectation
the whole creation yearns.
Shout! For liberation.
This is the day of his power,
(woa-oh) his power.

Shout together in the day of his power.
Sing together in the day of his power.
Walk together in the day of his power.
Serve together in the day of his power.
Pray together in the day of his power.
Work together in the day of his power.
Come together in the day of his power.
This is the day of his power,
(woa-oh) his power, (woa-oh) his power.
Shout!

© 1995 Make Way Music

453   Collette Dallas and Deborah Page

Shout unto God with a voice of triumph,
sing and proclaim his mighty name.
Shout unto God with a voice of triumph,
sing and proclaim that our God reigns.
(Repeat)

He is Lord over all the nation,
he is Lord over all the earth.
With high praises we shall sing
all the honour to the King.
With a two-edged sword in our hand
we are marching on to take the land.

He is Lord over all the nation,
he is Lord over all the earth.
We shall go out in one accord,
in the power of God's Word.
We proclaim liberty,
in Christ Jesus the victory.

© 1997 Kingdom Faith Ministries

454   Graham Kendrick

Show your pow'r, O Lord,
demonstrate the justice of your kingdom.
Prove your mighty word,
vindicate your name
before a watching world.
Awesome are your deeds, O Lord;
renew them for this hour.
Show your pow'r, O Lord,
among the people now.

Show your pow'r, O Lord,
cause your church to rise and take action.
Let all fear be gone,
powers of the age to come
are breaking through.
We your people are ready to serve,
to arise and to obey.
Show you pow'r, O Lord,
and set the people free.

(Last time)
Show your pow'r, O Lord,
and set the people –
show your pow'r, O Lord,
and set the people –
show your pow'r, O Lord,
and set the people free.

© 1988 Make Way Music

455   Joseph Mohr trans. John Freeman Young

Silent night, holy night.
All is calm, all is bright,
round yon virgin mother and child;
holy infant, so tender and mild,
sleep in heavenly peace,
sleep in heavenly peace.

Silent night, holy night.
Shepherds quake at the sight,
glories stream from heaven afar,
heav'nly hosts sing alleluia:
Christ the Saviour is born,
Christ the Saviour is born.

1. Sons and daughters of creation
       by God's will we came to be,
    like a poet dreaming marvels
       he has spun our history.
    Working, till from shapeless chaos
       He evoked humanity.

2. Dark within our first conceiving
       runs the rifts that still divide,
    Envy splits and anger hardens,
       Colour, gender, wealth collide.
    Sov'reign nations arm for conflict,
       Violence thrusting peace aside.

3. Yet God holds his steadfast purpose
       of humanity made one.
    Walls were breached and bounds transcended
       By the death of his own Son:
    And the way for love's encounter
       Through the Spirit's power begun.

Silent night, holy night.
Son of God, love's pure light,
radiant beams from thy holy face,
with the dawn of redeeming grace:
Jesus, Lord, at thy birth,
Jesus, Lord, at thy birth.

456 Pamela Hayes

Silent, surrendered, calm and still,
open to the word of God.
Heart humbled to his will,
offered is the servant of God.

Come, Holy Spirit, calm and still,
teach us, heal us, give us life.
Come, Lord, O let our hearts
flow with love and all that is true.

457 David Ruis

Sing a song of celebration,
lift up a shout of praise,
for the Bridegroom will come,
the glorious One.
And O, we will look on his face;
we'll go to a much better place.

Dance with all your might,
lift up your hands and clap for joy:
the time's drawing near
when he will appear.
And O, we will stand by his side;
a strong, pure, spotless bride.

> O, we will dance on the streets that are
>   golden,
> the glorious bride and the great Son of man,
> from every tongue and tribe and nation
> will join in the song of the Lamb.

Sing aloud for the time of rejoicing is near
(sing aloud for the time of rejoicing is near).
The risen King, our Groom, is soon to appear
(the risen King, our Groom, is soon to appear).

The wedding feast to come is now near at
    hand
(the wedding feast to come is now near at
    hand).
Lift up your voice, proclaim the coming Lamb
(lift up your voice, proclaim the coming Lamb).

458 Taizé Community

Sing, praise and bless the Lord.
Sing, praise and bless the Lord,
peoples! nations!
Alleluia!

459 Graham Kendrick

Soften my heart, Lord,
soften my heart.
From all indifference set me apart.
To feel your compassion,
to weep with your tears,
come soften my heart, O Lord,
soften my heart.

460 Andraé Crouch

Soon and very soon
we are going to see the King,
soon and very soon
we are going to see the King,
soon and very soon
we are going to see the King,
hallelujah, hallelujah,
we're going to see the King.

No more crying there,
we are going to see the King . . .

No more dying there,
we are going to see the King . . .

461 Dave Bilbrough

Sound the trumpet, strike the drum,
see the King of glory come,
join the praises rising from the people
   of the Lord.
Let your voices now be heard,
unrestrained and unreserved,
prepare a way for his return,
   you people of the Lord.
Sing Jesus is Lord, Jesus is Lord.
Bow down to his authority,
for he has slain the enemy.
Of heav'n and hell he holds the key.
Jesus is Lord, Jesus is Lord.

462 Daniel Iverson

Spirit of the living God,
fall afresh on me.
Spirit of the living God,
fall afresh on me.
Melt me, mould me,
fill me, use me,
Spirit of the living God,
fall afresh on me.

463 Paul Armstrong

Spirit of the living God,
fall afresh on me.
Spirit of the living God,
fall afresh on me.
Fill me anew,
fill me anew.
Spirit of the Lord,
fall afresh on me.

464 David Hadden

Streams of worship
and rivers of praise,
ascending to the One who is
the Ancient of Days:
to him who is worthy,
to him who was slain,
to him who sits upon the throne
and to the Lamb:

Thousands upon thousands
encircle the throne,
singing a new song
to the One who is to come:
to him who is worthy,
to him who was slain,
to him who sits upon the throne
and to the Lamb:

   You are worthy,
   you are holy –
   the Lord who was,
   the Lord who is,
   the Lord who is to come;
   you are mighty,
   you are awesome,
   be praise and honour and glory
   for evermore.

Streams of worship
and rivers of praise
flowing from the lips of those
who never cease to be amazed
with him who is worthy,
with him who was slain,
with him who sits upon the throne
and with the Lamb:

465 Graham Kendrick

Such love, pure as the whitest snow;
such love weeps for the shame I know;
such love, paying the debt I owe;
O Jesus, such love.

Such love, stilling my restlessness;
such love, filling my emptiness;
such love, showing me holiness;
O Jesus, such love.

Such love springs from eternity;
such love, streaming through history;
such love, fountain of life to me;
O Jesus, such love.

466 David and Liz Morris

*Surely our God is the God of gods
and the Lord of kings,
a revealer of mysteries.
Surely our God is the God of gods
and the Lord of kings,
a revealer of mysteries.*

He changes the times and the seasons,
he gives rhythm to the tides;
he knows what is hidden in the darkest
    of places,
brings the shadows into his light.

I will praise you always, my Father,
you are Lord of heaven and earth,
you hide your secrets from the wise and
    the learnèd
and reveal them to this your child.

Thank you for sending your only Son,
we may know the myst'ry of God;
he opens the treasures of wisdom and
    knowledge
to the humble, not to the proud.

467 Dave Browning

Take me past the outer courts,
and through the holy place,
past the brazen altar, Lord,
I want to see your face.

Pass me by the crowds of people,
and the priests who sing their praise;
I hunger and thirst for your righteousness,
but it's only found one place.

*So take me in to the Holy of holies,
take me in by the blood of the Lamb;
so take me in to the Holy of holies,
take the coal, cleanse my lips, here I am.*

468 Frances Ridley Havergal

Take my life, and let it be
consecrated, Lord, to thee;
take my moments and my days,
let them flow in ceaseless praise.

Take my hands, and let them move
at the impulse of thy love;
take my feet, and let them be
swift and beautiful for thee.

Take my voice, and let me sing
always, only, for my King;
take my lips, and let them be
filled with messages from thee.

Take my silver and my gold;
not a mite would I withhold;
take my intellect, and use
every pow'r as thou shalt choose.

Take my will, and make it thine:
it shall be no longer mine;
take my heart: it is thine own;
it shall be thy royal throne.

Take my love; my Lord, I pour
at thy feet its treasure-store;
take myself, and I will be
ever, only, all for thee.

468a Frances Ridley Havergal

Take my life, and let it be
consecrated, Lord, to thee;
take my hands, and let them move
at the impulse of thy love,
at the impulse of thy love.

Continued overleaf

Take my feet, and let them be
swift and beautiful for thee.
Take my voice, and let me sing
always, only, for my King,
always, only, for my King.

Take my lips, and let them be
filled with messages from thee.
Take my silver and my gold,
not a mite would I withhold,
not a mite would I withhold.

Take my love; my God I pour
at thy feet its treasure-store.
Take myself, and I will be
ever, only, all for thee,
ever, only, all for thee.

Take my life, and let it be
consecrated, Lord, to thee.
Take myself, and I will be
ever, only, all for thee,
ever, only, all for thee.

469   Graham Kendrick and Steve Thompson

*Teach me to dance
to the beat of your heart,
teach me to move
in the pow'r of your Spirit,
teach me to walk
in the light of your presence,
teach me to dance
to the beat of your heart.
Teach me to love
with your heart of compassion,
teach me to trust
in the word of your promise,
teach me to hope
in the day of your coming,
teach me to dance
to the beat of your heart.*

You wrote the rhythm of life,
created heaven and earth,
in you is joy without measure.

So, like a child in your sight,
I dance to see your delight,
for I was made for your pleasure,
pleasure.

Let all my movements express
a heart that loves to say 'yes',
a will that leaps to obey you.
Let all my energy blaze
to see the joy in your face;
let my whole being praise you,
praise you.

470   Eugene Greco

Teach me your ways,
O Lord, my God,
and I will walk in your truth.
Give me a totally undivided heart
that I may fear your name.

*Purify my heart,
cleanse me, Lord, I pray,
remove from me all
that is standing in the way.
Purify my heart,
cleanse me, Lord, I pray,
remove from me all
that is standing in the way
of your love.*

471   Timothy Dudley-Smith

Tell out, my soul,
the greatness of the Lord:
unnumbered blessings
give my spirit voice;
tender to me
the promise of his word;
in God my Saviour
shall my heart rejoice.

Tell out, my soul,
the greatness of his name:
make known his might,
the deeds his arm has done;
his mercy sure,
from age to age the same;
his holy name:
the Lord, the Mighty One.

Tell out, my soul,
the greatness of his might:
pow'rs and dominions
lay their glory by;
proud hearts and stubborn wills
are put to flight,
the hungry fed,
the humble lifted high.

Tell out, my soul,
the glories of his word:
firm is his promise,
and his mercy sure.
Tell out, my soul,
the greatness of the Lord
to children's children
and for evermore.

© Copyright Timothy Dudley-Smith

472 Martin Smith

Thank you for saving me;
what can I say?
You are my everything,
I will sing your praise.
You shed your blood for me;
what can I say?
You took my sin and shame,
a sinner called by name.

> Great is the Lord.
> Great is the Lord.
> For we know your truth has set us free;
> you've set your hope in me.

Mercy and grace are mine,
forgiv'n is my sin;
Jesus, my only hope,
the Saviour of the world.

'Great is the Lord,' we cry;
God, let your kingdom come.
Your word has let me see,
thank you for saving me.

© 1993 Curious? Music UK/Kingsway's Thankyou Music

473 Graham Kendrick

Thank you for the cross,
the price you paid for us,
how you gave yourself so completely,
precious Lord (precious Lord).
Now our sins are gone,
all forgiven,
covered by your blood,
all forgotten,
thank you, Lord (thank you, Lord).

> O I love you, Lord,
> really love you, Lord.
> I will never understand
> why you love me.
> You're my deepest joy,
> you're my heart's delight,
> and the greatest thing of all, O Lord, I see:
> you delight in me.

For our healing there,
Lord, you suffered,
and to take our fear
you poured out your love,
precious Lord (precious Lord).
Calvary's work is done,
you have conquered,
able now to save
so completely,
thank you, Lord (thank you, Lord).

© 1985 Kingsway's Thankyou Music

474 Don Moen

Thank you for your mercy,
thank you for your grace;
thank you for your blood
that's made a way
to come into your presence
and glorify your name.
Lord, I stand amazed at what I see.

Continued overleaf

Great is your mercy toward me,
your loving kindness toward me,
your tender mercies I see
day after day.
For ever faithful to me,
always providing for me,
great is your mercy toward me
great is your grace.

Your promises are ageless,
your love will never end,
for a thousand generations
your covenant will stand;
showing grace and mercy
to those who fear your name,
establishing your righteousness and praise.

475 Unknown

Thank you, Jesus, thank you, Jesus,
thank you, Lord, for loving me.
Thank you, Jesus, thank you, Jesus,
thank you, Lord, for loving me.

You went to Calvary,
and there you died for me.
Thank you, Lord, for loving me.
(Repeat)

You rose up from the grave,
to me new life you gave,
thank you, Lord, for loving me.
(Repeat)

You're coming back again,
and we with you shall reign.
Thank you, Lord, for loving me.
(Repeat)

476 Matt Redman

The angels, Lord, they sing around your throne;
and we will join their song: praise you alone.
(Repeat)

Holy, holy, holy, Lord our God,
who was and is and is to come.
Holy, holy, holy, Lord our God,
who was and is and is to come.

(Last time)
Amen. Amen.

The living creatures, Lord, speak endless praise;
and joining at your throne, we'll sing their sweet
 refrain.
(Repeat)

The elders, Lord, they fall before your throne;
our hearts we humbly bow to you alone.
(Repeat)

477 Samuel John Stone

The church's one foundation
is Jesus Christ, her Lord;
she is his new creation,
by water and the word;
from heav'n he came and sought her
to be his holy bride,
with his own blood he bought her,
and for her life he died.

Elect from every nation,
yet one o'er all the earth,
her charter of salvation,
one Lord, one faith, one birth;
one holy name she blesses,
partakes one holy food,
and to one hope she presses,
with every grace endued.

'Mid toil and tribulation,
and tumult of her war,
she waits the consummation
of peace for evermore;
till with the vision glorious
her longing eyes are blest,
and the great church victorious
shall be the church at rest.

Yet she on earth hath union
with God the Three in One,
and mystic sweet communion
with those whose rest is won:
O happy ones and holy!
Lord, give us grace that we
like them, the meek and lowly,
on high may dwell with thee.

478 Matt Redman and Martin Smith

The cross has said it all,
the cross has said it all.
I can't deny what you have shown,
the cross speaks of a God of love;
there displayed for all to see,
Jesus Christ, our only hope,
a message of the Father's heart,
'Come, my children, come on home.'

As high as the heavens are above the earth,
so high is the measure of your great love,
as far as the east is from the west,
so far have you taken our sins from us.
(Repeat)

The cross has said it all,
the cross has said it all.
I never recognised your touch,
until I met you at the cross.
We are fallen, dust to dust,
how could you do this for us?
Son of God shed precious blood,
who can comprehend this love?

How high, how wide, how deep.
How high, how wide, how deep.
How high, how wide, how deep.
How high, how wide, how deep.
How high!

479 Martin Smith

The crucible for silver
and the furnace for gold,
but the Lord tests the heart of this child.

Standing in all purity, God,
our passion is for holiness,
lead us to the secret place of praise.

Jesus, Holy One, you are my heart's desire.
King of kings, my everything,
you've set this heart on fire.
(Repeat)

Father, take our offering,
with our song we humbly praise you.
You have brought your holy fire to our lips.
Standing in your beauty, Lord,
your gift to us is holiness;
lead us to the place where we can sing:

480 Geoff Bullock

The heavens shall declare
the glory of his name,
all creation bows
at the coming of the King.
Every eye shall see,
every heart will know,
every knee shall bow,
every tongue confess:
Holy, holy, holy is the Lord.
See the coming of the King,
holy is the Lord.

481 Graham Kendrick

Men	The Lord is a mighty King,
Women	the Maker of everything.
Men	The Lord, he made the earth,
Women	he spoke and it came at once to birth.
Men	He said, 'Let us make mankind',
Women	the crown of his design,
Men	'in our own likeness',
Women	his image in every human face.

Continued overleaf

And he made us for his delight,
gave us the gift of life,
created us family to be his glory,
to be his glory.

Men	And yet we were deceived,
Women	in pride the lie believed,
Men	to sin and death's decay –
Women	the whole creation fell that day.
Men	Now all creation
Women	yearns for liberation;
Men	all things in Christ restored –
Women	the purchase of his precious blood.

Shout:
For by him
all things were created.
Things in heaven
and on earth.
Visible and invisible.
Whether thrones
or powers
or rulers
or authorities;
all things were created by him,
and for him.

© 1988 Make Way Music

482   Graham Kendrick

The Lord is marching out in splendour,
in awesome majesty he rides,
for truth, humility and justice,
his mighty army fills the skies.

> *O give thanks to the Lord*
> *for his love endures,*
> *O give thanks to the Lord*
> *for his love endures,*
> *O give thanks to the Lord*
> *for his love endures*
> *for ever, for ever.*

His army marches out with dancing
for he has filled our hearts with joy.
Be glad the kingdom is advancing,
the love of God, our battle cry!

© 1986 Kingsway's Thankyou Music

483   Colin Owen

The Lord is moving across this land,
it's time to rise up and take our stand
behind the banner of Jesus Christ
and claim the victory that's ours by right;
we're in God's army,
we're in God's army.

The Spirit's leading us out to war,
but we're not the same as we were before,
we are anointed to multiply;
the Lord has called us and that is why
we're in God's army,
we're in God's army.

> *We are marching out to take the land,*
> *strongholds fall beneath our feet.*
> *Satan, we proclaim your time's at hand;*
> *we're marching on to victory.*

The Devil's shakin', his time has come,
the powers of darkness are on the run;
we're standing firm by faith in our authority,
defeating all our foes and bringing liberty;
we're in God's army,
we're in God's army.

© 1995 Kingsway's Thankyou Music

484   Carol Owen

The Lord is our strength,
the Lord is our song,
with joy we draw
from the wells of salvation today.
(Repeat)

> *So let's sing to the Lord,*
> *he's done glorious things,*
> *let's shout aloud and dance for joy*
> *for great is the Holy One.*
> *So let's sing to the Lord,*
> *he's done glorious things,*
> *let's rejoice in our God*
> *for the things he has done.*

We give thanks to you, Lord,
and call on your name;
we proclaim that your name is exalted on high.
(Repeat)

So we sing to you, Lord,
you've done glorious things,
we shout aloud and dance for joy,
for great is the Holy One.
So we sing to you, Lord,
you've done glorious things,
we rejoice in our God
for the things you have done.

485   Dan C. Stradwick

The Lord reigns, the Lord reigns,
the Lord reigns,
let the earth rejoice, let the earth rejoice,
let the earth rejoice,
let the people be glad that our God reigns.
(Repeat)

A fire goes before him
and burns up all his enemies;
the hills melt like wax at the presence of the
Lord,
at the presence of the Lord.

The heav'ns declare his righteousness,
the peoples see his glory;
for you, O Lord, are exalted over all the earth,
over all the earth.

486   The Scottish Psalter

The Lord's my shepherd, I'll not want.
He makes me down to lie
in pastures green. He leadeth me
the quiet waters by.

My soul he doth restore again,
and me to walk doth make
within the paths of righteousness,
e'en for his own name's sake.

Yea, though I walk in death's dark vale,
yet will I fear none ill.
For thou art with me, and thy rod
and staff me comfort still.

My table thou hast furnishèd
in presence of my foes:
my head thou dost with oil anoint,
and my cup overflows.

Goodness and mercy all my life
shall surely follow me.
And in God's house for evermore
my dwelling-place shall be.

487   Graham Kendrick

The price is paid,
come, let us enter in
to all that Jesus died
to make our own.
For every sin
more than enough he gave,
and bought our freedom
from each guilty stain.

The price is paid,
alleluia,
amazing grace,
so strong and sure,
and so with all my heart,
my life in every part,
I live to thank you
for the price you paid.

The price is paid,
see Satan flee away;
for Jesus crucified
destroys his pow'r.
No more to pay,
let accusation cease,
in Christ there is
no condemnation now.

The price is paid
and by that scourging cruel
he took our sicknesses
as if his own.
And by his wounds
his body broken there,
his healing touch may now
by faith be known.

Continued overleaf

The price is paid,
'Worthy the Lamb!' we cry,
eternity shall never
cease his praise.
The church of Christ
shall rule upon the earth,
in Jesus' name
we have authority.

The price is paid,
alleluia,
amazing grace,
so strong and sure,
and so with all my heart,
my life in every part,
I live to thank you
for the price you paid.

© 1983 Kingsway's Thankyou Music

488   Richard Hubbard

The promise of the Holy Spirit
is for you.
The promise of the Holy Spirit
is for your children.
The promise of the Holy Spirit
is for all who are far off,
even as many as the Lord your God shall call.
O yeah!
Acts, chapter two, verse thirty-nine.

© 1991 Kingsway's Thankyou Music

489   Unknown

Therefore we lift our hearts in praise,
sing to the living God who saves,
for grace poured out for you and me.

There for everyone to see,
there on the hill at Calvary,
Jesus died for you and me.

For our sad and broken race,
he arose with life and grace,
and reigns on high for you and me.

There for such great pain and cost
the Spirit came at Pentecost
and comes in pow'r for you and me.

Therefore we lift our hearts in praise,
sing to the living God who saves,
for grace poured out for you and me.

490   Matt Redman

There is a louder shout to come,
there is a sweeter song to hear;
all the nations with one voice,
all the people with one fear.
Bowing down before your throne,
every tribe and tongue will be;
all the nations with one voice,
all the people with one King.
And what a song we'll sing upon that day!

O what a song we'll sing
and O what a tune we'll bear;
you deserve an anthem of the highest praise.
O what a joy will rise
and O what a sound we'll make;
you deserve an anthem of the highest praise.

Now we see a part of this,
one day we shall see in full;
all the nations with one voice,
all the people with one love.
No one else will share your praise,
nothing else can take your place;
all the nations with one voice,
all the people with one Lord.
And what a song we'll sing upon that day!

Even now upon the earth
there's a glimpse of all to come;
many people with one voice,
harmony of many tongues.
We will all confess your name,
you will be our only praise;
all the nations with one voice,
all the people with one God.
And what a song we'll sing upon that day!

© 1996 Kingsway's Thankyou Music

491 David Ruis

There is a place of commanded blessing
where brethren in unity dwell,
a place where anointing oil is flowing,
where we live as one.

You have called us to be a body,
you have called us as friends,
joined together in the bond of the Spirit,
unto the end.

Father, we join with the prayer of Jesus;
as you are, so let us be one,
joined together in unity and purpose,
all for the love of your Son.

We will break dividing walls,
we will break dividing walls,
we will break dividing walls
in the name of your Son.
We will break dividing walls,
we will break dividing walls
and we will be one.
(Repeat)

© 1994 Mercy/Vineyard Publishing/Music Services/CopyCare

492 Melody Green

There is a Redeemer,
Jesus, God's own Son,
precious Lamb of God, Messiah,
Holy One.

Thank you, O my Father,
for giving us your Son,
and leaving your Spirit
till the work on earth is done.

Jesus, my Redeemer,
Name above all names,
precious Lamb of God, Messiah,
O for sinners slain.

When I stand in glory,
I will see his face.
And there I'll serve my King for ever,
in that Holy Place.

© 1982 Birdwing Music/Ears to Hear Music/BMG Songs Inc./CopyCare

493 Lenny LeBlanc

There is none like you,
no one else can touch my heart like you do.
I could search for all eternity long
and find there is none like you.
(Repeat)

Your mercy flows like a river wide,
and healing comes from your hands.
Suffering children are safe in your arms;
there is none like you.

© 1991 Integrity's Hosanna! Music/Kingsway's Thankyou Music

494 Morris Chapman and Claire Cloninger

There is only one Lord that we cling to,
there is only one truth that we claim;
there is only one way that we walk in,
there is only power in one name.

And in the strong name of Jesus,
by the blood of the Lamb,
we are able to triumph,
we are able to stand.
In the power of his Spirit,
by the strength of his hand,
in the strong name of Jesus,
by the precious blood of the Lamb.

Though apart from him we can do nothing,
by his Spirit we can do all things;
covered by his blood we are made righteous,
lifting up the name of Christ, our King!

© 1991 Word Music Inc./CopyCare

495 Noel Richards

There is pow'r in the name of Jesus;
we believe in his name.
We have called on the name of Jesus;
we are saved! We are saved!
At his name the demons flee.
At his name captives are freed,
for there is no other name that is higher
than Jesus!

Continued overleaf

There is pow'r in the name of Jesus,
like a sword in our hands.
We declare in the name of Jesus
we shall stand! We shall stand!
At his name God's enemies
shall be crushed beneath our feet,
for there is no other name that is higher
than Jesus!

© 1989 Kingsway's Thankyou Music

496 J. B. Vaughn

There's a blessed time that's coming, coming
    soon,
it may be evening, morning or at noon.
There'll be a wedding of the Bride,
united with the Groom.
We shall see the King when he comes.

We shall see the King,
we shall see the King,
we shall see the King when he comes.
He is coming in pow'r,
he'll hail the blessed hour.
We shall see the King when he comes.

Are you ready should the Saviour call today?
Would Jesus say, 'Well done' or 'Go away'?
He's building a home for the pure,
the vile can never stay.
We shall see the King when he comes.

O my brother, are you ready for the call?
We'll crown our Saviour King and Lord of all.
All the kingdoms of this world
shall soon before him fall.
We shall see the King when he comes.

497 Richard Lewis

There's an awesome sound
    on the winds of heaven,
mighty thunder-clouds in the skies above.
The immortal King who will reign for ever
is reaching out with his arms of love,
his arms of love, his arms of love.

All creation sings of the Lamb of glory
who laid down his life for all the world.
What amazing love, that the King of heaven
should be crucified, stretching out his arms,
his arms of love, his arms of love.

Send revival to this land,
fill this nation with your love.
Send revival to this land,
fill this nation with your love.

© 1997 Kingsway's Thankyou Music

498 Paul Oakley

There's a place where the streets shine
with the glory of the Lamb.
There's a way, we can go there,
we can live there beyond time.

Because of you, because of you,
because of your love,
because of your blood.

No more pain, no more sadness,
no more suffering, no more tears.
No more sin, no more sickness,
no injustice, no more death.

Because of you . . .

All our sins are washed away,
and we can live for ever,
now we have this hope,
because of you.
O, we'll see you face to face,
and we will dance together
in the city of our God,
because of you.

There is joy everlasting,
there is gladness, there is peace.
There is wine everflowing,
there's a wedding, there's a feast.

Because of you . . .

All our sins are washed away . . .

© 1995 Kingsway's Thankyou Music

499 Taran Ash, James Mott and Matthew Pryce

There's a river of joy
that flows from your throne,
O river of joy, flow through me.
There's a river of joy
that flows from your throne,
come, Holy Spirit, with joy,
come, Holy Spirit, with joy.
(Repeat)

I will rise up on the wings of an eagle;
with joy I receive your love.
I will praise you with a song everlasting.
Thank you, Lord, for your love,
thank you, Lord, for your love.

500 Matt Redman and Paul Donnelly

There's a sound of singing in our midst,
there's an offering of praise.
We set our hearts towards you, Lord,
with our lips our songs we raise.
There is jubilation in the camp
for your promises are true,
and by your grace salvation comes
to bring us home to you.

We rejoice in you,
give our lives to you.
We rejoice in you
and we testify
that this love is true
with the sound of singing.

With our lives we humbly bow to you,
and standing in this place
our songs express our hearts' desire
to serve you all our days.
We will honour you and magnify
your name above all names,
for we know there is no other God,
yes, you are the King of kings.

Our hearts are filled with gladness
and a sacrifice of praise,
for you have done great things for us.

So glad that you have called us
and what else can we say,
you've saved us by your grace.

501 David Ruis

There's a wind a-blowing
all across the land;
fragrant breeze of heaven
blowing once again.
Don't know where it comes from,
don't know where it goes,
but let it blow over me.
O, sweet wind,
come and blow over me.

There's a rain a-pouring
showers from above;
mercy drops are coming,
mercy drops of love.
Turn your face to heaven,
let the water pour,
well, let it pour over me.
O, sweet rain,
come and pour over me.

There's a fire burning,
falling from the sky;
awesome tongues of fire,
consuming you and I.
Can you feel it burning,
burn the sacrifice?
Well, let it burn over me.
O, sweet fire,
come and burn over me.

502 Eddie Espinosa

There's no one like you, my Lord,
no one could take your place;
my heart beats to worship you,
I live just to seek your face.
There's no one like you, my Lord,
no one could take your place;
there's no one like you, my Lord,
no one like you.

Continued overleaf

You are my God.
You're everything to me,
there's no one like you, my Lord,
no one like you.
(Repeat)

There's no one like you, my Lord,
no one could take your place;
I long for your presence, Lord,
to serve you is my reward.
There's no one like you, my Lord,
no one could take your place;
there's no one like you, my Lord,
no one like you.

© 1990 Mercy/Vineyard Publishing/Music Services/CopyCare

503   Robin Mark

These are the days of Elijah,
declaring the word of the Lord;
and these are the days of your servant, Moses,
righteousness being restored.
And though these are days of great trial,
of famine and darkness and sword,
still we are the voice in the desert crying,
'Prepare ye the way of the Lord.'

Behold, he comes riding on the clouds,
shining like the sun at the trumpet call;
lift your voice, it's the year of jubilee,
out of Zion's hill salvation comes.

These are the days of Ezekiel,
the dry bones becoming as flesh;
and these are the days of your servant, David,
rebuilding a temple of praise.
These are the days of the harvest,
the fields are as white in the world,
and we are the labourers in your vineyard,
declaring the work of the Lord.

© 1996 Daybreak Music

504   Andy Park

The Spirit of the sovereign Lord is upon you
because he has anointed you
to preach good news;

the Spirit of the sovereign Lord is upon you
because he has anointed you
to preach good news.

He has sent you to the poor
(this is the year),
to bind up the broken-hearted
(this is the day);
to bring freedom to the captives
(this is the year),
and to release the ones in darkness.

This is the year
of the favour of the Lord,
this is the day
of the vengeance of our God;
this is the year,
of the favour of the Lord,
this is the day
of the vengeance of our God.

The Spirit of the sovereign Lord is upon us
because he has anointed us
to preach good news;
the Spirit of the sovereign Lord is upon us
because he has anointed us
to preach good news.

He will comfort all who mourn
(this is the year),
he will provide for those who grieve in Zion
(this is the day);
he will pour out the oil of gladness
(this is the year),
instead of mourning we will praise.

This is the year . . .

© 1994 Mercy/Vineyard Publishing/Music Services/CopyCare

505   Edith McNeil

The steadfast love of the Lord never ceases,
his mercies never come to an end.
They are new every morning,
new every morning;
great is thy faithfulness, O Lord,
great is thy faithfulness.

© 1974 Celebration/Kingsway's Thankyou Music

506 Graham Kendrick

The trumpets sound, the angels sing,
the feast is ready to begin;
the gates of heav'n are open wide,
and Jesus welcomes you inside.

Tables are laden with good things,
O taste the peace and joy he brings;
he'll fill you up with love divine,
he'll turn your water into wine.

Sing with thankfulness songs of pure delight,
come and revel in heaven's love and light;
take your place at the table of the King,
the feast is ready to begin,
the feast is ready to begin.

The hungry heart he satisfies,
offers the poor his paradise;
now hear all heav'n and earth applaud
the amazing goodness of the Lord.

Leader	Jesus,
All	Jesus,
Leader	we thank you,
All	we thank you,
Leader	for your love,
All	for your love,
Leader	for your joy,
All	for your joy.
Leader	Jesus,
All	Jesus,
Leader	we thank you,
All	we thank you,
Leader	for the good things,
All	for the good things,
Leader	you give to us,
All	you give to us.

© 1989 Make Way Music

507 Wes Sutton

The Word made flesh, full of truth and grace,
the light of men, God incarnate came.
He lived, he loved, a servant, humble, meek,
and in his voice we hear the Father speak.

We await a Saviour from heaven,
and he will surely come,
in his glory and with the angels
and the power of this throne.
The Christ from heaven returning,
his promise to fulfil
before the splendour of his presence,
let the earth be still.

Such hate, such scorn, and a traitor's kiss
led to the cross for such a world as this.
The death he died, the grave in which he laid
could not hold him; to life again he came.

Now death destroyed, the grave left open wide,
our Saviour reigns at the Father's side.
Where death your sting, where your power,
   O grave?
The Son of God prepares to come again.

© 1997 Sovereign Lifestyle Music

508 Noel and Tricia Richards

The world is looking for a hero;
we know the greatest one of all:
the mighty ruler of the nations,
King of kings and Lord of lords,
who took the nature of a servant,
and gave his life to save us all.

We will raise a shout,
we will shout it out,
he is the Champion of the world.
(Repeat)

The Lord Almighty is our hero,
he breaks the stranglehold of sin.
Through Jesus' love we fear no evil;
pow'rs of darkness flee from him.
His light will shine in every nation,
a sword of justice he will bring.

© 1994 Kingsway's Thankyou Music

509 Kevin Prosch

They that wait on the Lord
will renew their strength.
Run and not grow weary,
walk and not faint.
(Repeat)

Do you not know, have you not heard?
My Father does not grow weary.
He'll give passion to a willing heart.
Even the youths get tired and faint,
but strength will come for those who wait.

I will wait, I will wait,
I will wait on you.
I will run, I will run,
I will run with you.
My love, my love,
my love for you.

© 1995 7th Time Music/Kingsway's Thankyou Music

510 Edmond Louis Budry trans. Richard Birch Hoyle

Thine be the glory,
risen, conquering Son,
endless is the victory
thou o'er death hast won;
angels in bright raiment
rolled the stone away,
kept the folded grave-clothes
where thy body lay.

Thine be the glory,
risen, conquering Son,
endless is the victory
thou o'er death hast won.

Lo! Jesus meets us,
risen from the tomb;
lovingly he greets us,
scatters fear and gloom.
Let the church with gladness
hymns of triumph sing,
for her Lord now liveth;
death hast lost its sting.

No more we doubt thee,
glorious Prince of Life;
life is naught without thee:
aid us in our strife.
Make us more than conquerors
through thy deathless love;
bring us safe through Jordan
to thy home above.

© Copyright control (revived 1996)

511 Graham Kendrick

This Child, secretly comes in the night,
O this Child, hiding a heavenly light,
O this Child, coming to us like a stranger,
this heavenly Child.

This Child, heaven come down now
to be with us here,
heavenly love and mercy appear,
softly in awe and wonder come near –
to this heavenly Child.

This Child, rising on us like the sun,
O this Child, given to light everyone,
O this Child, guiding our feet on the pathway
to peace on earth.

This Child, raising the humble and poor,
O this Child, making the proud ones to fall;
O this child, filling the hungry with good things,
this heavenly Child.

© 1988 Make Way Music

512 Geoff Bullock

This grace is mine,
this glory, earth-bound heaven sent
this plan divine,
this life, this light that breaks my night,
the Spirit of God
heaven falls like a dove to my heart.

This love is mine,
so undeserved, this glorious name,
this Son, this God,
this life, this death, this victory won,
forgiveness has flowed and
this grace that is mine finds my heart.

The power and the glory of your name.
The power and the glory of your name.
The power and the glory of your name,
the name of the Lord, the Son of God.

This life is mine,
so perfect and so pure, this God in me,
this glorious hope
from earth to heaven, death to life,
this future assured and secured
by this love in my heart.

513   Gary Sadler and Lynn DeShazo

This, in essence, is the message
we heard from Christ.
This, in essence, is the message
we heard from Christ
and are passing on to you.
God is light, God is light,
pure light, pure light.
God is light, pure light.
There's not a trace of darkness in him.

514   Graham Kendrick

This is my beloved Son
who tasted death
that you, my child, might live.
See the blood he shed for you,
what suffering,
say what more could he give?
Clothed in his perfection
bring praise, a fragrant sweet,
garlanded with joy,
come worship at his feet.

That the Lamb who was slain
might receive the reward,
might receive the reward
of his suffering.

Look, the world's great harvest fields
are ready now
and Christ commands us: 'Go!'
Countless souls are dying
so hopelessly,
his wondrous love unknown.
Lord, give us the nations
for the glory of the King.
Father, send more labourers
the lost to gather in.

Come the day when we will stand
there face to face,
what joy will fill his eyes.
For at last his bride appears
so beautiful,
her glory fills the skies.
Drawn from every nation,
people, tribe and tongue;
all creation sings,
the wedding has begun.

515   Reuben Morgan

This is my desire, to honour you.
Lord, with all my heart,
I worship you.
All I have within me I give you praise.
All that I adore is in you.

Lord, I give you my heart,
I give you my soul;
I live for you alone.
Every breath that I take,
every moment I'm awake,
Lord, have your way in me.

516 Bob Fitts

This is the day that the Lord has made;
I will rejoice and celebrate.
This is the day that the Lord has made;
I will rejoice, I will rejoice and celebrate.
(Repeat)

He goes before me (he goes before me),
he walks beside me (he walks beside me),
he lives within me,
he's the lover of my soul.
He's my defender (he's my defender),
he's my provider (he's my provider),
his overflowing mercies
are brand new every day.

517 Les Garrett

This is the day,
this is the day that the Lord has made,
that the Lord has made;
we shall rejoice,
we shall rejoice and be glad in it,
and be glad in it.
This is the day that the Lord has made,
we shall rejoice and be glad in it;
this is the day,
this is the day that the Lord has made.

518 Martin Smith

This is the message of the cross,
that we can be free,
to live in the victory
and turn from our sin.
My precious Lord Jesus,
with sinners you died,
for there you revealed your love
and you laid down your life.

This is the message of the cross,
that we can be free,
to lay all our burdens here,
at the foot of the tree.
The cross was the shame of the world,
but the glory of God,
for Jesus you conquered sin
and you gave us new life.

You set me free
when I came to the cross,
poured out your blood
for I was broken and lost.
There I was healed
and you covered my sin.
It's there you saved me.
This is the message of the cross.

This is the message of the cross,
that we can be free,
to hunger for heaven,
to hunger for thee.
The cross is such foolishness
to the perishing,
but to us who are being saved,
it is the power of God.

You set us free
when we come to the cross,
you pour out your blood
for we are broken and lost.
Here we are healed
and you cover our sin.
It's here you save us.
You set me free
when I come to the cross,
pour out your blood
for I am broken and lost.
Here I am healed
and you cover my sin.
It's here you save me.
This is the message of the cross.

Let us rejoice at the foot of the cross;
we can be free, glory to God.
Let us rejoice at the foot of the cross;
we can be free, Glory to God.

Thank you, Lord, thank you, Lord,
you've set us free, glory to God.
Thank you, Lord, thank you, Lord,
you've set us free, glory to God.

519 Philip Lawson Johnston and Chris Bowater

This is the mystery,
that Christ has chosen you and me,
to be the revelation of his glory;
a chosen, royal, holy people
set apart and loved,
a bride preparing for her King.

> Let the Bride say, 'Come',
> let the Bride say, 'Come',
> let the Bride of the Lamb say,
>   'Come, Lord Jesus!'
> Let the Bride say, 'Come',
> let the Bride say, 'Come',
> let the Bride of the Lamb say,
>   'Come, Lord Jesus, come!'

She's crowned in splendour
and a royal diadem,
the King is enthralled by her beauty.
Adorned in righteousness,
arrayed in glorious light,
the Bride is waiting for her King.

Now hear the Bridegroom call,
'Beloved, come aside;
the time of betrothal is at hand.
Lift up your eyes and see
the dawning of the day,
when as King, I'll return to claim my Bride.'

520 Andy Piercy and Dave Clifton

This is the sweetest mystery
that you, O Lord, are One in Three;
majestic, glorious Trinity
of Father, Spirit, Son.

The heav'nly Father, great 'I Am',
the Son of God, the Son of Man,
and yet within this wondrous plan
the Spirit with us here.

Lord, may this truth become a flame
that burns within our hearts again,
that we may glorify your name
in all we do and say.
And so, dear Lord, we gladly come
to stand before the Three in One,
and worship Father, Spirit, Son;
accept the praise we bring.

521 Geoff Bullock

This love, this hope,
this peace of God, this righteousness,
this faith, this joy,
this life, complete in me.
Now healed and whole
and risen in his righteousness;
I live in him, he lives in me.
And filled with this hope in God,
reflecting his glory.

> Now is the time to worship you,
> now is the time to offer you
> all of my thoughts, my dreams and plans;
> I lay it down.
> Now is the time to live for you,
> now is the time I'm found in you,
> now is the time your kingdom comes.

522 Ian White

Though I feel afraid
of territory unknown,
I know that I can say
that I do not stand alone.
For Jesus, you have promised
your presence in my heart;
I cannot see the ending,
but it's here that I must start.

Continued overleaf

And all I know is you have called me,
and that I will follow is all I can say.
I will go where you will send me,
and your fire lights my way.

What lies across the waves
may cause my heart to fear;
will I survive the day,
must I leave what's known and dear?
A ship that's in the harbour
is still and safe from harm,
but it was not built to be there,
it was made for wind and storm.

523   Mark Altrogge

Though the earth should tremble
and the oceans roar
and the mountains slip into the sea,
I shall not fear any harm
with your powerful arms around me.

I worship you, eternal God,
I worship you, the unchanging One.
Before the angels ever sang one song,
before the morning stars had ever shone,
you were on the throne, eternal God.

Though earth's kingdoms crumble
and the nations rage
and rulers and kings come and go,
yours is the kingdom unshaken,
and you've never forsaken your own.

524   Noel Richards

To be in your presence,
to sit at your feet,
where your love surrounds me,
and makes me complete.

This is my desire,
O Lord, this is my desire.
This is my desire,
O Lord, this is my desire.

To rest in your presence,
not rushing away,
to cherish each moment,
here would I stay.

525   Bob Fitts

To every good thing God is doing
within me that I cannot see, amen.
And to the healing virtue of Jesus
that's flowing in me, amen.
For every hope that is still just a dream,
by trusting in you, Lord, becomes reality.
I stake my claim, seal it in faith,
I say amen.

Amen (amen), amen (amen).
So be it, Lord, your word endures, I say 'amen'.
Amen (amen), amen (amen).
So be it, Lord, amen.
So be it, Lord, amen.

526   Frances Jane van Alstyne

To God be the glory!
great things he hath done;
so loved he the world
that he gave us his Son;
who yielded his life
an atonement for sin,
and opened the life-gate
that all may go in.

Praise the Lord, praise the Lord!
let the earth hear his voice;
praise the Lord, praise the Lord!
let the people rejoice:
O come to the Father,
through Jesus the Son,
and give him the glory;
great things he hath done.

O perfect redemption,
the purchase of blood!
to every believer
the promise of God;

the vilest offender
who truly believes
that moment from Jesus
a pardon receives.

Great things he hath taught us,
great things he hath done,
and great our rejoicing
through Jesus the Son;
but purer, and higher,
and greater will be
our wonder, our rapture,
when Jesus we see.

527 Graham Kendrick

To keep your lovely face
ever before my eyes,
this is my prayer,
make it my strong desire;
that in my secret heart
no other love competes,
no rival throne survives,
and I serve only you.

© 1983 Kingsway's Thankyou Music

528 Graham Kendrick

Tonight, while all the world was sleeping,
a light exploded in the skies.
And then, as glory did surround us,
a voice, an angel did appear!

Glory to God in the highest,
and on the earth all peace from heav'n!
Glory to God in the highest,
and on the earth all peace from heav'n!

Afraid, we covered up our faces,
amazed at what our ears did hear.
Good news of joy for all the people –
today a Saviour has appeared!

And so to Bethlehem
to find it all was true;
despised and worthless shepherds,
we were the first to know.

© 1988 Make Way Music

529 Craig Musseau

To you, O Lord, I bring my worship,
an offering of love to you.
Surrounded in your holy presence,
all I can say is that I love you.

Give ear to the groaning in my spirit.
Hear the crying in my heart.
Release my soul to freely worship,
for I was made to give you honour.

Holy, holy, holy, holy.
Holy, holy, holy, holy.

© 1990 Mercy/Vineyard Publishing/Music Services/CopyCare

530 Graham Kendrick

To you, O Lord, I lift up my soul.
In you I trust, O my God.
Do not let me be put to shame,
nor let my enemies triumph over me.

No one whose hope is in you
will ever be put to shame;
that's why my eyes are on you, O Lord.
Surround me, defend me,
O how I need you.
To you I lift up my soul,
to you I lift up my soul.

Show me your ways and teach me your paths.
Guide me in truth, lead me on;
for you're my God, you are my Saviour.
My hope is in you each moment of the day.

Remember, Lord, your mercy and love
that ever flow from of old.
Remember not the sins of my youth
or my rebellious ways.
According to your love, remember me.
According to your love, for you are good,
O Lord.

© 1997 Make Way Music

531
Graham Kendrick

Turn our hearts, turn our hearts.

Turn our hearts to one another,
let your kindness show:
where our words or deeds have wounded,
let forgiveness flow.

Turn our hearts from pride and anger
to your ways of peace,
for you died and shed your blood
that enmity may cease.

Turn the hearts of generations
that we may be one:
make us partners in the kingdom
till your work is done.

As we all have been forgiven,
so must we forgive;
as we all have found acceptance,
so let us receive.

Turn our hearts, change our hearts,
join our hearts, turn our hearts.

532
Graham Kendrick

Turn to me and be saved,
all you nations.
Turn to me and be saved,
all you nations.

Turn to me (turn to me)
and be saved (and be saved),
all you nations.
Turn to me (turn to me)
and be saved (and be saved)
all you nations.
For I am God, and there is no other.
For I am God, and there is no other.
Turn to me (turn to me)
and be saved (and be saved),
all you people.

Turn to me (turn to me)
and be saved (and be saved),
all you people.
For he is God, and there is no other.
For he is God, and there is no other.
For you are God, and there is no other.
For you are God, and there is no other.

Shout:

Leader	Now, Lord, send your Holy Spirit.
All	Now, Lord, send your Holy Spirit.
Leader	Drench this land with your awesome presence.
All	Drench this land with your awesome presence.
Leader	Send your Holy Spirit more powerfully.
All	Send your Holy Spirit more powerfully.
Leader	Let grace and mercy flood this land.
All	Let grace and mercy flood this land.
Leader	Let mercy triumph over judgement.
All	Let mercy triumph over judgement.
Leader	Let mercy triumph over judgement.
All	Let mercy triumph over judgement.

533
Helen H. Lemmel

Turn your eyes upon Jesus,
look full in his wonderful face,
and the things of earth
will grow strangely dim
in the light of his glory and grace.

534
Matt Redman

Wake up, my soul,
worship the Lord of truth and life.
Have strength, my heart,
press on as one who seeks the prize.
I'll run for you, my God and King,
I'll run as one who runs to win.
I'm pressing on, not giving in.
I will run, I will run for you, my King.

And Spirit, come, give life to us,
come breathe the Father's love in us.
Won't you fill us once again?
And we will run and run with him.
We'll run with strength, with all our might,
we'll fix our eyes on Jesus Christ;
he has conquered death and sin.
And we will run and run and run with him.

535 Graham Kendrick

Wake up, O sleeper,
and rise from the dead,
and Christ will shine on you.
Wake up, O sleeper,
and rise from the dead,
and Christ will shine on you.

Once you were darkness, but now you are light,
now you are light in the Lord.
So as true children of light you must live,
showing the glory of God.

This is the beautiful fruit of the light,
the good, the righteous, the true.
Let us discover what pleases the Lord
in everything we do.

As days get darker, take care how you live,
not as unwise, but as wise,
making the most of each moment he gives,
and pressing on for the prize.

536 Trevor King

We are a people of power,
we are a people of praise;
we are a people of promise,
Jesus has risen, he's conquered the grave!
Risen, yes, born again,
we walk in the power of his name;
power to be the sons of God,
the sons of God! the sons of God!
we are the sons, sons of God!

537 Graham Kendrick

We are his children,
the fruit of his suffering,
saved and redeemed by his blood;
called to be holy, a light to the nations:
clothed with his power,
filled with his love.

Go forth in his name,
proclaiming, 'Jesus reigns!'
Now is the time for the church to arise
and proclaim him
'Jesus, Saviour, Redeemer and Lord'.
(Repeat)

Countless the souls
that are stumbling in darkness;
why do we sleep in the light?
Jesus commands us to go make disciples,
this is our cause,
this is our fight.

Listen, the wind
of the Spirit is blowing,
the end of the age is so near;
powers in the earth and heavens are shaking,
Jesus our Lord
soon shall appear.

538 Kevin Prosch

We are his people,
he gives us music to sing.
There is a sound now,
like the sound of the Lord
when his enemies flee.
But there is a cry in our hearts,
like when deep calls unto the deep,
for your breath of deliverance,
to breathe on the music we so desperately
need.
But without your power
all we have are these simple songs.
If you'd step down from heaven,
then the gates of hell would surely fall.

Continued overleaf

So we shout to the Lord,
shout to the Lord,
shout to the Lord of hosts.
Shout to the Lord, shout to the Lord,
shout to the Lord of hosts.
And it breaks the heavy yoke,
breaks the heavy yoke,
when you shout, you shout to the Lord.
It breaks the heavy yoke,
breaks the heavy yoke,
when you shout, you shout to the Lord.
Woa, you shout to the Lord,
yeah, you shout to the Lord,
woa, you shout to the Lord.

539   Traditional African

We are marching in the light of God,
we are marching in the light of God.
We are marching in the light of God,
we are marching in the light of God.

We are marching, marching,
we are marching, oh, we are marching
in the light of God.
(Repeat)

We are living in the love of God . . .

We are moving in the pow'r of God . . .

540   Kevin Prosch

We are the army of God,
children of Abraham,
we are a chosen generation.
Under a covenant,
washed by his precious blood,
filled with the mighty Holy Ghost.
And I hear the sound of the coming rain,
as we sing the praise to the great 'I Am'.

And the sick are healed,
and the dead shall rise,
and your church is the army
that was prophesied.

(Last time)
Your church is the army.
Your church is the army.
Your church is the army.
Your church is the army.

541   Graham Kendrick

We believe in God the Father,
Maker of the universe,
and in Christ his Son, our Saviour,
come to us by virgin birth.
We believe he died to save us,
bore our sins, was crucified.
Then from death he rose victorious,
ascended to the Father's side.

Jesus, Lord of all, Lord of all,
Jesus, Lord of all, Lord of all,
Jesus, Lord of all, Lord of all,
Jesus, Lord of all, Lord of all.
Name above all names.
Name above all names.

We believe he sends his Spirit
on his church with gifts of pow'r.
God, his word of truth affirming,
sends us to the nations now.
He will come again in glory,
judge the living and the dead.
Every knee shall bow before him,
then must every tongue confess.

542   Kirk Dearman

We bring the sacrifice of praise
into the house of the Lord.
We bring the sacrifice of praise
into the house of the Lord.

We bring the sacrifice of praise
into the house of the Lord.
We bring the sacrifice of praise
into the house of the Lord.

And we offer up to you
the sacrifices of thanksgiving,
and we offer up to you
the sacrifices of joy.

543   Robert Eastwood

We come into your presence
to sing a song to you,
a song of praise and honour
for all the things you've helped us through;
you gave a life worth living,
a life in love with you,
and now I just love giving
all my praises back to you.

You're the Father of creation,
the risen Lamb of God,
you're the One who walked away
from the empty tomb that day;
and you set your people free
with love and liberty,
and I can walk with you
every night and every day.

544   Malcolm du Plessis

We declare your majesty,
we proclaim that your name is exalted;
for you reign magnificently,
rule victoriously
and your pow'r is shown throughout the earth.
And we exclaim our God is mighty,
lift up your name, for you are holy.
Sing it again, all honour and glory,
in adoration we bow before your throne.

545   Andy Piercy

We do not presume
to come to your table
trusting in our own righteousness.
For we are not worthy so much
as to gather the crumbs
from under your table.
But trusting, O Lord,
in your great and manifold mercies.
For you are the same Lord
whose nature's always to have mercy.

So cleanse us and feed us
with the body and blood of your Son.
That we may live in him,
that he may live in us
for ever and ever. Amen.

546   Dave Clifton

We have a great priest
over the house of God.
So let us draw near to God
with a sincere heart,
in full assurance,
assurance of our faith,
having our hearts touched
to cleanse us from our guilt.

For he who promised is faithful,
for he who promised is faithful,
is faithful to me.

Give me a pure heart,
holding to your hope,
the hope I profess, Lord,
lead me in your way;
be now my strength, Lord,
and all of my trust, Lord,
I will fear no one,
for you are with me.

547 Paul Oakley

We have prayed that you would have mercy;
we believe from heaven you've heard.
Heal our land, so dry and so thirsty;
we have strayed so far from you, Lord.
Your cloud appeared on the horizon,
small as a man's hand.
But now you're near, filling our vision,
pour out your Spirit again.
I felt the touch of your wind on my face:
I feel the first drops of rain.

Let it rain, let it rain.
I will not be the same.
Let it rain, rain on me.
Let it pour down on me,
let it rain, let it rain,
let it rain, let it rain, let it rain on me.

© 1994 Kingsway's Thankyou Music

548 Noel Richards

Welcome, King of kings!
How great is your name.
You come in majesty
for ever to reign.

You rule the nations, they shake
at the sound of your name.
To you is given all pow'r
and you shall reign.

Let all creation bow down
at the sound of your name.
Let every tongue now confess,
the Lord God reigns.

© 1991 Kingsway's Thankyou Music

549 Graham Kendrick

Welcome the King, welcome the King,
welcome the King, welcome the King,
welcome the King
who comes in the name of the Lord.
(Repeat)

Clear the road before him,
open the ancient doors,
let every heart receive him:
welcome the King
who comes in the name of the Lord.

Who is this King, who is this King,
who is this King, who is this King,
who is this King
who comes in the name of the Lord?
(Repeat)

He is the King of Glory,
crucified and risen;
he is the Lord Almighty:
welcome the King
who comes in the name of the Lord;
welcome the King
who comes in the name of the Lord.

© 1996 Make Way Music

550 Martin Smith

Well, I hear they're singing in the streets
that Jesus is alive,
and all creation shouts aloud
that Jesus is alive;
now surely we can all be changed
'cos Jesus is alive;
and everybody here can know
that Jesus is alive.

And I will live for all my days
to raise a banner of truth and light,
to sing about my Saviour's love
and the best thing that happened –
it was the day I met you.

I've found Jesus, I've found Jesus,
I've found Jesus, I've found Jesus.

Well, I feel like dancing in the streets
'cos Jesus is alive,
to join with all who celebrate
that Jesus is alive.
The joy of God is in this town
'cos Jesus is alive;
for everybody's seen the truth
that Jesus is alive.

And I will live for all my days . . .

Well, you lifted me from where I was,
set my feet upon a rock,
humbled that you even know 'bout me.
Now I have chosen to believe,
believing that you've chosen me;
I was lost but now I've found —

551 Graham Kendrick

We'll walk the land with hearts on fire;
and every step will be a prayer.
Hope is rising, new day dawning;
sound of singing fills the air.

Two thousand years, and still the flame
is burning bright across the land.
Hearts are waiting, longing, aching,
for awakening once again.

Let the flame burn brighter
in the heart of the darkness,
turning night to glorious day.
Let the song grow louder,
as our love grows stronger;
let it shine! Let it shine!

We'll walk for truth, speak out for love;
in Jesus' name we shall be strong,
to lift the fallen, to save the children,
to fill the nation with your song.

552 Steven Fry

We march to the tune of a love-song,
singing the King's jubilee;
anointed to enter the hell-gate,
anointed to set captives free.
We lift up our banner of worship
and Jesus our Champion we praise;
an army of worshippers stand by his side,
baptised in his fire,
revealing his glorious light.

We lift up a shout,
a victory shout,
for we've overcome
by the blood of the Lamb
and the word of our mouth.
We've declared war
in the name of the Lord,
we've laid down our lives
that the triumph of Christ
may resound in the earth.

We sing the high praises of heaven
and fight with the sword of the Word;
to bind every stronghold of Satan,
preparing the way of the Lord.
We lift up a standard of worship
that shatters the darkness with light,
and God will arise on the wings of our praise
and march as a Warrior
who's mighty and able to save.

553 Ian Mizen and Andy Pressdee

We must work together,
bringing in the kingdom,
bringing heaven here on earth.
Start a new world order,
start a revolution,
let all people know their worth.

We'll see it all (we'll see it all),
we'll see it all (we'll see it all),
we'll see it all (we'll see it all),
we'll see it all,

when the kingdom comes,
when Jesus comes,
when the kingdom comes,
when Jesus comes,
when the kingdom comes.
When Jesus comes,
when the kingdom comes,
when Jesus comes.

Your kingdom come,
your will be done,
your kingdom come,
your will be done.

Continued overleaf

When the kingdom comes,
when Jesus comes . . .

We will see the dawning,
in this generation
see the start of a new day.
We'll know peace and freedom.
We will know true laughter,
we'll see sickness blown away.

554   Carol Owen

We rejoice in the goodness of our God,
we rejoice in the wonders of your favour.
You've set the captives free,
you've caused the blind to see,
hallelujah, you give us liberty,
hallelujah.

Always the same, you never change,
and your mercies are new every day.
Compassionate and gracious,
our faithful, loving God,
slow to anger, rich in love.

You give us hope, you give us joy,
you give us fullness of life to enjoy.
Our shepherd and provider,
our God who's always there,
never failing, always true.

555   Mark Altrogge

We serve a God of miracles,
you heal the sick and open blinded eyes;
we serve a God of miracles,
the demons flee the moment you arise,
arise, and show yourself strong,
arise, arise, and show yourself strong.
(Repeat)

We serve a God of power,
we serve a God of might,
we serve a God of signs and wonders;

we serve a God of power,
we serve a God of might.
You speak and all creation thunders.

556   Graham Kendrick

We shall stand
with our feet upon the Rock.
Whatever they may say,
we'll lift your name up high.
And we shall walk
through the darkest night;
setting our faces like flint,
we'll walk into the light.

Lord, you have chosen me
for fruitfulness,
to be transformed
into your likeness.
I'm gonna fight on through
till I see you face to face.

Lord, as your witnesses
you've appointed us.
And with your Holy Spirit
anointed us.
And so I'll fight on through
till I see you face to face.

557   Matt Redman

We've had a light shine in our midst,
we've felt your presence, we've known your
        peace,
and though this blessing comes to us free,
it carries a challenge to go.
We've had a feast laid on for us,
you have commanded, 'Bring in the lost',
there's food for all, any who'd come,
any who would know your Son.

We know it's time to go,
we've heard the cries of all of the earth.
Send us with pow'r,
we cannot do it alone.

With passion for the lost
we'll take the truth,
whatever the cost;
time is so short,
we cannot squander this love.

Surely the time has come
to bring the harvest home.
Surely the time has come
to bring the harvest home.

© 1995 Kingsway's Thankyou Music

558 Andy Piercy and Dave Clifton

We want to remain in your love,
we want to remain in your love.
O Lord, O Lord, we need you so.
I want to remain in your love,
I want to remain in your love.
O Lord, don't ever let us go.
(Repeat)

Love is patient, love is kind,
does not envy, does not boast,
is not proud, is not rude;
love does not rejoice in evil,
but rejoices with the truth.
Love protects, always trusts,
always hopes, and perseveres,
is slow to anger, never fails;
love does not delight in evil,
but rejoices with the truth.
Love does not delight in evil,
but rejoices with the truth.

I want to remain in your love,
I want to remain in your love.
O Lord, don't ever let us go.

© 1994 IQ Music Ltd

559 Doug Horley

We want to see Jesus lifted high,
a banner that flies across this land,
that all men might see the truth
and know he is the way to heaven.
(Repeat)

We want to see, we want to see,
we want to see Jesus lifted high.
We want to see, we want to see,
we want to see Jesus lifted high.

Step by step we're moving forward,
little by little taking ground,
every prayer a powerful weapon,
strongholds come tumbling down,
and down, and down, and down.

We're gonna see . . .

© 1993 Kingsway's Thankyou Music

560 Graham Kendrick

We will cross every border,
throw wide every door,
joining our hands across the nations,
we'll proclaim Jesus is Lord.

We will break sin's oppression,
speak out for the poor,
announce the coming of Christ's kingdom
from east to west and shore to shore.

We will gather in the harvest,
and work while it's day,
though we may sow with tears of sadness,
we will reap with shouts of joy.

Soon our eyes shall see his glory,
the Lamb, our risen Lord,
when he receives from every nation
his blood-bought Bride, his great reward.
Then we'll proclaim Jesus is Lord.
We shall proclaim Jesus is Lord.

© 1991 Make Way Music

561 Tricia Allen and Martin J. Nystrom

We will run and not grow weary,
we will walk and will not faint,
for the Lord will go before us
and his joy will be our strength.
Mounting up with wings as eagles,
as our spirits start to soar;
when we come into his presence,
and we wait upon the Lord.

Continued overleaf

We will wait upon the Lord,
for in his presence is fullness of joy;
and our strength will be restored,
as we wait upon the Lord.

562 Kath Hall

*We will turn the hearts of the fathers
so they will look again to their children.
We will turn the hearts of the children
so that together we can look to you.
(Repeat)*

The young and the old now,
standing together,
looking to Jesus to carry us through.
All different races, all different ages,
all of us here for your glory.
And we call on your Spirit,
keep us together and pour in your power.

563 Dennis Jernigan

We will worship the Lamb of glory,
we will worship the King of kings;
we will worship the Lamb of glory,
we will worship the King.

*And with our hands lifted high
we will worship and sing,
and with our hands lifted high
we come before you rejoicing.
With our hands lifted high to the sky,
when the world wonders why,
we'll just tell them
we're loving our King.
Oh, we'll just tell them
we're loving our King.
Yes, we'll just tell them
we're loving our King.*

Bless the name of the Lamb of glory,
I bless the name of the King of kings;
bless the name of the Lamb of glory,
bless the name of the King.

564 Andy Piercy (v. 3 Cecil Frances Alexander)

*We worship and adore you, Lord,
hear us when we call,
for there is no god above you,
you are the Lord of all.*

But how can we begin to express
what's on our hearts?
There are no words enough, Lord,
for us to even start.

The tongues of men and angels
we need, to sing your praise,
so that we may glorify your name
through heav'n's eternal days.

There was no other good enough
to pay the price of sin;
you only could unlock the gate
of heav'n, and let us in.

So, we worship and adore you . . .

565 Martin Smith

What a friend I've found,
closer than a brother.
I have felt your touch,
more intimate than lovers.

*Jesus, Jesus,
Jesus, friend for ever.*

What a hope I've found,
more faithful than a mother.
It would break my heart
to ever lose each other.

566 Joseph Medlicott Scriven

What a friend we have in Jesus,
all our sins and griefs to bear!
What a privilege to carry
everything to him in prayer!
O what peace we often forfeit,
O what needless pain we bear,
all because we do not carry
everything to God in prayer!

Have we trials and temptations?
Is there trouble anywhere?
We should never be discouraged:
take it to the Lord in prayer!
Can we find a friend so faithful,
who will all our sorrows share?
Jesus knows our every weakness –
take it to the Lord in prayer!

Are we weak and heavy-laden,
cumbered with a load of care?
Jesus only is our refuge,
take it to the Lord in prayer!
Do thy friends despise, forsake thee?
Take it to the Lord in prayer!
In his arms he'll take and shield thee,
thou wilt find a solace there.

567 Graham Kendrick

What kind of greatness can this be,
that chose to be made small?
Exchanging untold majesty
for a world so pitiful.
That God should come as one of us,
I'll never understand.
The more I hear the story told,
the more amazed I am.

O what else can I do
but kneel and worship you,
and come just as I am,
my whole life an offering.

The One in whom we live and move
in swaddling clothes lies bound.
The voice that cried, 'Let there be light',
asleep without a sound.
The One who strode among the stars,
and called each one by name,
lies helpless in a mother's arms
and must learn to walk again.

What greater love could he have shown
to shamed humanity,
yet human pride hates to believe
in such deep humility.
But nations now may see his grace
and know that he is near,
when his meek heart, his words, his works
are incarnate in us.

© 1994 Make Way Music

568 Bryn and Sally Haworth

What kind of love is this
that gave itself for me?
I am the guilty one,
yet I go free.
What kind of love is this,
a love I've never known?
I didn't even know his name.
What kind of love is this?

What kind of man is this
that died in agony?
He who had done no wrong
was crucified for me.
What kind of man is this
who laid aside his throne,
that I may know the love of God?
What kind of man is this?

By grace I have been saved;
it is the gift of God.
He destined me to be his child,
such is his love.
No eye has ever seen,
no ear has ever heard,
nor has the heart of man conceived
what kind of love is this.

© 1983 Signalgrade/Kingsway's Thankyou Music

569 Lucy East

*What noise shall we make
to say that God is great?
What noise shall we make
unto the Lord?*

Let's make a loud noise
to say that God is great.
Let's make a loud noise
unto the Lord.
Here is my loud noise,
here is my loud noise,
here is my loud noise
unto the Lord.

Let's make a quiet noise . . .
Here is my quiet noise . . .

Let's make a fast noise . . .
Here is my fast noise . . .

Let's make a slow noise . . .
He is my slow noise . . .

Let's make a joyful noise . . .
Here is my joyful noise . . .

Let's make a praising noise . . .
Here is my praising noise . . .

We love making noise
to say that God is great.
We love making noise
unto the Lord.

570 Keri Jones and David Matthew

When I feel the touch
of your hand upon my life,
it causes me to sing a song
that I love you, Lord.
So from deep within
my spirit singeth unto thee,
you are my King,
you are my God,
and I love you, Lord.

571 Wayne and Cathy Perrin

When I look into your holiness,
when I gaze into your loveliness,
when all things that surround
become shadows in the light of you;
when I've found the joy
of reaching your heart,
when my will becomes enthralled
in your love,
when all things that surround
become shadows in the light of you:

*I worship you, I worship you,
the reason I live is to worship you.
I worship you, I worship you,
the reason I live is to worship you.*

572 Isaac Watts

When I survey the wondrous cross
on which the Prince of Glory died,
my richest gain I count but loss,
and pour contempt on all my pride.

Forbid it, Lord, that I should boast,
save in the death of Christ, my God:
all the vain things that charm me most,
I sacrifice them to his blood.

See from his head, his hands, his feet,
sorrow and love flow mingling down:
did e'er such love and sorrow meet,
or thorns compose so rich a crown?

Were the whole realm of nature mine,
that were an offering far too small;
love so amazing, so divine,
demands my soul, my life, my all.

573 Lynn DeShazo

When my heart is overwhelmed,
hear my cry, give heed to my prayer;
and my eyes are dim with tears,
O Father, make them clear;

from the ends of all the earth,
when my heart is fainting,
let me know that you have heard,
lead me into safety.

And lead me to the rock,
the rock that's higher,
lead me to the rock
that's higher than I.
Lead me to the rock
the rock that's higher, higher than I.
(Repeat)

You, O Lord, have been for me
a refuge from my enemies,
let me live within your strength,
in the shelter of your wings;
from the ends of all the earth,
when my heart is fainting,
let me know that you have heard,
lead me into safety.

574   Horatio G. Spafford

When peace like a river
attendeth my way,
when sorrows like sea-billows roll,
whatever my lot,
thou hast taught me to know,
it is well, it is well with my soul.

It is well (it is well)
with my soul (with my soul),
it is well, it is well with my soul.

Though Satan should buffet,
though trials should come,
let this blest assurance control,
that Christ hath regarded
my helpless estate,
and hath shed his own blood for my soul.

For me be it Christ,
be it Christ, hence to live!
If Jordan above me shall roll,

no pang shall be mine,
for in death as in life,
thou wilt whisper thy peace to my soul.

But, Lord, 'tis for thee,
for thy coming we wait,
the sky, not the grave, is our goal;
oh, trump of the angel!
O voice of the Lord!
Blessed hope! Blessed rest of my soul!

575   Graham Kendrick

When the Lord brought us back
and restored our freedom,
we felt so good, we felt so strong,
at first we thought we were dreaming.
How we laughed! How we sang,
we were overflowing;
then we heard the nations say,
'Look what the Lord has done.'

The Lord has done great things for us,
and we are filled with joy.
The Lord has done great things for us,
and we are filled with joy,
with joy, with joy, with joy.

576   Matt Redman

When the music fades,
all is stripped away,
and I simply come.
Longing just to bring
something that's of worth
that will bless your heart.

I'll bring you more than a song,
for a song in itself
is not what you have required.
You search much deeper within,
through the way things appear;
you're looking into my heart.

Continued overleaf

I'm coming back to the heart of worship,
and it's all about you,
all about you, Jesus.
I'm sorry, Lord,
for the thing I've made it,
when it's all about you,
all about you, Jesus.

King of endless worth,
no one could express
how much you deserve.
Though I'm weak and poor,
all I have is yours,
every single breath.

I'll bring you . . .

577   Tommy Walker

Where there once was only hurt,
he gave his healing hand.
Where there once was only pain,
he brought comfort like a friend.
I feel the sweetness of his love
piercing my darkness.
I see the bright and morning sun
as it ushers in his joyful gladness.

    He's turned my mourning
    into dancing again,
    he's lifted my sorrow.
    I can't stay silent,
    I must sing for his joy has come.
    (Repeat)

His anger lasts for a moment in time;
but his favour is here
and will be on me for all my lifetime.

578   Graham Kendrick

Where two or three of you gather in my name,
I am there, I am there with you;
and if just two of you stand in agreement,
as you pray gathered in my name,

my Father will hear your prayer,
hear your prayer,
and answer and will give you
anything you ask in my name.

579   Graham Kendrick

Who can sound the depths of sorrow
in the Father heart of God,
for the children we've rejected,
for the lives so deeply scarred?
And each light that we've extinguished
has brought darkness to our land:
upon our nation, upon our nation
have mercy, Lord.

We have scorned the truth you gave us,
we have bowed to other lords.
We have sacrificed the children
on the altar of our gods.
O let truth again shine on us,
let your holy fear descend:
upon our nation, upon our nation
have mercy, Lord.

(Men)
Who can stand before your anger?
Who can face your piercing eyes?
For you love the weak and helpless,
and you hear the victims' cries.
(All)
Yes, you are a God of justice,
and your judgement surely comes:
upon our nation, upon our nation
have mercy, Lord.

(Women)
Who will stand against the violence?
Who will comfort those who mourn?
In an age of cruel rejection,
who will build for love a home?
(All)
Come and shake us into action,
come and melt our hearts of stone:
upon your people, upon your people
have mercy, Lord.

Who can sound the depths of mercy
in the Father heart of God?
For there is a Man of sorrows
who for sinners shed his blood.
He can heal the wounds of nations,
he can wash the guilty clean:
because of Jesus, because of Jesus
have mercy, Lord.

580   Graham Kendrick

Who sees it all, before whose gaze
is darkest night bright as the day;
watching as in the secret place
his likeness forms upon a face?

Who sees it all, the debt that's owed
of lives unlived, of love unknown?
Who weighs the loss of innocence,
or feels the pain of our offence?

God sees, God knows,
God loves the broken heart;
and holds, and binds,
and heals the broken heart.

Who knows the fears that drive a choice,
unburies pain and gives it a voice?
And who can wash a memory,
or take the sting of death away?

God sees, God knows . . .

Whose anger burns at what we've done,
then bears our sin as if his own?
Who will receive us as we are,
whose arms are wide and waiting now?

Whose broken heart upon a cross
won freedom, joy and peace for us?
Whose blood redeems, who ever lives
and all because of love forgives?

God sees, God knows . . .

581   Steve McGregor

With all my heart,
I will put my trust in you.
With all my heart,
I will put my trust in you.
I will lean on you,
depend on you,
I will look to the one I love
with all my heart.

When in despair,
and no one else cares,
storms all around,
no friends can be found;
you're always there,
you're always there for me.

Nothing compares
to your faithfulness,
no greater love
in earth or above:
so I'll declare,
my heart is safe in your arms.

582   Graham Kendrick

With my whole heart I will praise you,
holding nothing back, hallelujah!
You have made me glad and now
I come with open arms to thank you,
with my heart embrace, hallelujah!
I can see your face is smiling.
With my whole life I will serve you,
captured by your love, hallelujah!
O amazing love! O amazing love!

Lord, your heart is overflowing
with a love divine, hallelujah!
And this love is mine for ever.
Now your joy has set you laughing
as you join the song, hallelujah!
Heaven sings along, I hear the
voices swell to great crescendos,
praising your great love, hallelujah!
O amazing love! O amazing love!

Continued overleaf

Come, O Bridegroom, clothed in splendour,
my Beloved One, hallelujah!
How I long to run and meet you.
You're the fairest of ten thousand,
you're my life and breath, hallelujah!
Love as strong as death has won me.
All the rivers, all the oceans
cannot quench this love, hallelujah!
O amazing love! O amazing love!

© 1981 Kingsway's Thankyou Music

583 Geoff Baker

With this bread we will remember him,
Son of God, broken and suffering;
for our guilt – innocent offering.
As we eat, remember him.

With this wine we will remember him,
on the cross, paying the price for sin –
blood of Christ cleansing us deep within.
As we drink, remember him.

© 1994 Sovereign Music UK

584 Eddie Espinosa

Worthy is the Lamb,
worthy is the Lamb,
worthy is the Lamb
that was slain.
(Repeat)

> *To receive wisdom and honour,*
> *to receive power and strength,*
> *to receive wealth and all glory,*
> *worthy is the Lamb.*

Jesus is the Lamb,
Jesus is the Lamb,
Jesus is the Lamb
that was slain.
Worthy is the Lamb,
worthy is the Lamb,
worthy is the Lamb
that was slain.

© 1993 Mercy/Vineyard Publishing/Music Services/CopyCare

585 Mark S. Kinzer

Worthy, O worthy are you, Lord,
worthy to be thanked and praised
and worshipped and adored.
(Repeat)

Singing hallelujah,
Lamb upon the throne,
we worship and adore you,
make your glory known.
Hallelujah, glory to the King:
you're more than a conqueror,
you're Lord of everything.

© 1976 Word of God Music/The Copyright Co./CopyCare

586 Andy Park

Yahweh, Yahweh, Ancient One,
yet you're here today.
Ageless One, Changeless One,
showing love to all generations.
Show us your glory, O Lord,
let your goodness pass before us,
right before our eyes.

> *And we will worship,*
> *and we will bow down,*
> *and we will call you Lord.*
> *And we will kneel*
> *before the Maker of the universe,*
> *and we will call you Lord.*

Yahweh, Yahweh, Faithful One,
you have shown us the way.
Through the years, through all our lives,
you have shown you are faithful to the end.
Show us your glory, O Lord,
let your goodness pass before us,
right before our eyes.

© 1994 Mercy/Vineyard Publishing/Music Services/CopyCare

587 Carl Tuttle

Yet this will I call to mind,
and therefore I will hope,
because of the Lord's great love
I've been redeemed.

The Lord is gracious and kind
to all who call on his name,
because of the Lord's great love
I've been redeemed.

Because of the Lord's great love,
because of the Lord's great love,
because of the Lord's great love,
I've been redeemed.

I know of his steadfast love,
his mercy renewed each day,
because of the Lord's great love
I've been redeemed.
Washed in the blood of the Lamb,
guiltless for ever I stand,
because of the Lord's great love
I've been redeemed.

© 1992 Mercy/Vineyard Publishing/Music Services/CopyCare

588 Carol Owen

You alone, Lord, are wonderful.
Father, you alone are wise.
Your love, Lord, is eternal,
your faithfulness reaches to the skies.

And I adore you, Lord.
I stand in awe of you,
for all of your ways are so great.
Yes, I adore you, Lord.
I stand in awe of you,
for all of your ways are so great.

And I exalt you, my Lord,
I exalt you, my Lord,
I exalt you, my Lord and my King.
I exalt you, my Lord,
I exalt you, my Lord,
for you are my God and King.

© 1996 Kingsway's Thankyou Music

589 Mark Altrogge

You are beautiful beyond description,
too marvellous for words,
too wonderful for comprehension,
like nothing ever seen or heard.

Who can grasp your infinite wisdom?
Who can fathom the depth of your love?
You are beautiful beyond description,
majesty, enthroned above.

And I stand, I stand in awe of you.
I stand, I stand in awe of you.
Holy God, to whom all praise is due,
I stand in awe of you.

© 1987 PDI Music/CopyCare

590 John Sellers

You are crowned with many crowns,
and rule all things in righteousness.
You are crowned with many crowns,
upholding all things by your word.
You rule in power and reign in glory!
You are Lord of heaven and earth!
You are Lord of all.
You are Lord of all.

© 1984 Integrity's Hosanna! Music/Kingsway's Thankyou Music

591 Carol Owen

You are God, you are great,
you are Lord over all.
You are good, you are kind,
you are Lord over all.
You are God, you are great,
you are Lord over all.
You are good, you are kind,
you are Lord over all.
My God, my Friend, my King.

Nothing can compare with all your mighty
    ways.
You sustain the heavens and the earth.
You've revealed your glory
to the sons of men through Jesus.

You're the God of wisdom and of majesty,
the earth is like a footstool at your feet,
yet you came down and dwelt
among the sons of men in Jesus.

© 1996 Kingsway's Thankyou Music

592 Trish Morgan

You are Lord of our hearts,
you are Lord of our lives,
and you reign, and you reign.

His wave of love will wash away
our prejudice and shame,
our brokenness and pain.
Faith will rise,
faith instead of fear,
connected in his love,
anointed from above.

593 Ian White

You are merciful to me,
you are merciful to me,
you are merciful to me, my Lord.
You are merciful to me,
you are merciful to me,
you are merciful to me, my Lord.

Every day my disobedience
grieves your loving heart,
but then redeeming love breaks through,
and causes me to worship you.

Redeemer (Redeemer),
Saviour (Saviour),
Healer (Healer)
and Friend (and Friend).
Every day (every day)
renew my ways (renew my ways),
fill me with love (fill me with love)
that never ends (that never ends).

594 Craig Musseau

You are mighty,
you are holy,
you are awesome in your power;
you have risen,
you have conquered,
you have beaten the power of death.

Hallelujah, we will rejoice;
hallelujah, we will rejoice!

595 Brian Doerksen

You are my King (you are my King),
and I love you.
You are my King (you are my King)
and I worship you,
kneeling before you now,
all of my life I gladly give to you.

You are my King (you are my King),
and I love you.
You are my King (you are my King)
and I worship you,
kneeling before you now,
all of my life I gladly give to you,
placing my hopes and dreams in your hands,
I give my heart to you.

I love you, love you, Jesus.
Yes, I love you, love you, Jesus, my King.

596 Noel and Tricia Richards

You are my passion, love of my life,
friend and companion, my Lover.
All of my being longs for your touch;
with all my heart I love you.
Now will you draw me close to you,
gather me in your arms;
let me hear the beating of your heart,
O my Jesus, O my Jesus.

597 Jarrod Cooper and Sharon Pearce

You are my rock, you are my fortress,
you are my strength, I will not fear.
You are my shield and my strong tower,
you are my refuge in the storm.

You are the invincible God,
mighty in power and great in splendour.
You are the invincible God,
mighty in power and great in splendour.
King of kings,
Lord of lords,
God of all the earth.

You are my light and my salvation,
I run to you, my hiding-place.
Your name is Jesus and you are mighty.
You are my stronghold, you are my life.

598   Lynn DeShazo and Martin J. Nystrom

You have called us out of darkness,
out of darkness into your glorious light.
You have saved us from the darkness,
we rejoice in your power and might.
(Repeat)

We are a chosen race,
a royal priesthood by your grace.
We are a holy nation
set apart for you.

We are to take your light
to every nation, tongue and tribe;
so they may see your glory
shining through our lives.

599   Brian Thiessen

You have shown me favour unending;
you have given your life for me.
And my heart knows of your goodness,
your blood has covered me.

I will arise and give thanks to you,
Lord, my God,
and your name I will bless
with my whole heart.
You have shown mercy,
you have shown mercy to me.
I give thanks to you, Lord.

You have poured out your healing upon us;
you have set the captives free.
And we know it's not what we've done,
but by your hand alone.

We will arise and give thanks to you,
Lord, our God,
and your name we will bless
with all our hearts.
You have shown mercy,
you have shown mercy to us.
We give thanks to you, Lord.

You, O Lord, are the healer of my soul.
You, O Lord, are the gracious Redeemer,
you come to restore us again.
Yes, you come to restore us again, and again.

600   Kevin Prosch and Tom Davis

You have taken the precious
from the worthless
and given us beauty for ashes, love for hate.
You have chosen the weak things of the world
to shame that which is strong,
and the foolish things to shame the wise.

You are help to the helpless,
strength to the stranger,
and a father to the child that's left alone.
And the thirsty are invited
to come to the waters,
and those who have no money come and buy.

So come, so come.

Behold, the days are coming,
for the Lord has promised
that the ploughman will overtake the reaper.
And our hearts shall be the threshing floor,
and the move of God we've cried out for
will come, it will surely come.

Continued overleaf

For you will shake the heavens,
and fill your house with glory,
and turn the shame of the outcast into praise.
And all creation groans and waits
for the Spirit and the bride to say
the word that your heart has longed to hear.

So come, so come.

601   Noel Richards

You laid aside your majesty,
gave up everything for me,
suffered at the hands of those you had created.
You took all my guilt and shame,
when you died and rose again;
now today you reign,
in heav'n and earth exalted.

I really want to worship you, my Lord,
you have won my heart and I am yours
for ever and ever;
I will love you.
You are the only one who died for me,
gave your life to set me free,
so I lift my voice to you in adoration.

602   Russell Fragar

You love me as you found me;
your love keeps following me.
You wrapped your arms around me,
your love keeps following me.
By grace I'm what I should be;
your love keeps following me.
You saw me as I could be;
your love keeps following me.

And it's higher (reaches from heaven to man),
it's wider (anyone can come in),
it's deeper (it covers any sin),
and I know this one thing:
wherever I go I know
your love keeps following me.

603   Patricia Morgan and Sue Rinaldi

You make my heart feel glad,
you make my heart feel glad;
Jesus, you bring me joy,
you make my heart feel glad.

Lord, your love brings healing
and a peace into my heart;
I want to give myself in praise to you.
Though I've been through heartache,
you have understood my tears:
O Lord, I will give thanks to you.

When I look around me
and I see the life you made,
all creation shouts aloud in praise;
I realise your greatness –
how majestic is your name!
O Lord, I love you more each day.

604   Darlene Zschech and Russell Fragar

You make your face to shine on me,
and that my soul knows very well.
You lift me up, I'm cleansed and free,
and that my soul knows very well.

When mountains fall I'll stand
by the power of your hand
and in your heart of hearts I'll dwell,
and that my soul knows very well.

Joy and strength each day I find,
and that my soul knows very well.
Forgiveness, hope, I know is mine,
and that my soul knows very well.

605   Geoff Bullock

You rescued me, and picked me up,
a living hope of grace revealed
a life transformed in righteousness.
O Lord, you have rescued me.

Forgiving me, you healed my heart,
and set me free from sin and death.
You brought me life, you made me whole,
O Lord, you have rescued me.

And you loved me before I knew you,
and you knew me for all time.
I've been created in your image, O Lord.
And you bought me, and you sought me,
your blood poured out for me;
a new creation in your image, O Lord.
You rescued me, you rescued me.

606   Robin Mark

You're the Lion of Judah,
the Lamb that was slain,
you ascended to heaven
and evermore will reign;
at the end of the age
when the earth you reclaim,
you will gather the nations before you.
And the eyes of all men
will be fixed on the Lamb
who was crucified,
for with wisdom and mercy
and justice he reigns
at the Father's side.

And the angels will cry:
'Hail the Lamb who was slain
for the world – rule in pow'r.'
And the earth will reply:
'You shall reign
as the King of all kings
and the Lord of all lords.'

There's a shield in our hand
and a sword at our side,
there's a fire in our spirit
that cannot be denied;
as the Father has told us:
for these you have died,
for the nations that gather before you.

And the ears of all men
need to hear of the Lamb
who was crucified,
who descended to hell
yet was raised up to reign
at the Father's side.

607   Scott and Michele Brenner

Your love flows like a river,
flows like a fountain into the sea.
Your love washes me over,
filling my spirit, making me clean.

As I worship you,
come fill me with your love,
flow over me.
As I lift your name
for all the world to see,
flow over me.
As I bless you, Lord,
with all that's in my heart.
Jesus, my King,
O eternal One,
my sacrificial Lamb,
flow over me.

Your touch, taking me over,
leading me gently into your arms.
Your touch, holding me closer,
healing my spirit, restoring my soul.

Flow over me,
river, flow over me,
river, flow over me,
flow over me.
Jesus, wash over me,
wash over me,
wash over me,
flow over me.
Fill me with your love,
Spirit, fill me with your love,
fill me with your love,
flow over me.

608 Wes Sutton

Your mercy flows upon us like a river.
Your mercy stands unshakable and true.
Most holy God, of all good things the giver,
we turn and lift our fervent prayer to you.

> *Hear our cry (hear our cry),*
> *O Lord (O Lord),*
> *be merciful (be merciful)*
> *once more (once more).*
> *Let your love (let your love)*
> *your anger stem (your anger stem),*
> *remember mercy, O Lord, again.*

Your Church once great, though standing
    clothed in sorrow,
is even still the bride that you adore;
revive your church, that we again may honour
our God and King, our Master and our Lord.

As we have slept, this nation has been taken
by every sin we have ever known,
so at its gates, though burnt by fire and broken,
in Jesus' name we come to take our stand.

609 Steffi Geiser Rubin and Stuart Dauermann

You shall go out with joy
and be led forth with peace,
and the mountains and the hills
shall break forth before you.
There'll be shouts of joy
and the trees of the field
shall clap, shall clap their hands.
And the trees of the field
shall clap their hands,
and the trees of the field
shall clap their hands,
and the trees of the field
shall clap their hands,
and you'll go out with joy.

610 David Palmer

This is the time,
this is the place;
we're living in a season of amazing grace.
We are the people,
born for this hour,
and we will be willing in the day of his pow'r.
Can you hear him saying
that the prophecy's fulfilled.
Now a Holy Ghost revival
is gonna gather every field.

> *I hear the sound of a distant thunder,*
> *I hear the sound of a coming rain.*
> *I hear the wind blowing through the harvest,*
> *he's coming, he's coming again.*

Though the mountains tremble,
though the oceans roar,
all the earth will be filled
with the glory of the Lord.

Indexes

Key Word Index

The key word categories appear alphabetically and are cross-referenced to make it as easy as possible for worship leaders to find songs and hymns suitable for various themes and occasions.

ADORATION AND PRAISE – GODHEAD

All people that on earth do dwell	13
All things bright and beautiful	14
Almighty God, we bring you praise	16
Almighty God, my Redeemer	17
Among the gods	19
Ascribe greatness	25
As I come into your presence	26
As the deer pants (Lewis)	28
As we seek your face	31
Be glorified	42
Be still, for the presence of the Lord	47
Blessing and honour	54
Bless the Lord, my soul	56
Exalt the Lord	87
Faithful God	88
Father, I come to you	95
Father in heaven, how we love you	96
For thou, O Lord, art high	112
From the ends of the earth	115
Gloria	119
God is good	124
God is good all the time	125
God is great	126
God of glory, we exalt your name	130
God's not dead	133
Great and mighty is he	135
Great is the Lord and most worthy of praise	137
Great is your name	139
Hallelujah, hallelujah	141
He's given me a garment of praise	166
Holy, holy, Lord God Almighty	177
Holy, holy, Lord, you're worthy	178
How lovely is your dwelling-place	188
I am standing beneath your wings	193
I give you all the honour	203
I have come to love you	204
I have made you too small	205
I just want to be where you are	207
I just want to praise you	208
I love to be in your presence	213
I'm gonna click	218
Immortal, invisible, God only wise	220
In heavenly armour	228
In the presence of a holy God	232
I sing praises	240
I stand before your throne	245
I will enter his gates	262
I will praise you all my life	266
I will wave my hands	269
I worship you, Almighty God	271
Let the righteous sing	316
Look what God has done	325
Lord, for the years	327

Lord, my heart cries out	331
Lord of lords	332
Lord, we long to see your glory	338
Lord, you are more precious	339
Lord, you are so precious to me	340
Lord, you have my heart	341
Lord, you put a tongue in my mouth	342
Make a joyful noise, all ye people	347
May our worship be as fragrance	351
Mighty is our God	357
More love, more power	359
My heart will sing to you	364
Now unto the King	378
O give thanks	384
O Lord, how majestic is your name	395
O Lord our God	398
On this day	409
O the glory of your presence	415
Our God is an awesome God	418
O worship the King	425
O worship the Lord in the beauty of holiness	426
Praise, my soul, the King of heaven	433
Praise the Lord, O my soul	434
Salvation belongs to our God	443
See his glory	446
Sing, praise and bless the Lord	458
Streams of worship	464
Surely our God	466
Teach me to dance	469
Tell out, my soul	471
Thank you for your mercy	474
The angels, Lord, they sing	476
The Lord is our strength	484
The Lord reigns	485
Therefore we lift our hearts in praise	489
There is none like you	493
The steadfast love of the Lord	505
They that wait on the Lord	509
This is my desire	515
This is the day that the Lord has made	516
This is the day	517
Though the earth should tremble	523
To every good thing God is doing	525
To God be the glory!	526
To keep your lovely face	527
Tonight	528
To you, O Lord, I bring my worship	529
We bring the sacrifice of praise	542
We declare your majesty	544
We rejoice in the goodness of our God	554

What noise shall we make	569
When I feel the touch	570
When I look into your holiness	571
Yahweh	586
You alone, Lord, are wonderful	588
You are beautiful	589
You are God, you are great	591
You are Lord	592
You are merciful to me	593
You are my rock	597
You rescued me	605

ADORATION AND PRAISE – JESUS CHRIST

Alleluia, alleluia, give thanks to the risen Lord	4
All hail King Jesus!	5
All hail the Lamb	6
All hail the power of Jesus' name	7
All heaven declares	8
All I once held dear	11
Almighty God, we bring you praise	16
Almighty God, my Redeemer	17
And he shall reign	22
As the deer pants (Nystrom)	27
At the foot of the cross	32
At the name of Jesus	33
At your feet we fall	35
Behold his love	43
Behold the Lord	44
Blessed be the name of the Lord	53
Blessing, honour, glory to the Lamb	55
By his grace	59
By your side	60
Come and see	70
Come, let us worship Jesus	73
Come on, all us singers, sing	74
Crown him with many crowns	77
Every nation, power and tongue	86
Far and near	90
Father, you are my portion	104
For all that you've done	108
From heaven you came	114
From the sun's rising	116
From where the sun rises	117
Glory	120
Glory to the King of kings	121
Hail, Jesus, you're my King	140
Hallelujah! Jesus is alive	142
Hallelujah, my Father	143
He is exalted	156
He is here	157
He is Lord	158
Here in your presence	162
Higher, higher	170
Holy One of God	179
Hosanna	182
How can I not love you?	184

How deep the Father's love
  for us 185
How sweet the name of Jesus
  sounds 190
I am a new creation 191
I am so thankful 192
I bow my knee before your
  throne 197
I lift my hands 212
I love you, Lord, and I lift
  my voice 214
I love you, Lord, with all of
  my heart 215
I love your presence 216
I'm accepted, I'm forgiven 217
Immanuel, O Immanuel 219
I'm special 222
In Christ alone 225
In moments like these 229
I reach up high 235
I sing a simple song of love 239
Isn't he beautiful 242
I stand amazed in the presence 243
I stand before the presence 244
I've got a love song 252
I will dance, I will sing 261
I will lift my voice 263
I will offer up my life 265
I will worship 270
I worship you, O Lamb of God 272
Jesus, at your name 273
Jesus Christ 274
Jesus Christ is risen today 276
Jesus Christ is the Lord of all 277
Jesus, God's righteousness
  revealed 278
Jesus, how lovely you are 279
Jesus! I am resting, resting 280
Jesus is greater 282
Jesus is King 283
Jesus is Lord! 284
Jesus is the name we honour 285
Jesus, Jesus (Holy and anointed
  one) 286
Jesus, Jesus, you have the name 288
Jesus, lover of my soul 290
Jesus, name above all names 291
Jesus shall take the highest
  honour 296
Jesus, what a beautiful name 301
Jesus, your loving kindness 303
Jesus, your name is power 304
King of kings, majesty 309
Lamb of God 310
Led like a lamb 312
Lift up your heads 321
Living under the shadow of
  his wing 323
Lo, he comes with clouds
  descending 324
Look what the Lord has done 326
Lord, I lift your name on high 330
Lord of the heavens 333
Lord, the light of your love 335
Lord, we lift you high 336
Majesty 346
Make way, make way 349

Man of sorrows 350
May the fragrance 352
Meekness and majesty 353
My heart is full 363
My Jesus, I love thee 366
My Jesus, my Saviour 367
My life is in you, Lord 368
My lips shall praise you 369
My Lord, what love is this 370
No one but you, Lord 373
No other name 374
No scenes of stately majesty 375
O for a thousand tongues to sing 383
O let the sun of God enfold you 392
O Lord our God 398
O Lord, you're beautiful 401
O the deep, deep love of Jesus! 414
O, what a morning 424
Praise the name of Jesus 435
Shout for joy 449
Shout for joy and sing 450
Sing a song of celebration 457
Sound the trumpet 461
Streams of worship 464
Such love 465
Thank you for saving me 472
Thank you for the cross 473
Thank you, Jesus 475
The heavens shall declare 480
The price is paid 487
There is a louder shout to come 490
There is only one Lord 494
There is power in the name
  of Jesus 495
There's an awesome sound 497
There's a sound of singing 500
The trumpets sound, the angels
  sing 506
The world is looking for a hero 508
Thine be the glory 510
This Child 511
This is my beloved Son 514
To every good thing God
  is doing 525
To God be the glory! 526
Tonight 528
We come into your presence 543
Welcome the King 549
Well, I hear they're singing in
  the streets 550
We will cross every border 560
We will worship the Lamb
  of glory 563
We worship and adore you 564
What kind of greatness 567
When the music fades 576
With my whole heart 582
Worthy is the Lamb 584
Worthy, O worthy are you, Lord 585
You are crowned with many
  crowns 590
You are mighty 594
You are my King 595
You are my passion 596
You are my rock 597
You have called us 598
You laid aside your majesty 601

You make my heart feel glad 603
You're the Lion of Judah 606

ADORATION AND PRAISE – THE FATHER

Father God, I wonder 91
Father, we adore you 101
Father, you are my portion 104
God is good 124
Hallelujah, my Father 143
How deep the Father's love
  for us 185
It is to you 247
No one but you, Lord 373
O Father of the fatherless 382
Surely our God 466
We come into your presence 543

ADORATION AND PRAISE – TRINITY

All honour, all glory 10
Father God, we worship you 92
Father, we adore you, you've
  drawn us 102
Father, we love you 103
Holy, holy, holy! Lord God
  Almighty 176
I'm your child 224
Lead us, heavenly Father, lead us 311
Let your living water flow 318
Praise God from whom all
  blessings flow 432
River, wash over me 441
There is a Redeemer 492
This is the sweetest mystery 520
We believe 541

ADVENT

See **Jesus – Advent and Birth**

ASCENSION

See **Jesus – Ascension**

ASSURANCE

Blessed assurance, Jesus is mine 52
I am a new creation 191
I know it 210
I'm so secure 221
In heavenly armour 228
Jesus, we celebrate the victory 299
Jesus, you're my firm foundation 302
My Jesus, my Saviour 367
My life is in you, Lord 368
My lips shall praise you 369
Nothing shall separate us 377
Our confidence is in the Lord 417
Salvation belongs to our God 443
There is only one Lord 494
This grace is mine 512
This is the day that the Lord
  has made 516
Though I feel afraid 522
Though the earth should tremble 523
We are a people of power 536
We have a great priest 546
You make your face to shine
  on me 604

ATONEMENT

See **Jesus – Atonement, Suffering and Death**

BENEDICTIONS

See **Closing of Service**

CALL TO WORSHIP

As I come into your presence	26
As we are gathered	29
Be glorified	42
Blessed be the name of the Lord	53
Celebrate, celebrate	66
Come on, all us singers, sing	74
Come on and celebrate	75
Crown him with many crowns	77
Exalt the Lord	87
Far and near	90
For this purpose	111
From the ends of the earth	115
Glory	120
God is good	124
God is here, God is present	127
God of all comfort	129
Hail, Jesus, you're my King	140
Heaven invites you to a party	150
Here in your presence	162
He's given me a garment of praise	166
Holy, holy, holy! Lord God Almighty	176
Hosanna	182
I believe in Jesus	195
I have come to love you	204
I will enter his gates	262
Jesus is Lord!	284
Jesus, the name high over all	298
Joy to the world	305
King of kings and Lord of lords	307
King of kings	308
Lift up your heads	321
Lord, I lift your name on high	330
Lord of lords	332
Lord, you put a tongue in my mouth	342
Make a joyful noise, all ye people	347
Make way, make way	349
My lips shall praise you	369
O, heaven is in my heart	388
Oh, I was made for this	389
On this day	409
Praise God from whom all blessings flow	432
Praise, my soul, the King of heaven	433
Praise the Lord, O my soul	434
Rejoice!	438
Righteousness, peace, joy in the Holy Ghost	440
Shout for joy	449
Shout for joy and sing	450
Sing, praise and bless the Lord	458
Sound the trumpet	461
Tell out, my soul	471
The Lord is marching out	482
We are marching	539
We believe	541
We bring the sacrifice of praise	542
We come into your presence	543
Welcome, King of kings	548

CELEBRATION

Celebrate, celebrate	66
Celebrate Jesus	67
Come on, all us singers, sing	74
Come on and celebrate	75
Down the mountain the river flows	83
Far and near	90
From where the sun rises	117
God is good	124
Great and mighty is he	135
Hail, Jesus, you're my King	140
Hallelujah! Jesus is alive	142
Heaven invites you to a party	150
He has clothed us with his righteousness	153
He is the Lord	159
He's given me a garment of praise	166
I am a new creation	191
I could sing unending songs	200
In the tomb so cold	234
I reach up high	235
I will wave my hands	269
Jesus' love has got under our skin	289
Jesus, we celebrate the victory	299
Joy to the world	305
Let the righteous sing	316
Look what the Lord has done	326
Lord of lords	332
Lord, you put a tongue in my mouth	342
Low in the grave he lay	345
Make way, make way	349
O come and join the dance	381
O give thanks	384
O, heaven is in my heart	388
Oh, I was made for this	389
O, what a morning	424
Righteousness, peace, joy in the Holy Ghost	440
Shout for joy	449
Shout for joy and sing	450
Shout, shout for joy	451
Shout! The Lord is risen!	452
Shout unto God	453
Sing a song of celebration	457
Teach me to dance	469
Tell out, my soul	471
The Lord is marching out	482
The Lord is our strength	484
The price is paid	487
There's a sound of singing	500
The trumpets sound, the angels sing	506
This is the day that the Lord has made	516
This is the day	517
Welcome, King of kings	548
Welcome the King	549
Well, I hear they're singing in the streets	550
What noise shall we make	569
Where there once was only hurt	577
You shall go out with joy	609

CHILDREN AND FAMILY WORSHIP

All things bright and beautiful	14
Be bold, be strong	38
Earth lies spellbound	85
Father God, I wonder	91
5000+ hungry folk	107
God's not dead	133
Have you got an appetite?	145
Heaven invites you to a party	150
Higher, higher	170
I'm gonna click	218
I'm special	222
I'm your child	224
I reach up high	235
I've got a love song	252
I want to be a tree that's bearing fruit	254
I will wave my hands	269
Jesus put this song into our hearts	292
Like a candle flame	322
Lord, we lift you high	336
Lord, you put a tongue in my mouth	342
O come and join the dance	381
O give thanks	384
Once in royal David's city	404
Our God is so great	420
Righteousness, peace, joy in the Holy Ghost	440
Seek ye first	447
Teach me to dance	469
The promise of the Holy Spirit	488
This Child	511
We are marching	539
We will turn the hearts	562
What noise shall we make	569

CHRISTINGLE

Can you see what we have made	65

CHRISTMAS

At this time of giving	34
Away in a manger	36
Earth lies spellbound	85
Gloria	119
Hark, the herald-angels sing	144
Heaven invites you to a party	150
He is here	157
Immanuel, O Immanuel	219
Like a candle flame	322
O come, all ye faithful	380
O come and join the dance	381
O little town of Bethlehem	393
Once in royal David's city	404
Silent night	455
This Child	511
Tonight	528
What kind of greatness	567

CHURCH – FELLOWSHIP AND UNITY

All over the world	12
An army of ordinary people	20

A new commandment 23
As we are gathered 29
Bind us together 51
Called to a battle 61
Did you feel the mountains tremble? 80
God is here, God is present 127
God of all comfort 129
He brought me to his banqueting table 152
Here is bread 163
How good and how pleasant 187
I believe in Jesus 195
If you are encouraged 202
I love to be in your presence 213
Jesus put this song into our hearts 292
Jesus, restore us again 295
Let there be love 317
Let your word go forth 320
Living under the shadow of his wing 323
Look what God has done 325
May the fragrance 352
One heart, one voice, one mind 405
O the glory of your presence 415
Peace I give to you 428
Rejoice! 438
Righteousness, peace, joy in the Holy Ghost 440
The church's one foundation 477
There is a place of commanded blessing 491
To every good thing God is doing 525
Turn our hearts 531
We are his people 538
We are marching 539
We must work together 553
We want to remain in your love 558
We will turn the hearts 562
Where two or three 578

CHURCH – IN PRAYER

All heaven waits 9

CHURCH – NATURE

An army of ordinary people 20
As we are gathered 29
For I'm building a people of power 109
Here I am 161
I went to the enemy's camp 257
I will build my church 259
Jesus put this song into our hearts 292
Jesus, we enthrone you 300
Look what God has done 325
May the fragrance 352
O, heaven is in my heart 388
One heart, one voice, one mind 405
O the glory of your presence 415
Our God is awesome in power 419
Rejoice! 438
Shout for joy 449
Show your power, O Lord 454
The church's one foundation 477

We are marching 539
We are the army of God 540
We must work together 553
You have called us 598
Your mercy flows 608

CLOSING OF SERVICE

Be patient, be ready 46
In my life, Lord 230
Now unto the King 378
O Jesus, I have promised 391
Peace to you 431
The steadfast love of the Lord 505
This is the sweetest mystery 520
To every good thing God is doing 525

COMFORT AND ENCOURAGEMENT

See **Faith and Hope**

COMMITMENT AND CONSECRATION

Abba, Father, let me be 1
All I once held dear 11
All to Jesus I surrender 15
A new commandment 23
At the name of Jesus 33
Be thou my vision 50
Blessed assurance, Jesus is mine 52
Breathe on me, Breath of God 57
By your side 60
Can I ascend 63
Change my heart, O God 68
Come and see 70
Come, let us return 72
Come on, all us singers, sing 74
Do something new, Lord 82
Draw me closer 84
Father, hear our prayer 93
Fire 106
From heaven you came 114
God is here, God is present 127
Have you got an appetite? 145
Have you not said 147
He has fire in his eyes 154
Here I am 161
Here we stand in total surrender 165
How can I be free from sin? 183
How can I not love you? 184
I bow my knee before your throne 197
I bow my knee 198
I have come to love you 204
I lift my hands 212
I love you, Lord, with all of my heart 215
In the morning when I rise 231
I reach up high 235
Is it true today 241
I, the Lord of sea and sky 246
I want to be a tree that's bearing fruit 254
I want to be out of my depth in your love 255
I want to serve the purpose of God 256
I will be yours 258

I will lift my voice 263
I will never be the same again 264
I will offer up my life 265
I will praise you all my life 266
I will worship 270
Jesus! I am resting, resting 280
Jesus, Jesus, you have the name 288
Jesus, lover of my soul 290
Jesus, take me as I am 297
Jesus, your loving kindness 303
Just as I am, without one plea 306
King of kings, majesty 309
Lamb of God 310
Let it be to me 313
Let me be a sacrifice 315
Let your word go forth 320
Lord, for the years 327
Lord, I come to you 329
Lord, my heart cries out 331
Lord, prepare me 334
Lord, the light of your love 335
Lord, you are more precious 339
Lord, you have my heart 341
May our worship be as fragrance 351
More about Jesus 358
More love, more power 359
More of your glory 360
My Jesus, I love thee 366
O happy day 387
O Jesus, I have promised 391
O Lord, my heart is not proud 397
O Lord, you're beautiful 401
One thing I ask 407
On this day 409
O thou who camest from above 416
Purify my heart 436
Reign in me 437
Restore, O Lord 439
River, wash over me 441
Ruach 442
Seek ye first 447
Show your power, O Lord 454
Silent, surrendered 456
Spirit of the living God (Iverson) 462
Take me past the outer courts 467
Take my life, and let it be 468
Teach me to dance 469
Teach me your ways 470
Thank you for saving me 472
The crucible for silver 479
There's a sound of singing 500
There's a wind a-blowing 501
There's no one like you 502
This is my desire 515
This is the sweetest mystery 520
This love 521
Though I feel afraid 522
To every good thing God is doing 525
To keep your lovely face 527
Wake up, my soul 534
Wake up, O sleeper 535
We are a people of power 536
We shall stand 556
We've had a light 557
We will run and not grow weary 561

When I look into your holiness 571
When I survey the wondrous
   cross 572
When the music fades 576
With my whole heart 582
You are my King 595

COMMUNION

As we are gathered 29
Broken for me 58
Here is bread 163
We do not presume 545
With this bread 583

CONFESSION

See **Repentance and Forgiveness**

CREATION

See **God – Creation**

CREEDS

The Lord is a mighty King 481
We believe 541

DELIVERANCE

I give you all the honour 203
I know it 210
O God, most high 385
O the blood of my Saviour 413
This is the message of the cross 518
We are his people 538
When the Lord brought us back 575

DESIRE FOR GOD

Abba, Father, let me be 1
All I once held dear 11
Anointing, fall on me 24
As the deer pants (Nystrom) 27
As the deer pants (Lewis) 28
As we seek your face 31
Be still, for the presence of
   the Lord 47
Be thou my vision 50
Blessed assurance, Jesus is mine 52
By your side 60
Can I ascend 63
Change my heart, O God 68
Come down, O Love divine 71
Come, let us return 72
Come on, all us singers, sing 74
Come, Spirit, come 76
Dear Lord and Father of mankind 79
Don't let my love grow cold 81
Draw me closer 84
Father, here I am 94
Father, I want you to hold me 98
Father of life, draw me closer 100
Father, you are my portion 104
God of all comfort 129
He brought me to his
   banqueting table 152
Hold me closer to you 172
Hold me, Lord 173
Holiness unto the Lord 175
Holy Spirit, come 180

Holy Spirit, we welcome you 181
How lovely is your dwelling-
   place 188
I bow my knee before your
   throne 197
I bow my knee 198
I cry out for your hand 201
I just want to be where you are 207
I just want to praise you 208
I lift my eyes up to the mountains 211
I love to be in your presence 213
I love you, Lord, with all of
   my heart 215
I love your presence 216
Immanuel, O Immanuel 219
I'm special 222
I need you more 226
In my life, Lord 230
In the morning when I rise 231
In the secret 233
I receive your love 236
Is anyone thirsty? 237
I sing a simple song of love 239
Isn't he beautiful 242
I stand before your throne 245
I want to be a tree that's
   bearing fruit 254
I want to be out of my depth
   in your love 255
I want to serve the purpose
   of God 256
I will never be the same again 264
I will seek your face, O Lord 268
I will worship 270
Jesus! I am resting, resting 280
Jesus, I am thirsty 281
Jesus, Jesus, Jesus 287
Jesus, Jesus, you have the name 288
Jesus, lover of my soul 290
Jesus, take me as I am 297
Jesus, your loving kindness 303
Just as I am, without one plea 306
Let your living water flow 318
Lord, I come to you 329
Lord, the light of your love 335
Lord, we long for you 337
Lord, we long to see your glory 338
Lord, you are more precious 339
Lord, you are so precious to me 340
Lord, you have my heart 341
Love divine, all loves excelling 343
Love of Christ, come now 343
May the fragrance 352
More about Jesus 358
More love, more power 359
More of your glory 360
More than oxygen 361
My first love 362
My heart is full 363
My heart will sing to you 364
My spirit rests in you alone 371
Nearer, my God, to thee 372
No one but you, Lord 373
O Breath of Life 379
O Father of the fatherless 382
O God of burning, cleansing
   flame 386

Oh, lead me 390
O Jesus, I have promised 391
O let the sun of God enfold you 392
O Lord, hear my prayer 394
O Lord, you're beautiful 401
O Lord, your tenderness 402
One thing I ask 407
O thou who camest from above 416
Over the mountains and the sea 421
Peace like a river 429
Purify my heart 436
Righteousness, peace, joy in
   the Holy Ghost 440
River, wash over me 441
Ruach 442
Silent, surrendered 456
Soften my heart, Lord 459
Spirit of the living God (Iverson) 462
Spirit of the living God
   (Armstrong) 463
Take me past the outer courts 467
Teach me to dance 469
Teach me your ways 470
Thank you for the cross 473
The crucible for silver 479
There's a wind a-blowing 501
There's no one like you 502
This is my desire 515
This is the mystery 519
This love 521
To be in your presence 524
To keep your lovely face 527
To you, O Lord, I bring my
   worship 529
Turn your eyes upon Jesus 533
Wake up, my soul 534
Wake up, O sleeper 535
We have a great priest 546
We want to remain in your love 558
What a friend I've found 565
When I feel the touch 570
When I look into your holiness 571
When the music fades 576
With my whole heart 582
Yahweh 586
You are merciful to me 593
You are my King 595
You are my passion 596
You laid aside your majesty 601
Your love flows like a river 607

DISCIPLESHIP

See **Commitment and Consecration**

EASTER

At the foot of the cross 32
Beneath the cross of Jesus 45
Celebrate Jesus 67
Come and see 70
For this purpose 111
From heaven you came 114
Hallelujah! Jesus is alive 142
Hallelujah, my Father 143
He has risen 155
He is Lord 158
He is the mighty God 160

Here is love	164
He was pierced	169
Holy One of God	179
How can I be free from sin?	183
How deep the Father's love for us	185
I am so thankful	192
I believe in Jesus	195
I know a place	209
In the tomb so cold	234
I stand amazed in the presence	243
It's your blood	250
I will offer up my life	265
I worship you, O Lamb of God	272
Jesus Christ	274
Jesus Christ is risen today	276
Jesus is Lord!	284
Lamb of God	310
Led like a lamb	312
Low in the grave he lay	345
Man of sorrows	350
Meekness and majesty	353
My Lord, what love is this	370
No scenes of stately majesty	375
On a hill far away	403
Only by grace	408
O the blood of Jesus	412
O the blood of my Saviour	413
O, what a morning	424
Thank you for saving me	472
Thank you for the cross	473
Thank you, Jesus	475
The cross has said it all	478
The price is paid	487
There is a Redeemer	492
The Word made flesh	507
Thine be the glory	510
This is my beloved Son	514
This is the message of the cross	518
To God be the glory!	526
What kind of love is this	568
When I survey the wondrous cross	572
You laid aside your majesty	601

ETERNAL LIFE

Called to a battle	61
This grace is mine	512

EVANGELISM

See **Mission**

FAITH AND HOPE

Almighty God, my Redeemer	17
And can it be	21
Be bold, be strong	38
Beneath the cross of Jesus	45
Be still, my soul	49
Called to a battle	61
Can we walk upon the water	64
Draw me closer	84
Faithful God	88
Faithful One	89
Father in heaven, how we love you	96
Father, I place into your hands	97

For the joys and for the sorrows	110
Give thanks with a grateful heart	118
God is good all the time	125
Great is thy faithfulness	138
Have you heard the good news	146
Have you not said	147
He is the Lord	159
He that is in us	167
He walked where I walked	168
His love	171
How can I be free from sin?	183
How firm a foundation	186
I am standing beneath your wings	193
I believe the promise	196
I heard the voice of Jesus say	206
I lift my eyes up to the mountains	211
In Christ alone	225
I need you more	226
In every circumstance	227
Is it true today	241
I've found a friend	251
I walk by faith	253
I will be yours	258
I will change your name	260
I will never be the same again	264
I will praise you all my life	266
Jesus, God's righteousness revealed	278
Jesus, you're my firm foundation	302
Let your love come down	319
Living under the shadow of his wing	323
Men of faith	354
My life is in you, Lord	368
O Jesus, I have promised	391
O Lord, you lead me	400
One thing I ask	407
Our confidence is in the Lord	417
Our God is awesome in power	419
O, we are more than conquerors	423
Peace I give to you	428
Peace, perfect peace	430
Salvation belongs to our God	443
Say the word	445
Soon and very soon	460
Tell out, my soul	471
The Lord is moving across this land	483
The Lord is our strength	484
The Lord's my shepherd	486
There is a louder shout to come	490
There is only one Lord	494
There is power in the name of Jesus	495
There's a place where the streets shine	498
The Word made flesh	507
The world is looking for a hero	508
They that wait on the Lord	509
Thine be the glory	510
This grace is mine	512
This is the day that the Lord has made	516
This is the time	610
This love	521
To every good thing God is doing	525

To you, O Lord, I lift up my soul	530
Wake up, my soul	534
We are his people	538
We are the army of God	540
We march to the tune of a love-song	552
We must work together	553
We serve a God of miracles	555
We will run and not grow weary	561
We will turn the hearts	562
When peace like a river	574
Where two or three	578
With all my heart	581
Yet this will I call to mind	587
You are Lord	592
You are my rock	597
You have taken the precious	600
You love me as you found me	602
You make your face to shine on me	604

FELLOWSHIP OF BELIEVERS

See **Church – Fellowship and Unity**

FELLOWSHIP WITH GOD

See **Desire for God** and **God – Presence**

FORGIVENESS

See **Repentance and Forgiveness**

GOD – CREATION

All things bright and beautiful	14
From the ends of the earth	115
God is great	126
He is the Lord	159
I, the Lord of sea and sky	246
Jesus is Lord!	284
Mighty is our God	357
No scenes of stately majesty	375
O give thanks	384
O Lord, my God	396
Our God is so great	420
O worship the King	425
The heavens shall declare	480
The Lord is a mighty King	481
We believe	541

GOD – FAITHFULNESS

All people that on earth do dwell	13
Almighty God, my Redeemer	17
Ascribe greatness	25
Be bold, be strong	38
Faithful God	88
Faithful One	89
Great is thy faithfulness	138
Have you not said	147
I am standing beneath your wings	193
I'm so secure	221
I'm standing here to testify	223
In every circumstance	227
I walk by faith	253
I will be yours	258
I will praise you all my life	266
Look what God has done	325

My Jesus, my Saviour	367
O Lord, you lead me	400
On this day	409
O the deep, deep love of Jesus!	414
Our confidence is in the Lord	417
O, we are more than conquerors	423
The Lord's my shepherd	486
There is none like you	493
The steadfast love of the Lord	505
To you, O Lord, I lift up my soul	530
We have a great priest	546
We rejoice in the goodness of our God	554
We shall stand	556
What a friend I've found	565
What a friend we have in Jesus	566
When peace like a river	574
When the Lord brought us back	575
Where two or three	578
With all my heart	581
Yahweh	586
Yet this will I call to mind	587
You alone, Lord, are wonderful	588
You love me as you found me	602

GOD – FATHER

Abba, Father, let me be	1
Father God, I wonder	91
Father God, we worship you	92
Father, hear our prayer	93
Father, I come to you	95
Father, I place into your hands	97
Father, I want you to hold me	98
Father, we adore you	101
God is good	124
I'm accepted, I'm forgiven	217
I'm your child	224
O Father of the fatherless	382
One shall tell another	406
Praise, my soul, the King of heaven	433
We will turn the hearts	562
Where two or three	578

GOD – GLORY

Be glorified	42
Be still, for the presence of the Lord	47
Father, we adore you, you've drawn us	102
Glory to the King of kings	121
God of glory, we exalt your name	130
God of glory	131
Great and mighty is he	135
Here in your presence	162
I love you, Lord, with all of my heart	215
Immortal, invisible, God only wise	220
In my life, Lord	230
I sing praises	240
Lord, my heart cries out	331
Lord of lords	332
Lord of the heavens	333
Lord, we long to see your glory	338
Now unto the King	378
O Lord, how majestic is your name	395

O the glory of your presence	415
Praise God from whom all blessings flow	432
Salvation belongs to our God	443
See his glory	446
There's no one like you	502
This grace is mine	512
This, in essence, is the message	513
We declare your majesty	544
When I look into your holiness	571
Yahweh	586

GOD – GRACE

Amazing grace	18
And can it be	21
Behold his love	43
By his grace	59
Father, I come to you	95
For the joys and for the sorrows	110
God, be gracious	122
God of grace	132
He brought me to his banqueting table	152
He has clothed us with his righteousness	153
Here is bread	163
How can I not love you?	184
I am a new creation	191
I could sing unending songs	200
I cry out for your hand	201
I heard the voice of Jesus say	206
In the presence of a holy God	232
I will change your name	260
Jesus, what a beautiful name	301
Just as I am, without one plea	306
Look what God has done	325
Love divine, all loves excelling	343
Love of Christ, come now	343
Make me a channel of your peace	348
Meekness and majesty	353
O Lord, you're beautiful	401
O Lord, your tenderness	402
One shall tell another	406
Only by grace	408
O worship the Lord in the beauty of holiness	426
Peace be to these streets	427
Praise, my soul, the King of heaven	433
Such love	465
Surely our God	466
Thank you for your mercy	474
The cross has said it all	478
Therefore we lift our hearts in praise	489
There's an awesome sound	497
The Spirit of the sovereign Lord	504
The trumpets sound, the angels sing	506
This grace is mine	512
This is the message of the cross	518
Turn to me and be saved	532
We rejoice in the goodness of our God	554
We worship and adore you	564
What kind of love is this	568
You rescued me	605

GOD – HOLINESS

Ascribe greatness	25
Holiness is your life in me	174
Holiness unto the Lord	175
Holy, holy, holy! Lord God Almighty	176
Holy, holy, Lord God Almighty	177
Holy, holy, Lord, you're worthy	178
I love you, Lord, with all of my heart	215
In the presence of a holy God	232
I see the Lord	238
I will seek your face, O Lord	268
Lord, we long to see your glory	338
O God of burning, cleansing flame	386
O worship the Lord in the beauty of holiness	426
The crucible for silver	479
The heavens shall declare	480
This, in essence, is the message	513
We declare your majesty	544
You are mighty	594

GOD – JUDGEMENT

O Lord, the clouds are gathering	399
Tell out, my soul	471
The Lord reigns	485
We believe	541
Who can sound the depths of sorrow	579
Who sees it all	580
Your mercy flows	608

GOD – MAJESTY AND POWER

Among the gods	19
Ascribe greatness	25
As the deer pants (Lewis)	28
Be glorified	42
Be still, for the presence of the Lord	47
Did you feel the mountains tremble?	80
Father, we adore you, you've drawn us	102
Glory to the King of kings	121
God of glory, we exalt your name	130
Great and mighty is he	135
He is the Lord	159
I have made you too small	205
Immortal, invisible, God only wise	220
In the presence of a holy God	232
I see the Lord	238
I sing praises	240
King of kings, majesty	309
Lo, he comes with clouds descending	324
Majesty	346
Meekness and majesty	353
Mighty is our God	357
My heart is full	363
My Jesus, my Saviour	367
Now unto the King	378
O God, most high	385
O Lord, how majestic is your name	395
O Lord our God	398
Our God is an awesome God	418

Our God is so great	420
O worship the King	425
Rejoice!	438
Salvation belongs to our God	443
Shout! The Lord is risen!	452
Show your power, O Lord	454
Streams of worship	464
Surely our God	466
Tell out, my soul	471
Thank you for saving me	472
The Lord is our strength	484
The Lord reigns	485
They that wait on the Lord	509
This grace is mine	512
Though the earth should tremble	523
We are his people	538
We are the army of God	540
We declare your majesty	544
We serve a God of miracles	555
What kind of greatness	567
What noise shall we make	569
You alone, Lord, are wonderful	588
You are God, you are great	591
You are Lord	592
You are mighty	594
You are my rock	597
You make my heart feel glad	603
You're the Lion of Judah	606

GOD – MERCY

And can it be	21
Come, let us return	72
Day of favour	78
Father, hear our prayer	93
Father, here I am	94
Hear, O Lord, our cry	148
Hear our cry	149
It's our confession, Lord	248
I will seek your face, O Lord	268
Jesus, take me as I am	297
Just as I am, without one plea	306
Lamb of God	310
Let it rain	314
Lord, have mercy	328
Love of Christ, come now	343
Mercy is falling	355
O Lord, the clouds are gathering	399
O Lord, your tenderness	402
Restore, O Lord	439
Save the people	444
See his glory	446
See, your Saviour comes	448
Soften my heart, Lord	459
Take me past the outer courts	467
Tell out, my soul	471
Thank you for the cross	473
Thank you for your mercy	474
The cross has said it all	478
There is none like you	493
There's an awesome sound	497
The steadfast love of the Lord	505
This is the message of the cross	518
To you, O Lord, I lift up my soul	530
Turn to me and be saved	532
We do not presume	545
We have prayed that you would have mercy	547

We rejoice in the goodness of our God	554
We worship and adore you	564
What kind of love is this	568
Who can sound the depths of sorrow	579
Who sees it all	580
You are merciful to me	593
You have shown me	599
Your mercy flows	608

GOD – PRESENCE

Abide with me	2
As I come into your presence	26
As we are gathered	29
As we seek your face	31
At your feet we fall	35
Be bold, be strong	38
Be still, for the presence of the Lord	47
Be still and know	48
By your side	60
Can I ascend	63
Come down, O Love divine	71
Dear Lord and Father of mankind	79
Down the mountain the river flows	83
Draw me closer	84
Father, I want you to hold me	98
Father, we adore you	101
For the joys and for the sorrows	110
God is here, God is present	127
God of all comfort	129
He brought me to his banqueting table	152
He has fire in his eyes	154
He is here	157
Here is bread	163
He walked where I walked	168
Hold me closer to you	172
Hold me, Lord	173
How lovely is your dwelling-place	188
I believe in Jesus	195
I have come to love you	204
I heard the voice of Jesus say	206
I just want to be where you are	207
I love to be in your presence	213
I love your presence	216
Immanuel, O Immanuel	219
I'm your child	224
I need you more	226
In every circumstance	227
In the morning when I rise	231
In the presence of a holy God	232
In the secret	233
I receive your love	236
I sing a simple song of love	239
I stand before the presence	244
I stand before your throne	245
I've found a friend	251
I will be yours	258
I will seek your face, O Lord	268
Lift up your heads	321
Like a candle flame	322
Living under the shadow of his wing	323
Lord, I come to you	329

My first love	362
My heart will sing to you	364
My Jesus, I love thee	366
My spirit rests in you alone	371
Nearer, my God, to thee	372
No one but you, Lord	373
O, heaven is in my heart	388
Oh, I was made for this	389
Oh, lead me	390
O Lord, hear my prayer	394
O Lord, my heart is not proud	397
O Lord, you lead me	400
One thing I ask	407
Only by grace	408
O the glory of your presence	415
Peace be to these streets	427
See his glory	446
Take me past the outer courts	467
Thank you for your mercy	474
The angels, Lord, they sing	476
The crucible for silver	479
There's a place where the streets shine	498
There's a wind a-blowing	501
There's no one like you	502
This grace is mine	512
This is the mystery	519
Though I feel afraid	522
Though the earth should tremble	523
To be in your presence	524
To keep your lovely face	527
To you, O Lord, I bring my worship	529
We come into your presence	543
We have a great priest	546
Welcome, King of kings	548
We want to remain in your love	558
We will run and not grow weary	561
What a friend I've found	565
What a friend we have in Jesus	566
When I feel the touch	570
When my heart is overwhelmed	573
Yahweh	586
You love me as you found me	602
You make your face to shine on me	604

GOD – PROTECTION, CARE AND GUIDANCE

Abide with me	2
All people that on earth do dwell	13
Amazing grace	18
Because of your love	39
Be free	41
Be still and know	48
Be still, my soul	49
Father, I place into your hands	97
Father, I want you to hold me	98
God is good all the time	125
God will make a new way	134
His love	171
How firm a foundation	186
I cry out for your hand	201
I lift my eyes up to the mountains	211
I'm so secure	221
I'm your child	224
In heavenly armour	228

I will change your name 260
I will praise you all my life 266
Jesus, you're my firm foundation 302
Lead us, heavenly Father, lead us 311
Living under the shadow of
his wing 323
My life is in you, Lord 368
My spirit rests in you alone 371
O Jesus, I have promised 391
O Lord, you lead me 400
O the deep, deep love of Jesus! 414
Our confidence is in the Lord 417
O, we are more than conquerors 423
O worship the King 425
Rejoice! 438
Say the word 445
The Lord's my shepherd 486
There is none like you 493
This is the day that the Lord
has made 516
Though I feel afraid 522
Though the earth should tremble 523
To you, O Lord, I lift up my soul 530
We come into your presence 543
What a friend we have in Jesus 566
When my heart is overwhelmed 573
You are my rock 597
You make your face to shine
on me 604

GOD – PROVISION

Father, we adore you 101
He brought me to his
banqueting table 152
Lead us, heavenly Father, lead us 311
My spirit rests in you alone 371
O give thanks 384
Say the word 445
The Lord's my shepherd 486
The trumpets sound, the
angels sing 506
This is the day that the Lord
has made 516
We rejoice in the goodness of
our God 554
We will run and not grow weary 561
Where two or three 578

HARVEST

O give thanks 384

HEALING

Be still and know 48
For this purpose 111
Here is bread 163
Holy Spirit, come 180
I am the God that healeth thee 194
I believe in Jesus 195
I know it 210
I love your presence 216
Look what the Lord has done 326
Lord, we long for you 337
Make way, make way 349
O let the sun of God enfold you 392
One shall tell another 406
Peace like a river 429

Say the word 445
Thank you for the cross 473
There is none like you 493
This is the message of the cross 518
This love 521
To every good thing God is doing 525
We serve a God of miracles 555
Where there once was only hurt 577
Who sees it all 580
You are Lord 592
You have shown me 599
You make my heart feel glad 603
You rescued me 605
Your love flows like a river 607

HEAVEN

Abide with me 2
All hail the power of Jesus' name 7
He has risen 155
I will be yours 258
O, heaven is in my heart 388
O the deep, deep love of Jesus! 414
Soon and very soon 460
Streams of worship 464
The angels, Lord, they sing 476
There is a louder shout to come 490
There's a place where the
streets shine 498
This is my beloved Son 514
This is the mystery 519
You're the Lion of Judah 606

HOLINESS AND PURITY

All to Jesus I surrender 15
Be still, for the presence of
the Lord 47
Can I ascend 63
Come down, O Love divine 71
God of glory 131
Hold me, Lord 173
Holiness is your life in me 174
Holiness unto the Lord 175
Holy, holy, holy! Lord God
Almighty 176
Holy, holy, Lord God Almighty 177
How can I be free from sin? 183
Lamb of God 310
Lord, prepare me 334
Lord, the light of your love 335
O God of burning, cleansing
flame 386
Only by grace 408
O the blood of Jesus 412
Purify my heart 436
Take me past the outer courts 467
Teach me your ways 470
The crucible for silver 479

HOLY SPIRIT – GIFTS

I've found a friend 251
O thou who camest from above 416

**HOLY SPIRIT – PRESENCE AND
POWER**

All honour, all glory 10
All over the world 12

Anointing, fall on me 24
As we lift up your name 30
Breathe on me, Breath of God 57
Come down, O Love divine 71
Come, Spirit, come 76
Down the mountain the river flows 83
Father God, we worship you 92
Hold me, Lord 173
Holy Spirit, come 180
Holy Spirit, we welcome you 181
I believe the promise 196
I love your presence 216
I'm your child 224
I receive your love 236
Is anyone thirsty? 237
I've found a friend 251
I will never be the same again 264
Jesus, restore to us again 295
Lord, we long for you 337
More of your glory 360
O Breath of Life 379
O God of burning, cleansing
flame 386
O thou who camest from above 416
Peace like a river 429
Ruach 442
Silent, surrendered 456
Spirit of the living God (Iverson) 462
Spirit of the living God
(Armstrong) 463
The promise of the Holy Spirit 488
Therefore we lift our hearts
in praise 489
There's an awesome sound 497
There's a wind a-blowing 501
The Spirit of the sovereign Lord 504
We are marching 539

HOPE

See **Faith and Hope**

INTERCESSION

See **Prayer**

INTIMACY

See **Desire for God**

JESUS – ADVENT AND BIRTH

At this time of giving 34
Away in a manger 36
Earth lies spellbound 85
For unto us a child is born 113
Hark, the herald-angels sing 144
Heaven invites you to a party 150
He is here 157
I cannot tell 199
Immanuel, O Immanuel 219
Joy to the world 305
King of kings 308
Let it be to me 313
Like a candle flame 322
Mighty God 356
O come, all ye faithful 380
O come and join the dance 381
O little town of Bethlehem 393
Once in royal David's city 404

Silent night	455
This Child	511
Tonight	528
What kind of greatness	567

JESUS – ASCENSION

Lift up your heads	321
Lord, I lift your name on high	330
Nothing shall separate us	377
Shout! The Lord is risen!	452
Therefore we lift our hearts in praise	489

JESUS – ATONEMENT, SUFFERING AND DEATH

At the foot of the cross	32
At the name of Jesus	33
Beneath the cross of Jesus	45
Broken for me	58
Come and see	70
Filled with compassion	105
For this purpose	111
From heaven you came	114
Hallelujah, my Father	143
He is the mighty God	160
Here is love	164
He walked where I walked	168
He was pierced	169
Holiness is your life in me	174
Holy One of God	179
How can I be free from sin?	183
How deep the Father's love for us	185
I am so thankful	192
I believe in Jesus	195
I cannot tell	199
I know a place	209
Immanuel, O Immanuel	219
I stand amazed in the presence	243
It's your blood	250
I will offer up my life	265
I worship you, O Lamb of God	272
Jesus Christ	274
Jesus Christ is risen today	276
Jesus is Lord!	284
Jesus, remember me	294
Lamb of God	310
Led like a lamb	312
Lord, I lift your name on high	330
Man of sorrows	350
Meekness and majesty	353
My Lord, what love is this	370
No scenes of stately majesty	375
Nothing shall separate us	377
O Lord, my God	396
On a hill far away	403
Only by grace	408
O the blood of Jesus	412
O the blood of my Saviour	413
Thank you for saving me	472
Thank you for the cross	473
Thank you, Jesus	475
The cross has said it all	478
The Lord is a mighty King	481
The price is paid	487
Therefore we lift our hearts in praise	489

There is a Redeemer	492
The Word made flesh	507
This is my beloved Son	514
This is the message of the cross	518
To God be the glory!	526
What kind of love is this	568
When I survey the wondrous cross	572
With this bread	583
You laid aside your majesty	601

JESUS – INCARNATION

Behold his love	43
Let it be to me	313
Meekness and majesty	353
Mighty God	356
O come, all ye faithful	380
O come and join the dance	381
O little town of Bethlehem	393
Silent night	455
The Word made flesh	507
This Child	511
What kind of greatness	567
You are God, you are great	591

JESUS – KINGSHIP AND KINGDOM

All heaven waits	9
And he shall reign	22
At the name of Jesus	33
Beauty for brokenness	37
Behold the Lord	44
Blessed be the name of the Lord	53
Blessing and honour	54
Can we walk upon the water	64
Come, let us worship Jesus	73
Come on, all us singers, sing	74
Come on and celebrate	75
Crown him with many crowns	77
Day of favour	78
Did you feel the mountains tremble?	80
Every nation, power and tongue	86
Father God, we worship you	92
Father of creation	99
Filled with compassion	105
For I'm building a people of power	109
From the sun's rising	116
God forgave my sin	123
God is working his purpose out	128
God of glory, we exalt your name	130
Great is the darkness	136
Hallelujah, hallelujah	141
Have you not said	147
Heaven shall not wait	151
He has fire in his eyes	154
He is exalted	156
How lovely on the mountains	189
I cannot tell	199
Is it true today	241
It's rising up	249
I want to serve the purpose of God	256
I will build my church	259
I will worship	270
Jesus Christ is Lord of all	275

Jesus, God's righteousness revealed	278
Jesus is King	283
Jesus is the name we honour	285
Jesus' love has got under our skin	289
Jesus put this song into our hearts	292
Jesus reigns	293
Jesus, remember me	294
Jesus, we enthrone you	300
Jesus, what a beautiful name	301
Joy to the world	305
King of kings and Lord of lords	307
King of kings	308
King of kings, majesty	309
Let it rain	314
Let the righteous sing	316
Let your love come down	319
Lift up your heads	321
Lord, we lift you high	336
Majesty	346
Make me a channel of your peace	348
Make way, make way	349
Meekness and majesty	353
Men of faith	354
My heart is full	363
No scenes of stately majesty	375
Not by might	376
O for a thousand tongues to sing	383
O God, most high	385
O, heaven is in my heart	388
Oh, I was made for this	389
Once in royal David's city	404
One shall tell another	406
Open the doors of praise	411
Our God is awesome in power	419
Peace I give to you	428
Peace, perfect peace	430
Reign in me	437
Rejoice!	438
Restore, O Lord	439
Righteousness, peace, joy in the Holy Ghost	440
See, your Saviour comes	448
Shout for joy	449
Shout for joy and sing	450
Shout! The Lord is risen!	452
Shout unto God	453
Show your power, O Lord	454
Sing a song of celebration	457
Sound the trumpet	461
The Lord is marching out	482
The Lord is moving across this land	483
There is a place of commanded blessing	491
There is power in the name of Jesus	495
There's a blessed time that's coming	496
There's a place where the streets shine	498
These are the days	503
The Spirit of the sovereign Lord	504
The trumpets sound, the angels sing	506

This love	521
Though the earth should tremble	523
We are a people of power	536
We are his children	537
We are the army of God	540
We believe	541
Welcome the King	549
Well, I hear they're singing in the streets	550
We'll walk the land	551
We march to the tune of a love-song	552
We must work together	553
We serve a God of miracles	555
We've had a light	557
We will cross every border	560
Where there once was only hurt	577
You are my King	595
You have called us	598
You have taken the precious	600
You laid aside your majesty	601
You're the Lion of Judah	606
You shall go out with joy	609

JESUS – LIFE

5000+ hungry folk	107
He walked where I walked	168
Hosanna	182
I cannot tell	199
Immanuel, O Immanuel	219
Once in royal David's city	404
Welcome the King	549

JESUS – LORDSHIP

All hail King Jesus!	5
All hail the Lamb	6
All to Jesus I surrender	15
A new commandment	23
At the name of Jesus	33
At your feet we fall	35
Come, let us worship Jesus	73
Do something new, Lord	82
From the sun's rising	116
Heaven shall not wait	151
He is Lord	158
He is the mighty God	160
He that is in us	167
I lift my hands	212
I'm your child	224
In the tomb so cold	234
I want to be out of my depth in your love	255
I went to the enemy's camp	257
I will build my church	259
Jesus, at your name	273
Jesus Christ is Lord of all	275
Jesus Christ is the Lord of all	277
Jesus is greater	282
Jesus is King	283
Jesus is Lord!	284
Jesus is the name we honour	285
Jesus, Jesus, you have the name	288
Jesus shall take the highest honour	296
Jesus, the name high over all	298
Jesus, we enthrone you	300
King of kings and Lord of lords	307

King of kings	308
King of kings, majesty	309
Led like a lamb	312
Majesty	346
Men of faith	354
My heart is full	363
No other name	374
O God, most high	385
O Lord, how majestic is your name	395
O Lord our God	398
Open the doors of praise	411
Shout for joy	449
Shout, shout for joy	451
Silent, surrendered	456
Sound the trumpet	461
Take my life, and let it be	468
The world is looking for a hero	508
We believe	541
Welcome, King of kings	548
We want to see Jesus lifted high	559
We will worship the Lamb of glory	563
When the music fades	576
You are crowned with many crowns	590

JESUS – NAME AND GLORY

All heaven declares	8
Almighty God, we bring you praise	16
At the name of Jesus	33
At your feet we fall	35
Behold the Lord	44
Blessing, honour, glory to the Lamb	55
Celebrate, celebrate	66
Come, let us worship Jesus	73
Crown him with many crowns	77
For unto us a child is born	113
He is exalted	156
Holy One of God	179
How sweet the name of Jesus sounds	190
Jesus, Jesus (Holy and anointed one)	286
Jesus, restore to us again	295
Jesus shall take the highest honour	296
Jesus, the name high over all	298
Jesus, your name is power	304
Mighty God	356
More about Jesus	358
No other name	374
Shout for joy and sing	450
Shout! The Lord is risen!	452
Streams of worship	464
There is a Redeemer	492
There is only one Lord	494
The world is looking for a hero	508
Turn your eyes upon Jesus	533
We want to see Jesus lifted high	559
You are crowned with many crowns	590
You laid aside your majesty	601

JESUS – RESURRECTION

Alleluia, alleluia, give thanks to the risen Lord	4

Blessing, honour, glory to the Lamb	55
Celebrate Jesus	67
For this purpose	111
Hallelujah! Jesus is alive	142
He has risen	155
He is Lord	158
He is the mighty God	160
Holy One of God	179
In the tomb so cold	234
Jesus is Lord!	284
Jesus, we celebrate the victory	299
Led like a lamb	312
Lord, I lift your name on high	330
Low in the grave he lay	345
Nothing shall separate us	377
O God, most high	385
O, what a morning	424
Shout! The Lord is risen!	452
Thank you, Jesus	475
Therefore we lift our hearts in praise	489
Thine be the glory	510
You are mighty	594
You laid aside your majesty	601

JESUS – SAVIOUR

Above the clash of creeds	3
For all that you've done	108
For the joys and for the sorrows	110
How firm a foundation	186
I went to the enemy's camp	257
Jesus, Jesus, Jesus	287
Jesus, lover of my soul	290
Jesus reigns	293
Jesus, what a beautiful name	301
Jesus, your name is power	304
Men of faith	354
My Jesus, I love thee	366
My Jesus, my Saviour	367
O for a thousand tongues to sing	383
Oh, I was made for this	389
Oh, lead me	390
Save the people	444
See, your Saviour comes	448
Shout for joy and sing	450
There's a place where the streets shine	498
The Word made flesh	507
This is the message of the cross	518
We believe	541
We have a great priest	546
Well, I hear they're singing in the streets	550
Who can sound the depths of sorrow	579
You rescued me	605
Your love flows like a river	607

JESUS – SECOND COMING

All heaven waits	9
And he shall reign	22
At the name of Jesus	33
Be patient, be ready	46
Great is the darkness	136
He has fire in his eyes	154
He has risen	155

He is the mighty God 160
I cannot tell 199
Joy to the world 305
King of kings 308
Lo, he comes with clouds
  descending 324
Man of sorrows 350
O Lord, my God 396
Sing a song of celebration 457
Soon and very soon 460
Sound the trumpet 461
The heavens shall declare 480
There's a blessed time that's
  coming 496
These are the days 503
The Word made flesh 507
This is the mystery 519
This is the time 610
We are his children 537
We believe 541
We will cross every border 560
You have taken the precious 600
You're the Lion of Judah 606

JOY

Down the mountain the river flows 83
God is good 124
Hallelujah! Jesus is alive 142
Heaven invites you to a party 150
He has clothed us with his
  righteousness 153
He's given me a garment of
  praise 166
I could sing unending songs 200
In every circumstance 227
In the tomb so cold 234
I've found a friend 251
I've got a love song 252
I will enter his gates 262
I will wave my hands 269
Jesus' love has got under
  our skin 289
Jesus put this song into our
  hearts 292
Jesus, we celebrate the victory 299
Joy to the world 305
Let the righteous sing 316
Lord, I lift your name on high 330
Make a joyful noise, all ye people 347
Make way, make way 349
My first love 362
O come and join the dance 381
O happy day 387
O, heaven is in my heart 388
Oh, I was made for this 389
One shall tell another 406
Over the mountains and the sea 421
O, what a morning 424
Peace be to these streets 427
Peace I give to you 428
Peace like a river 429
Peace, perfect peace 430
Rejoice! 438
Righteousness, peace, joy in
  the Holy Ghost 440
Shout for joy 449
Shout for joy and sing 450

Shout, shout for joy 451
Sing a song of celebration 457
Teach me to dance 469
The Lord is marching out 482
The Lord is our strength 484
There's a sound of singing 500
The trumpets sound, the
  angels sing 506
This is the day that the Lord
  has made 516
This is the day 517
Well, I hear they're singing in
  the streets 550
We rejoice in the goodness of
  our God 554
When the Lord brought us back 575
Where there once was only hurt 577
With my whole heart 582
You are mighty 594
You make my heart feel glad 603
You shall go out with joy 609

JUSTICE

Beauty for brokenness 37
Have you heard the good news 146
Heaven shall not wait 151
Make me a channel of your
  peace 348
O Lord, the clouds are gathering 399
See, your Saviour comes 448
Who can sound the depths of
  sorrow 579

LORD'S SUPPER

See **Communion**

LOVE – GOD'S LOVE

And can it be 21
A new commandment 23
Because of your love 39
Before the world began 40
Be free 41
Behold his love 43
Bind us together 51
Come on, all us singers, sing 74
Father, I come to you 95
Father, I want you to hold me 98
Filled with compassion 105
God is good 124
Here is love 164
His love 171
How can I not love you? 184
How deep the Father's love
  for us 185
I am so thankful 192
I'm special 222
I receive your love 236
I stand amazed in the presence 243
I've got a love song 252
I want to be out of my depth
  in your love 255
Jesus! I am resting, resting 280
Jesus, Jesus, Jesus 287
Jesus' love has got under
  our skin 289
Jesus, your loving kindness 303

Let it rain 314
Let there be love 317
Let your love come down 319
Look what God has done 325
Lord, I come to you 329
Lord, you are so precious to me 340
Love divine, all loves excelling 343
Love of Christ, come now 343
Make me a channel of your
  peace 348
My heart will sing to you 364
My Lord, what love is this 370
Nothing shall separate us 377
O give thanks 384
Oh, I was made for this 389
O Lord, your tenderness 402
One shall tell another 406
O the deep, deep love of Jesus! 414
Over the mountains and the sea 421
Overwhelmed by love 422
Peace be to these streets 427
Peace I give to you 428
Peace, perfect peace 430
Righteousness, peace, joy in
  the Holy Ghost 440
Soften my heart, Lord 459
Such love 465
Thank you for your mercy 474
Thank you, Jesus 475
The cross has said it all 478
The Lord is marching out 482
There's an awesome sound 497
The steadfast love of the Lord 505
This grace is mine 512
To you, O Lord, I lift up my soul 530
We are marching 539
We march to the tune of a
  love-song 552
We rejoice in the goodness of
  our God 554
We want to remain in your love 558
What a friend I've found 565
What kind of love is this 568
With my whole heart 582
Yet this will I call to mind 587
You alone, Lord, are wonderful 588
You are my passion 596
You love me as you found me 602
Your love flows like a river 607
Your mercy flows 608

LOVE – OUR LOVE FOR OTHERS

A new commandment 23
Bind us together 51
Filled with compassion 105
Let there be love 317
Make me a channel of your
  peace 348
Peace I give to you 428
Righteousness, peace, joy in
  the Holy Ghost 440
We are marching 539
We want to remain in your love 558

MARCH FOR JESUS

And he shall reign 22
Celebrate, celebrate 66

Come, let us worship Jesus	73
Far and near	90
From where the sun rises	117
Hail, Jesus, you're my King	140
I will build my church	259
Jesus Christ is Lord of all	275
Jesus' love has got under our skin	289
Jesus put this song into our hearts	292
King of kings	308
Lift up your heads	321
Make way, make way	349
O give thanks	384
O, heaven is in my heart	388
Peace to these streets	427
The Lord is marching out	482
Welcome the King	549

MARRIAGE

On this day of happiness	410

MISSION

Above the clash of creeds	3
All over the world	12
As we lift up your name	30
At this time of giving	34
Before the world began	40
Colours of day	69
Come on, all us singers, sing	74
Day of favour	78
Did you feel the mountains tremble?	80
Every nation, power and tongue	86
Far and near	90
Father of creation	99
Filled with compassion	105
Fire	106
From the sun's rising	116
God forgave my sin	123
Great is the darkness	136
Have you heard the good news	146
Have you not said	147
Heaven invites you to a party	150
He is the Lord	159
Here I am	161
Here we stand in total surrender	165
How lovely on the mountains	189
I heard the voice of Jesus say	206
I'm standing here to testify	223
Is anyone thirsty?	237
Is it true today	241
I, the Lord of sea and sky	246
It's rising up	249
I want to serve the purpose of God	256
Just as I am, without one plea	306
Let your word go forth	320
Lord, the light of your love	335
Lord, we lift you high	336
Make way, make way	349
Not by might	376
O Breath of Life	379
O Father of the fatherless	382
O for a thousand tongues to sing	383
O God of burning, cleansing flame	386

Oh, I was made for this	389
One shall tell another	406
O thou who camest from above	416
Peace be to these streets	427
Rejoice!	438
Show your power, O Lord	454
The Lord is moving across this land	483
These are the days	503
The Spirit of the sovereign Lord	504
This is my beloved Son	514
This is the message of the cross	518
This is the time	610
To God be the glory!	526
Turn to me and be saved	532
We are his children	537
We are the army of God	540
We believe	541
Well, I hear they're singing in the streets	550
We'll walk the land	551
We march to the tune of a love-song	552
We've had a light	557
We will cross every border	560
You have called us	598
You're the Lion of Judah	606

NATURE

See **God – Creation**

OFFERING

Give thanks with a grateful heart	118

OPENING OF SERVICE

See **Call to Worship**

PALM SUNDAY

See **Jesus – Life**

PEACE

Father, we adore you	101
Here is bread	163
Hold me closer to you	172
Jesus! I am resting, resting	280
Make me a channel of your peace	348
O Lord, my heart is not proud	397
Peace to these streets	427
Peace I give to you	428
Peace like a river	429
Peace, perfect peace	430
Peace to you	431
Righteousness, peace, joy in the Holy Ghost	440
To be in your presence	524
You shall go out with joy	609

PENTECOST

All honour, all glory	10
All over the world	12
Anointing, fall on me	24
As we lift up your name	30
Breathe on me, Breath of God	57
Come down, O Love divine	71
Come, Spirit, come	76
Down the mountain the river flows	83

Holy Spirit, come	180
Holy Spirit, we welcome you	181
I believe the promise	196
Is anyone thirsty?	237
I've found a friend	251
Jesus, restore to us again	295
Lord, we long for you	337
More of your glory	360
O Breath of Life	379
O God of burning, cleansing flame	386
O thou who camest from above	416
Peace like a river	429
Ruach	442
Spirit of the living God (Iverson)	462
Spirit of the living God (Armstrong)	463
The promise of the Holy Spirit	488
Therefore we lift our hearts in praise	489
There's an awesome sound	497
There's a wind a-blowing	501
The Spirit of the sovereign Lord	504

PERSEVERANCE AND DETERMINATION

All I once held dear	11
Be bold, be strong	38
Be patient, be ready	46
Called to a battle	61
Far and near	90
Fire	106
For I'm building a people of power	109
For this purpose	111
Give thanks with a grateful heart	118
Hail, Jesus, you're my King	140
Have you got an appetite?	145
He has fire in his eyes	154
He that is in us	167
How can I be free from sin?	183
I need you more	226
In the morning when I rise	231
Is it true today	241
I walk by faith	253
I want to serve the purpose of God	256
I went to the enemy's camp	257
I will never be the same again	264
O Jesus, I have promised	391
On this day	409
O thou who camest from above	416
Salvation belongs to our God	443
They that wait on the Lord	509
Wake up, my soul	534
We shall stand	556
We've had a light	557
We want to see Jesus lifted high	559
We will cross every border	560

PRAISE

See **Adoration and Praise**

PRAYER

All heaven waits	9
Be thou my vision	50
Can a nation be changed?	62

Draw me closer 84
Father, hear our prayer 93
Father, here I am 94
Father of creation 99
Father of life, draw me closer 100
God, be gracious 122
God of glory 131
Hear, O Lord, our cry 148
Hear our cry 149
Here we stand in total surrender 165
Holy Spirit, come 180
I cry out for your hand 201
I lift my eyes up to the
  mountains 211
In my life, Lord 230
Let it rain 314
Let me be a sacrifice 315
Let there be love 317
Let your living water flow 318
Let your love come down 319
Let your word go forth 320
Lord, have mercy 328
Lord, the light of your love 335
Lord, we long for you 337
Love of Christ, come now 343
Make me a channel of your peace 348
May the fragrance 352
More love, more power 359
More of your glory 360
Oh, lead me 390
O Lord, hear my prayer 394
One thing I ask 407
Peace be to these streets 427
Restore, O Lord 439
Ruach 442
Save the people 444
See, your Saviour comes 448
Soften my heart, Lord 459
Teach me your ways 470
There's a wind a-blowing 501
To every good thing God is
  doing 525
Turn our hearts 531
Turn to me and be saved 532
We are his people 538
We have prayed that you would
  have mercy 547
We'll walk the land 551
We want to see Jesus lifted high 559
We will turn the hearts 562
What a friend we have in Jesus 566
When my heart is overwhelmed 573
Where two or three 578
Who can sound the depths of
  sorrow 579
Your mercy flows 608

PROCLAMATION

Above the clash of creeds 3
Be glorified 42
Blessed be the name of the Lord 53
Celebrate, celebrate 66
Come, let us worship Jesus 73
Day of favour 78
Every nation, power and tongue 86
Far and near 90
Father in heaven, how we love you 96

For I'm building a people of
  power 109
For this purpose 111
From the ends of the earth 115
From the sun's rising 116
Glory to the King of kings 121
God is good all the time 125
Great is thy faithfulness 138
Hail, Jesus, you're my King 140
Hallelujah, hallelujah 141
Hallelujah! Jesus is alive 142
Have you heard the good news 146
He has clothed us with his
  righteousness 153
He is the Lord 159
He is the mighty God 160
He that is in us 167
How lovely on the mountains 189
I am a new creation 191
I believe in Jesus 195
I'm standing here to testify 223
In every circumstance 227
In heavenly armour 228
In the tomb so cold 234
It's rising up 249
I walk by faith 253
I will build my church 259
Jesus, at your name 273
Jesus Christ is Lord of all 275
Jesus Christ is the Lord of all 277
Jesus, God's righteousness
  revealed 278
Jesus is greater 282
Jesus is Lord! 284
Jesus reigns 293
Jesus, we celebrate the victory 299
Jesus, you're my firm foundation 302
Jesus, your name is power 304
Joy to the world 305
King of kings and Lord of lords 307
King of kings 308
Led like a lamb 312
Lift up your heads 321
Lord of lords 332
Lord of the heavens 333
Low in the grave he lay 345
Make way, make way 349
Men of faith 354
Mighty God 356
Mighty is our God 357
My life is in you, Lord 368
Nothing shall separate us 377
O God, most high 385
One heart, one voice, one mind 405
Open the doors of praise 411
Our God is an awesome God 418
O, we are more than conquerors 423
Salvation belongs to our God 443
See his glory 446
Seek ye first 447
Shout, shout for joy 451
Shout! The Lord is risen! 452
Shout unto God 453
Tell out, my soul 471
The cross has said it all 478
The Lord is a mighty King 481
The Lord is marching out 482

The Lord is moving across
  this land 483
The Lord is our strength 484
The Lord reigns 485
The price is paid 487
There is a place of commanded
  blessing 491
There is a Redeemer 492
There is only one Lord 494
There is power in the name of
  Jesus 495
The world is looking for a hero 508
This, in essence, is the message 513
This is my beloved Son 514
This is the message of the cross 518
To every good thing God is
  doing 525
We are marching 539
We are the army of God 540
We believe 541
We declare your majesty 544
Welcome, King of kings 548
We serve a God of miracles 555
We shall stand 556
We want to see Jesus lifted high 559
We will cross every border 560
We will run and not grow weary 561
You are crowned with many
  crowns 590
You are God, you are great 591
You are mighty 594
You are my King 595
You are my rock 597
You're the Lion of Judah 606

RENEWAL

All over the world 12
Don't let my love grow cold 81
Do something new, Lord 82
Down the mountain the river flows 83
How lovely on the mountains 189
Is anyone thirsty? 237
It's our confession, Lord 248
I've found a friend 251
Jesus, restore to us again 295
Let it rain 314
Lord, have mercy 328
Love of Christ, come now 343
May the fragrance 352
Men of faith 354
Mercy is falling 355
More of your glory 360
My first love 362
Not by might 376
O Breath of Life 379
Oh, lead me 390
O let the sun of God enfold you 392
O Lord, the clouds are gathering 399
Restore, O Lord 439
River, wash over me 441
Ruach 442
Show your power, O Lord 454
Spirit of the living God (Iverson) 462
Spirit of the living God
  (Armstrong) 463
There's a wind a-blowing 501
These are the days 503

The Spirit of the sovereign Lord	504
They that wait on the Lord	509
Turn our hearts	531
We are his people	538
We will turn the hearts	562
When the Lord brought us back	575
You have shown me	599
You have taken the precious	600
Your love flows like a river	607
Your mercy flows	608

REPENTANCE AND FORGIVENESS

And can it be	1
Come and see	70
Come, let us return	72
Come on, all us singers, sing	74
Dear Lord and Father of mankind	79
Father, here I am	94
God forgave my sin	123
God of grace	132
Here we stand in total surrender	165
Holiness is your life in me	174
Holy Spirit, come	180
I believe in Jesus	195
I bow my knee	198
I have made you too small	205
I know a place	209
I'm special	222
I'm standing here to testify	223
It's our confession, Lord	248
I worship you, O Lamb of God	272
Just as I am, without one plea	306
Lamb of God	310
Lord, have mercy	328
My Lord, what love is this	370
O Father of the fatherless	382
Oh, I was made for this	389
O Lord, the clouds are gathering	399
O Lord, you're beautiful	401
Only by grace	408
O the blood of Jesus	412
O the blood of my Saviour	413
Restore, O Lord	439
Soften my heart, Lord	459
The cross has said it all	478
This is the message of the cross	518
Turn our hearts	531
Turn to me and be saved	532
We have a great priest	546
We have prayed that you would have mercy	547
Well, I hear they're singing in the streets	550
We will turn the hearts	562
What kind of love is this	568
With this bread	583
You are merciful to me	593
You rescued me	605

REVIVAL

As we lift up your name	30
Can a nation be changed?	62
Can we walk upon the water	64
Don't let my love grow cold	81
Down the mountain the river flows	83
God of glory	131
Great is the darkness	136

Hear, O Lord, our cry	148
Hear our cry	149
Here we stand in total surrender	165
I believe the promise	196
Is it true today	241
It's rising up	249
Let it rain	314
Lord, we long for you	337
Not by might	376
O Breath of Life	379
O God of burning, cleansing flame	386
O Lord, the clouds are gathering	399
Save the people	444
See, your Saviour comes	448
There's an awesome sound	497
There's a wind a-blowing	501
These are the days	503
The Spirit of the sovereign Lord	504
This is the time	610
We are his people	538
We are the army of God	540
We have prayed that you would have mercy	547
We'll walk the land	551
You have taken the precious	600
Your mercy flows	608

ROUNDS/ANTIPHONAL SONGS

From the ends of the earth	115
Glory	120
Hail, Jesus, you're my King	140
Hear our cry	149
Heaven invites you to a party	150
I believe in Jesus	195
I'm standing here to testify	223
In the tomb so cold	234
I will worship	270
I worship you, O Lamb of God	272
Jesus Christ is Lord of all	275
Jesus' love has got under our skin	289
Jesus, you're my firm foundation	302
King of kings and Lord of lords	307
Led like a lamb	312
Lord, you have my heart	341
Make way, make way	349
My heart is full	363
O, heaven is in my heart	388
O Lord, the clouds are gathering	399
The Lord is a mighty King	481
The Spirit of the sovereign Lord	504
Turn to me and be saved	532
You are merciful to me	593

SALVATION AND REDEMPTION

Above the clash of creeds	3
Amazing grace	18
And can it be	21
At the foot of the cross	32
Because of your love	39
Before the world began	40
Beneath the cross of Jesus	45
Come and see	70
Crown him with many crowns	77
Did you feel the mountains tremble?	80

Filled with compassion	105
God of grace	132
Hallelujah, my Father	143
He has clothed us with his righteousness	153
He is the Lord	159
Here is love	164
He's given me a garment of praise	166
He was pierced	169
Holiness is your life in me	174
How lovely on the mountains	189
How sweet the name of Jesus sounds	190
I am a new creation	191
I believe in Jesus	195
I could sing unending songs	200
I cry out for your hand	201
I give you all the honour	203
I heard the voice of Jesus say	206
I know a place	209
I know it	210
I'm accepted, I'm forgiven	217
I'm special	222
I stand amazed in the presence	243
I stand before the presence	244
I, the Lord of sea and sky	246
It's your blood	250
I went to the enemy's camp	257
I will change your name	260
I will offer up my life	265
I worship you, O Lamb of God	272
Jesus! I am resting, resting	280
Jesus, the name high over all	298
Jesus, what a beautiful name	301
Jesus, your name is power	304
Just as I am, without one plea	306
Like a candle flame	322
Meekness and majesty	353
Mighty God	356
My Jesus, I love thee	366
My lips shall praise you	369
My Lord, what love is this	370
O Father of the fatherless	382
O for a thousand tongues to sing	383
O happy day	387
O, heaven is in my heart	388
Oh, I was made for this	389
O Lord, my God	396
O Lord, your tenderness	402
O the blood of my Saviour	413
Overwhelmed by love	422
Peace be to these streets	427
Praise, my soul, the King of heaven	433
See, your Saviour comes	448
Shout! The Lord is risen!	452
Such love	465
Thank you for saving me	472
Thank you for the cross	473
The cross has said it all	478
The Lord is a mighty King	481
The price is paid	487
The promise of the Holy Spirit	488
There is a Redeemer	492
There's a place where the streets shine	498

There's a sound of singing 500
The trumpets sound, the
angels sing 506
The Word made flesh 507
The world is looking for a hero 508
This is my beloved Son 514
This is the message of the cross 518
This love 521
To every good thing God
is doing 525
To God be the glory! 526
Turn to me and be saved 532
We believe 541
We rejoice in the goodness of
our God 554
We serve a God of miracles 555
What kind of love is this 568
Where there once was only hurt 577
Who sees it all 580
With this bread 583
Yet this will I call to mind 587
You are Lord 592
You have called us 598
You have shown me 599
You laid aside your majesty 601
You rescued me 605

SANCTIFICATION

All I once held dear 11
All to Jesus I surrender 15
As we lift up your name 30
At the name of Jesus 33
Breathe on me, Breath of God 57
Can I ascend 63
Change my heart, O God 68
Come down, O Love divine 71
Come, let us return 72
Come, Spirit, come 76
Do something new, Lord 82
Father, here I am 94
God of glory 131
Hold me, Lord 173
Holiness is your life in me 174
Holiness unto the Lord 175
Holy Spirit, come 180
Holy Spirit, we welcome you 181
How can I be free from sin? 183
I bow my knee before your
throne 197
I bow my knee 198
If you are encouraged 202
In my life, Lord 230
It's your blood 250
I will never be the same again 264
Jesus, take me as I am 297
Lamb of God 310
Lord, I come to you 329
Lord, prepare me 334
Lord, the light of your love 335
Nothing shall separate us 377
O God of burning, cleansing
flame 386
O Jesus, I have promised 391
Purify my heart 436
Reign in me 437
Teach me your ways 470
This is the message of the cross 518

This love 521
Wake up, O sleeper 535
We shall stand 556

SECOND COMING

See **Jesus – Second Coming**

SOCIAL CONCERN

Beauty for brokenness 37
Can a nation be changed? 62
Heaven shall not wait 151
I, the Lord of sea and sky 246
Let your love come down 319
Lord, for the years 327
Lord, we long for you 337
Make me a channel of your peace 348
O Lord, the clouds are gathering 399
One shall tell another 406
Peace be to these streets 427
Save the people 444
See, your Saviour comes 448
The Spirit of the sovereign Lord 504
We'll walk the land 551
Who can sound the depths of
sorrow 579
Who sees it all 580
Your mercy flows 608

SPIRITUAL WARFARE

All heaven waits 9
Called to a battle 61
Can a nation be changed? 62
In heavenly armour 228
I went to the enemy's camp 257
I will build my church 259
Open the doors of praise 411
Our God is awesome in power 419
The Lord is moving across this
land 483
The price is paid 487
There is power in the name of
Jesus 495
We march to the tune of a
love-song 552
We shall stand 556
We want to see Jesus lifted hig 559
You're the Lion of Judah 606

SUBMISSION TO GOD

All to Jesus I surrender 15
By your side 60
Come down, O Love divine 71
Come, let us return 72
Do something new, Lord 82
Father, I place into your hands 97
God is here, God is present 127
Here I am 161
Here we stand in total surrender 165
I bow my knee before your
throne 197
I bow my knee 198
Jesus! I am resting, resting 280
King of kings, majesty 309
Let it be to me 313
Let me be a sacrifice 315
O Lord, my heart is not proud 397

Reign in me 437
River, wash over me 441
Silent, surrendered 456
Take my life, and let it be 468
To keep your lovely face 527

TEMPTATIONS AND TRIALS

Be patient, be ready 46
For the joys and for the sorrows 110
How firm a foundation 186
When peace like a river 574

THANKSGIVING

Alleluia, alleluia, give thanks to
the risen Lord 4
For all that you've done 108
Give thanks with a grateful heart 118
Great is the Lord and most
worthy of praise 137
Great is thy faithfulness 138
He has clothed us with his
righteousness 153
How can I not love you? 184
I am so thankful 192
I could sing unending songs 200
I give you all the honour 203
Immanuel, O Immanuel 219
I'm special 222
I sing a simple song of love 239
Jesus Christ 274
Look what God has done 325
Look what the Lord has done 326
Lord, for the years 327
O give thanks 384
Oh, I was made for this 389
Teach me to dance 469
Thank you for saving me 472
Thank you for the cross 473
Thank you for your mercy 474
Thank you, Jesus 475
The Lord is marching out 482
The Lord is our strength 484
The price is paid 487
Therefore we lift our hearts in
praise 489
There's a sound of singing 500
The trumpets sound, the angels
sing 506
Thine be the glory 510
This Child 511
When the Lord brought us back 575

TRINITY

See **Adoration and Praise**

TRUST

Almighty God, my Redeemer 17
Because of your love 39
Be still and know 48
Be still, my soul 49
Bless the Lord, my soul 56
Can we walk upon the water 64
Faithful God 88
Faithful One 89
Father, I place into your hands 97
For the joys and for the sorrows 110

God is good all the time 125
God will make a new way 134
Great is the Lord and most
worthy of praise 137
Great is thy faithfulness 138
Have you not said 147
He walked where I walked 168
Higher, higher 170
His love 171
Hold me closer to you 172
How firm a foundation 186
I am standing beneath your wings 193
I cry out for your hand 201
I lift my eyes up to the mountains 211
I'm so secure 221
I'm your child 224
In Christ alone 225
I need you more 226
In every circumstance 227
In heavenly armour 228
I walk by faith 253
I will praise you all my life 266
I will worship 270
Jesus! I am resting, resting 280
Jesus, lover of my soul 290
Jesus, you're my firm foundation 302
Lead us, heavenly Father, lead us 311
Let your living water flow 318
Living under the shadow of
his wing 323
My Jesus, my Saviour 367
My life is in you, Lord 368
My lips shall praise you 369
My spirit rests in you alone 371
O Jesus, I have promised 391
O Lord, you lead me 400
One thing I ask 407
Our confidence is in the Lord 417
Praise the name of Jesus 435
Say the word 445
Tell out, my soul 471
Thank you for your mercy 474
The Lord's my shepherd 486
There is none like you 493
They that wait on the Lord 509
This grace is mine 512
This is the day that the Lord
has made 516

Though I feel afraid 522
Though the earth should tremble 523
To you, O Lord, I lift up my soul 530
What a friend we have in Jesus 566
When my heart is overwhelmed 573
When peace like a river 574
With all my heart 581
You are my rock 597
You love me as you found me 602
You make your face to shine
on me 604

UNITY

See **Church**

VICTORY

Be bold, be strong 38
Called to a battle 61
Father of creation 99
For this purpose 111
Hallelujah! Jesus is alive 142
He that is in us 167
Higher, higher 170
I am a new creation 191
In every circumstance 227
In heavenly armour 228
I went to the enemy's camp 257
Nothing shall separate us 377
O God, most high 385
Open the doors of praise 411
Our God is awesome in power 419
O, we are more than conquerors 423
Rejoice! 438
Shout, shout for joy 451
Shout unto God 453
The Lord is moving across
this land 483
The price is paid 487
There is only one Lord 494
There is power in the name
of Jesus 495
The world is looking for a hero 508
Thine be the glory 510
We are a people of power 536
We are the army of God 540
We march to the tune of a
love-song 552
We must work together 553

VISION

Can we walk upon the water 64
Don't let my love grow cold 81
Father of creation 99
Great is the darkness 136
I believe the promise 196
I see the Lord 238
Is it true today 241
It's rising up 249
I want to serve the purpose
of God 256
I will change your name 260
I will never be the same again 264
Jesus, God's righteousness
revealed 278
Men of faith 354
No scenes of stately majesty 375
Rejoice! 438
Soon and very soon 460
There is a louder shout to
come 490
These are the days 503
The Spirit of the sovereign Lord 504
The world is looking for a hero 508
This is my beloved Son 514
Wake up, my soul 534
We are a people of power 536
We are the army of God 540
We must work together 553
We want to see Jesus lifted
high 559
We will turn the hearts 562
You have taken the precious 600
You're the Lion of Judah 606

WORD OF GOD

Have you got an appetite? 145
Jesus, restore to us again 295
Jesus, you're my firm foundation 302
Let your word go forth 320
Say the word 445
Seek ye first 447
Silent, surrendered 456
The Lord is a mighty King 481

WORSHIP

See **Adoration and Praise**

Index of First Lines and Titles

*This index gives the first line of each hymn. If a hymn is known by an alternative title,
this is also given, but indented and in italics.*

A

Abba, Father, let me be	1
Abide with me	2
Above the clash of creeds	3
Acts chapter 2, verse 39	488
A living sacrifice	351
Alleluia, alleluia, give thanks to the risen Lord	4
All hail King Jesus!	5
All hail the Lamb	6
All hail the power of Jesus' name	7
All heaven declares	8
All heaven waits	9
All honour, all glory	10
All I know	522
All I once held dear	11
All I want	231
All over the world	12
All people that on earth do dwell	13
All the earth shall worship	102
All the glory	363
All things are possible	17
All things bright and beautiful	14
All to Jesus I surrender	15
Almighty God, we bring you praise	16
Almighty God, my Redeemer	17
Amazing grace	18
Amazing love	370
Amen	525
Among the gods	19
An army of ordinary people	20
Ancient of Days	54
And can it be	21
And he shall reign	22
And his love goes on and on	325
And that my soul knows very well	604
A new commandment	23
Anointing, fall on me	24
Arms of love	239
Army of God	540
Ascribe greatness	25
As I come into your presence	26
As the deer pants (Nystrom)	27
As the deer pants (Lewis)	28
As we are gathered	29
As we lift up your name	30
As we seek your face	31
At the cross	209
At the foot of the cross	32
At the name of Jesus	33
At this time of giving	34
At your feet we fall	35
Away in a manger	36
Awesome God	418
Awesome in this place	26

B

Beauty for brokenness	37
Be bold, be strong	38

Because of the Lord's great love	587
Because of you	498
Because of your love	39
Before the world began	40
Be free	41
Be glorified	42
Behold his love	43
Behold the Lord	44
Be magnified	205
Beneath the cross of Jesus	45
Be patient, be ready	46
Be still, for the presence of the Lord	47
Be still and know	48
Be still, my soul	49
Be thou my vision	50
Better is one day	188
Bind us together	51
Blessed assurance, Jesus is mine	52
Blessed be the Lord God Almighty	96
Blessed be the name	193
Blessed be the name of the Lord	53
Blessing and honour	54
Blessing, honour, glory to the Lamb	55
Bless the Lord, my soul	56
Break dividing walls	491
Breathe on me, Breath of God	57
Broken for me	58
By his grace	59
By your side	60

C

Called to a battle	61
Can a nation be changed?	62
Can I ascend	63
Can we walk upon the water	64
Can you see what we have made	65
Cast your burdens	170
Celebrate	75
Celebrate, celebrate	66
Celebrate Jesus	67
Champion	508
Change my heart, O God	68
Christ is risen! (In the tomb so cold)	234
Christ is risen (O, what a morning)	424
Colours of day	69
Come and see	70
Come down, O Love divine	71
Come, let us return	72
Come, let us worship Jesus	73
Come, Lord Jesus	136
Come on, all us singers, sing	74
Come on and celebrate	75
Come, Spirit, come	76
Come to the light	223
Creation creed	481

D

Cross every border	560
Crown him with many crowns	77
Day of favour	78
Days of Elijah	503
Dear Lord and Father of mankind	79
Did you feel the mountains tremble?	80
Distant thunder	610
Don't let my love grow cold	81
Do something new, Lord	82
Down the mountain the river flows	83
Draw me closer	84

E

Earth lies spellbound	85
Enemy's camp	257
Eternity	258
Every nation, power and tongue	86
Exalt the Lord	87

F

Faithful God	88
Faithful One	89
Far and near	90
Father God, I wonder	91
Father God, we worship you	92
Father, hear our prayer	93
Father, here I am	94
Father, I come to you	95
Father in heaven, how we love you	96
Father, I place into your hands	97
Father, I want you to hold me	98
Father of creation	99
Father of creation (We come into your presence)	543
Father of life, draw me closer	100
Father me	382
Father, we adore you	101
Father, we adore you, you've drawn us	102
Father, we love you	103
Father, you are my portion	104
Filled with compassion	105
Fill us up and send us out	147
Fire	106
Fire of God's glory	131
Firm foundation	302
5000+ hungry folk	107
For all that you've done	108
For all the people who live on earth	105
For I'm building a people of power	109
For the joys and for the sorrows	110
For this I have Jesus	110
For this purpose	111
For thou, O Lord, art high	112
For unto us a child is born	113

Fountain of life 101
Freely, freely 123
From heaven you came 114
From the ends of the earth 115
From the sun's rising 116
From where the sun rises 117

G

Give thanks with a grateful heart 118
Gloria 119
Glorify your name 103
Glory 120
Glory to God 528
Glory to the King 331
Glory to the King of kings 121
Glory to the Lamb 55
God, be gracious 122
God forgave my sin 123
God is good 124
God is good all the time 125
God is great 126
God is here, God is present 127
God is light 513
God is working his purpose out 128
God of all comfort 129
God of glory, we exalt your name 130
God of glory 131
God of grace 132
God of the poor 37
God's not dead 133
God will make a new way 134
God with us 168
Go forth in his name 537
Good to me 201
Great and mighty is he 135
Great is the darkness 136
Great is the Lord and most
  worthy of praise 137
Great is thy faithfulness 138
Great is your mercy 474
Great is your name 139
Great love 364

H

Hail, Jesus, you're my King 140
Hallelujah, hallelujah 141
Hallelujah! Jesus is alive 142
Hallelujah, my Father 143
Hallowed be your name 178
Hark, the herald-angels sing 144
Have faith in God 400
Have you got an appetite? 145
Have you heard the good news 146
Have you not said 147
Heal our nation 337
Hear, O Lord, our cry 148
Hear our cry 149
Hearts on fire 288
Heaven invites you to a party 150
Heaven is in my heart 388
Heaven shall not wait 151
He brought me to his
  banqueting table 152
He has clothed us with his
  righteousness 153
He has fire in his eyes 154
He has made me glad 262

He has risen 155
He is exalted 156
He is here 157
He is Lord 158
He is the Lord 159
He is the mighty God 160
Here I am 161
Here I am, Lord 246
Here in your presence 162
Here is bread 163
Here is love 164
Here we stand in total surrender 165
He's given me a garment of praise 166
He that is in us 167
He walked where I walk 168
He was pierced 169
Higher, higher 170
His banner over me is love 152
His love 171
History maker 241
Hold me closer to you 172
Hold me, Lord 173
Holiness is your life in me 174
Holiness unto the Lord 175
Holy and anointed one 286
Holy, holy, holy! Lord God
  Almighty 176
Holy, holy, Lord God Almighty 177
Holy, holy, Lord, you're worthy 178
Holy is your name 215
Holy One of God 179
Holy Spirit, come 180
Holy Spirit, we welcome you 181
Hosanna 182
How can I be free from sin? 183
How can I not love you? 184
How deep the Father's love for us 185
How firm a foundation 186
How good and how pleasant 187
How great thou art 396
How lovely is your dwelling-place 188
How lovely on the mountains 189
How majestic 395
How sweet the name of Jesus
  sounds 190

I

I am a new creation 191
I am so thankful 192
I am standing beneath your wings 193
I am the God that healeth thee 194
I believe in Jesus 195
I believe the promise 196
I bow my knee before your throne 197
I bow my knee 198
I cannot tell 199
I could sing of your love for ever 421
I could sing unending songs 200
I cry out for your hand 201
I exalt thee 112
If you are encouraged 202
I give thanks 599
I give you all the honour 203
I give you my heart 515
I have come to love you 204
I have made you too small 205
I heard the voice of Jesus say 206

I just want to be where you are 207
I just want to praise you 208
I know a place 209
I know it 210
I lift my eyes up to the mountains 211
I lift my hands 212
I'll love you more 198
I love to be in your presence 213
I love you, Lord, and I lift
  my voice 214
I love you, Lord, with all of
  my heart 215
I love your presence 216
I'm accepted, I'm forgiven 217
I'm coming up the mountain 63
I'm gonna click 218
Immanuel, O Immanuel 219
Immortal, invisible, God only wise 220
I'm so secure 221
I'm special 222
I'm standing here to testify 223
I'm your child 224
In Christ alone 225
I need you more 226
In every circumstance 227
In heavenly armour 228
In moments like these 229
In my generation 256
In my life, Lord 230
In the morning when I rise 231
In the presence of a holy God 232
In the secret 233
In the tomb so cold 234
In your hands 221
I reach up high 235
I really want to worship you,
  my Lord 601
I receive your love 236
Is anyone thirsty? 237
I see the Lord 238
I sing a simple song of love 239
I sing praises 240
Is it true today 241
Isn't he beautiful 242
I stand amazed in the presence 243
I stand before the presence 244
I stand before your throne 245
I stand complete in you 132
I stand in awe 589
I surrender all 15
I, the Lord of sea and sky 246
It is to you 247
It's our confession, Lord 248
It's rising up 249
It's your blood 250
I've found a friend 251
I've found Jesus 550
I've got a love song 252
I walk by faith 253
I want to be a blooming tree 254
I want to be a tree that's
  bearing fruit 254
I want to be out of my depth
  in your love 255
I want to serve the purpose
  of God 256
I was made for this 389

I went to the enemy's camp 257
I will be yours 258
I will build my church 259
I will change your name 260
I will dance, I will sing 261
I will enter his gates 262
I will lift my voice 263
I will never be the same again 264
I will offer up my life 265
I will praise you all my life 266
I will seek you 267
I will seek your face, O Lord 268
I will serve no foreign god 212
I will sing your praises 91
I will wave my hands 269
I will worship 270
*I worship you (I give you all
the honour)* 203
I worship you, Almighty God 271
I worship you, eternal God 523
I worship you, O Lamb of God 272

J

Jesus, at your name 273
Jesus Christ 274
Jesus Christ is Lord of all 275
Jesus Christ is risen today 276
Jesus Christ is the Lord of all 277
Jesus, friend for ever 565
Jesus, God's righteousness
revealed 278
Jesus, how lovely you are 279
Jesus! I am resting, resting 280
Jesus, I am thirsty 281
Jesus is alive 142
Jesus is greater 282
Jesus is King 283
Jesus is Lord! 284
Jesus is our battle cry 275
Jesus is our God 285
Jesus is the name we honour 285
Jesus, Jesus (Holy and
anointed one) 286
Jesus, Jesus, Jesus 287
Jesus, Jesus, you have the name 288
Jesus' love has got under
our skin 289
Jesus, lover of my soul 290
Jesus, name above all names 291
Jesus put this song into
our hearts 292
Jesus reigns 293
Jesus, remember me 294
Jesus, restore to us again 295
Jesus shall take the highest
honour 296
Jesus, take me as I am 297
Jesus, the name high over all 298
Jesus, we celebrate the victory 299
Jesus, we enthrone you 300
Jesus, what a beautiful name 301
Jesus, you're my firm foundation 302
Jesus, your loving kindness 303
Jesus, your name is power 304
Joy in the Holy Ghost 251
Joy to the world 305
Just as I am, without one plea 306

K

King of kings and Lord of lords 307
King of kings 308
King of kings, majesty 309
King of the nations 73
Knowing you 11

L

Lamb of God 310
Laudate Dominum 458
Lead me to the cross 183
Lead me to the rock 573
Lead us, heavenly Father,
lead us 311
Led like a lamb 312
Let forgiveness flow 94
Let it be to me 313
Let it rain 314
Let it rain (We have prayed . . .) 547
Let me be a sacrifice 315
Let the bride say, 'Come' 519
Let the flame burn brighter 551
Let the peace of God reign 100
Let the righteous sing 316
Let there be love 317
Let your glory fall 99
Let your living water flow 318
Let your love come down 319
Let your word go forth 320
Lift up your heads 321
Light the fire again 81
Light up the fire 69
Like a candle flame 322
Like a child 362
Like a lamb 169
Lion of Judah 606
Living under the shadow of
his wing 323
Living water 318
Lo, he comes with clouds
descending 324
Look what God has done 325
Look what the Lord has done 326
Lord, be glorified 230
Lord, for the years 327
Lord, have mercy 328
Lord, I come to you 329
Lord, I lift your name on high 330
Lord most high 115
Lord, my heart cries out 331
Lord of lords 332
Lord of the heavens 333
Lord of the years 327
Lord, prepare me 334
Lord, the light of your love 335
Lord, we lift you high 336
Lord, we long for you 337
Lord, we long to see your glory 338
Lord, you are more precious 339
Lord, you are so precious to me 340
Lord, you have my heart 341
Lord, you put a tongue in
my mouth 342
Love divine, all loves excelling 343
Love of Christ, come now 344
Low in the grave he lay 345

M

Majesty 346
Make a joyful noise, all
ye people 347
Make me a channel of
your peace 348
Make way, make way 349
Man of sorrows 350
May I never lose sight of you 172
May our worship be as fragrance 351
May the fragrance 352
Meekness and majesty 353
Men of faith 354
Mercy is falling 355
Mighty God 356
Mighty is our God 357
More about Jesus 358
More of you 281
More love, more power 359
More of your glory 360
More than oxygen 361
Mourning into dancing 577
My delight 104
My desire 524
My first love 362
My God is so big 420
My heart is full 363
My heart will sing to you 364
My hope is built 365
My Jesus, I love thee 366
My Jesus, my Saviour 367
My life is in you, Lord 368
My lips shall praise you 369
My Lord, what love is this 370
My spirit rests in you alone 371

N

Nearer, my God, to thee 372
No one but you, Lord 373
No other name 374
No other way 3
No scenes of stately majesty 375
Not by might 376
Nothing shall separate us 377
Now is the time 521
Now unto the King 378

O

O Breath of Life 379
O come, all ye faithful 380
O come and join the dance 381
O faithful God 266
O Father of the fatherless 382
O for a thousand tongues to sing 383
O give thanks 384
*O give thanks (The Lord is
marching out)* 482
O God, most high 385
O God of burning, cleansing
flame 386
O happy day 387
O, heaven is in my heart 388
O I love you, Lord 473
Oh, I was made for this 389
Oh, lead me 390
O Jesus, I have promised 391

O let the sun of God enfold you 392
O little town of Bethlehem 393
O Lord, hear my prayer 394
O Lord, how majestic is your name 395
O Lord, my God 396
O Lord, my heart is not proud 397
O Lord our God 398
O Lord, the clouds are gathering 399
O Lord, you lead me 400
O Lord, you're beautiful 401
O Lord, your tenderness 402
On a hill far away 403
   Once again 274
Once in royal David's city 404
One heart, one voice, one mind 405
One shall tell another 406
One thing I ask 407
Only by grace 408
   Only the blood 174
   Only you 373
   Only you deserve the glory 139
On this day 409
On this day of happiness 410
Open the doors of praise 411
O the blood of Jesus 412
O the blood of my Saviour 413
O the deep, deep love of Jesus! 414
O the glory of your presence 415
O thou who camest from above 416
Our confidence is in the Lord 417
Our God is an awesome God 418
Our God is awesome in power 419
Our God is so great 420
   Our God reigns 189
Over the mountains and the sea 421
Overwhelmed by love 422
O, we are more than conquerors 423
O, what a morning 424
O worship the King 425
O worship the Lord in the
   beauty of holiness 426
   O you gates 321

P

Peace be to these streets 427
Peace I give to you 428
Peace like a river 429
Peace, perfect peace 430
Peace to you 431
   People just like us 86
   Power of your love 329
Praise God from whom all
   blessings flow 432
Praise, my soul, the King of heaven 433
Praise the Lord, O my soul 434
Praise the name of Jesus 435
   Prayer of humble access 545
   Prayer song 328
   Psalm 121 211
   Psalm 126 575
Purify my heart 436
   *Purify my heart (Teach me
   your ways)* 470

R

   Refiner's fire 436
Reign in me 437

Rejoice! 438
   Release my soul 529
Restore, O Lord 439
   Restorer of my soul 369
   Revealer of mysteries 466
   Revival fire, fall 30
   Revive us again 148
Righteousness, peace, joy in
   the Holy Ghost 440
River, wash over me 441
Ruach 442

S

Salvation belongs to our God 443
   Sanctuary 334
Save the people 444
   Say it loud 90
Say the word 445
See his glory 446
Seek ye first 447
See, your Saviour comes 448
   Send revival 497
   Send the fire 386
   Seven reasons to celebrate 66
   Shadow of your wings 371
   Shine, Jesus, shine 335
Shout for joy 449
Shout for joy and sing 450
Shout, shout for joy 451
Shout! The Lord is risen! 452
   *Shout to the Lord (My Jesus,
   my Saviour)* 367
   *Shout to the Lord (We are
   his people)* 538
   Shout to the North 354
Shout unto God 453
   Show your power 159
Show your power, O Lord 454
Silent night 455
Silent, surrendered 456
Sing a song of celebration 457
   Singers' song 74
Sing, praise and bless the Lord 458
   So come 600
Soften my heart, Lord 459
Soon and very soon 460
   Song for Christingle 65
Sound the trumpet 461
   So you would come 40
Spirit of the living God (Iverson) 462
Spirit of the living God
   (Armstrong) 463
   Spirit of the sovereign Lord 504
   Spirit song 392
Streams of worship 464
Such love 465
Surely our God 466
   Surely the time has come 557
   Sweet mercies 248
   Sweet wind 501

T

   Take me in 467
Take me past the outer courts 467
Take my life, and let it be 468
Teach me to dance 469
Teach me your ways 470

Tell out, my soul 471
Thank you for saving me 472
Thank you for the cross 473
Thank you for your mercy 474
Thank you, Jesus 475
   Thank you, Lord 108
   That the Lamb who was slain 514
The angels, Lord, they sing 476
   The battle belongs to the Lord 228
   The candle song 322
The church's one foundation 477
The cross has said it all 478
The crucible for silver 479
   The day of his power 452
   The feast is ready 506
   The giving song 34
   The happy song 200
   The heart of worship 576
The heavens shall declare 480
   The King of glory comes 308
   The Lord Almighty reigns 141
The Lord is a mighty King 481
The Lord is marching out 482
The Lord is moving across this
   land 483
The Lord is our strength 484
The Lord reigns 485
The Lord's my shepherd 486
   The old rugged cross 403
   The power and the glory 512
The price is paid 487
The promise of the Holy Spirit 488
Therefore we lift our hearts
   in praise 489
There is a louder shout to come 490
There is a place of commanded
   blessing 491
There is a Redeemer 492
There is none like you 493
There is only one Lord 494
There is power in the name
   of Jesus 495
There's a blessed time that's
   coming 496
There's an awesome sound 497
There's a place where the
   streets shine 498
There's a river of joy 499
There's a sound of singing 500
There's a wind a-blowing 501
There's no one like you 502
   The river is here 83
These are the days 503
   The Servant King 114
   The solid Rock 365
The Spirit of the sovereign Lord 504
The steadfast love of the Lord 505
   The strong name of Jesus 494
   The trees of the field 609
The trumpets sound, the angels
   sing 506
   The wine of the kingdom 406
The Word made flesh 507
The world is looking for a hero 508
They that wait on the Lord 509
Thine be the glory 510
This Child 511

This grace is mine	512
This, in essence, is the message	513
This is my beloved Son	514
This is my desire	515
This is the day that the Lord has made	516
This is the day	517
This is the message of the cross	518
This is the mystery	519
This is the sweetest mystery	520
This is the time	610
This is your God	353
This kingdom	278
This love	521
This thankful heart	265
Though I feel afraid	522
Though the earth should tremble	523
Three-part harmony	410
Thunder in the skies	61
To be in your presence	524
To every good thing God is doing	525
To God be the glory!	526
To keep your lovely face	527
Tonight	528
To seek your face	129
To you, O Lord, I bring my worship	529
To you, O Lord, I lift up my soul	530
Turn our hearts	531
Turn the hearts	562
Turn to me and be saved	532
Turn your eyes upon Jesus	533

U

Under our skin	289
Undignified	261
Unending love	95
Unto the King	378

V

Victory chant	140

W

Wake up, my soul	534
Wake up, O sleeper	535
Warrior	419
We are a people of power	536
We are his children	537
We are his people	538
We are marching	539

We are the army of God	540
We await a Saviour from Heaven	507
We believe	541
We bring the sacrifice of praise	542
We come into your presence	543
We declare your majesty	544
We do not presume	545
We have a great priest	546
We have prayed that you would have mercy	547
Welcome, King of kings	548
Welcome the King	549
We lift up a shout	552
Well, I hear they're singing in the streets	550
We'll see it all	553
We'll walk the land	551
We march to the tune of a love-song	552
We must work together	553
We're in God's army	483
We rejoice in the goodness of our God	554
We rejoice in the grace of God	153
We serve a God of miracles	555
We serve a God of power	555
We shall see the King	496
We shall stand	556
We've had a light	557
We want to remain in your love	558
We want to see Jesus lifted high	559
We will cross every border	560
We will dance	457
We will magnify	398
We will ride	154
We will run and not grow weary	561
We will turn the hearts	562
We will wait	561
We will worship the Lamb of glory	563
We worship and adore you	564
We worship at your feet	70
What a friend I've found	565
What a friend we have in Jesus	566
What kind of greatness	567
What kind of love is this	568
What noise shall we make	569
When I feel the touch	570
When I look into your holiness	571
When I survey the wondrous cross	572
When my heart is overwhelmed	573
When peace like a river	574

When the Lord brought us back	575
When the music fades	576
Where there once was only hurt	577
Where two or three	578
White horse	46
Who can sound the depths of sorrow	579
Who sees it all	580
With all my heart	581
With my whole heart	582
With this bread	583
Worship the Lord	347
Worthy is the Lamb	584
Worthy, O worthy are you, Lord	585

Y

Yahweh	586
Yet this will I call to mind	587
You alone are God	19
You alone are worthy of my praise	270
You alone, Lord, are wonderful	588
You are beautiful	589
You are crowned with many crowns	590
You are God, you are great	591
You are Lord	592
You are merciful to me	593
You are mighty	594
You are my King	595
You are my passion	596
You are my rock	597
You are the Christ	273
You came from heaven to earth	330
You have broken the chains	385
You have called us	598
You have shown me	599
You have taken the precious	600
You laid aside your majesty	601
You loved me as you found me	602
You make my heart feel glad	603
You make your face to shine on me	604
You're alive	312
You rescued me	605
You're the Lion of Judah	606
Your love	303
Your love flows like a river	607
Your love keeps following me	602
Your mercy flows	608
Your waves of love	28
You shall go out with joy	609

Acknowledgements

The publishers wish to express their gratitude to the following for permission to include copyright material in this publication. Details of copyright owners are given underneath each individual hymn.

Ateliers et Presses de Taizé, F-71250 Taizé-Communauté, France.

Brown Bear Music, c/o Jax Records, 55 Avignon Road, Brockley, London, SE4 2JT.

Christian Life Publications, PO Box 157, Folkestone, Kent, CT20 2YS.

Jarrod Cooper (Ministries), New Life Christian Centre, Bridlington Avenue, Hull, HU2 0DU, UK.

CopyCare Ltd, PO Box 77, Hailsham, East Sussex, BN27 3EF, UK, on behalf of Mercy/Vineyard Publishing/Music Services; Deep Fryed Music/Music Services; Word Music Inc.; Glory Alleluia Music/Word Music; Springtide/Word Music; Dancing Heart Music/Word Music; CA Music/Word Music; The Rodeheaver Co./Word Music; Shepherds Heart Music/Word Music; Maranatha! Music; Chris Falson Music/Maranatha! Music; Shade Tree Music/Maranatha! Music; Word of God Music/ The Copyright Company; John T. Benson Publishing Co./Universal Songs; Bud John Songs/Universal Songs; Straightway/Mountain Spring/Universal Songs; Latter Rain Music/Universal Songs; Birdwing Music/BMG Songs Inc./ Universal Songs; Singspiration Music/Universal Songs; Stamps Baxter Music/ Universal Songs; BMG Songs Inc.; Body Songs; Hope Publishing; PDI Music; Sound III/Tempo Music Publications; Fairhill Music; Bob Kilpatrick Music; Ampelos Music; Lillenas Publishing Co. and HarperCollins Religious. Used by permission.

Daybreak Music Ltd, Silverdale Road, Eastbourne, East Sussex, BN20 7AB.

Bishop Timothy Dudley-Smith, 9 Ashlands, Ford, Salisbury, Wiltshire, SP4 6DY.

Far Lane Music Publishing, PO Box 2164, Florence, AL 35630, USA.

FLAMME, 5 Rue Erik Satie, Apt. 278, 31100 Toulouse, France.

Gabriel Music Inc., PO Box 840999, Houston, Texas 77284, USA, on behalf of Pete Sanchez Jr.

Pamela Hayes RSCJ, Marden Lodge, Marden Park, Woldingham, Surrey, CR3 7YA.

Ice Music, Bayley's Plantation, St Philip, Barbados, West Indies.

IQ Music, Orchard House, Tyler's Green, Cuckfield, West Sussex, RH17 5DZ. (For the world.)

Jubilate Hymns, 4 Thorne Park Road, Chelston, Torquay, Devon, TQ2 6RX.

Kingdom Faith Ministries, Foundry Lane, Horsham, West Sussex, RU13 5PX.

Kingsway's Thankyou Music, PO Box 75, Eastbourne, East Sussex, BN23 6NW, UK, on behalf of Kingsway's Thankyou Music; Russell Fragar/Hillsongs Australia; Darlene Zschech/Hillsongs Australia; Integrity's Hosanna! Music; Peter West/ Integrity's Hosanna! Music; Integrity's Praise! Music; Curious? Music UK; Scripture in Song; Celebration (for Europe and British Commonwealth, excl. Canada, Australasia and Africa); Debbie and Rob Eastwood/Hillsongs Australia; Acts Music (Worldwide, excl. South Africa); Kempen Music (for Europe and British Commonwealth, excl. Canada); Reuben Morgan/Hillsongs Australia; 7th Time

the source will be developed into a major resource for the churches. It is already available in the following editions

- **Complete Music Book**

- **Words Only**

- **Arrangements for Music Groups**

- **Acetate Masters**

If you would like to be kept informed, please let us have your name and address.

Write to us   Kevin Mayhew Ltd
Rattlesden
Bury St Edmunds
Suffolk
IP30 0SZ

or

phone   01449 737978

fax   01449 737834

e-mail   info@kevinmayhewltd.com